VERG

G000245297

AENEID VI

EDITED WITH INTRODUCTION,
NOTES AND VOCABULARY BY

H.E. GOULD & J.L. WHITELEY

Published by Bristol Classical Press
General Editor: John H. Betts
(by arrangement with Macmillan Education Ltd.)

Cover Illustration: Vergil from the Ara Pietatis Augustae
of Claudian date (41-54 A.D.), Villa Medici,
Rome (*drawing by Jean Bees*).

Printed in Great Britain by
Antony Rowe Ltd, Chippenham, Wiltshire
ISBN 0-86292-146-5

First Published by Macmillan Education Ltd., 1946
Reprinted, with permission, 1984, 1990 by

Bristol Classical Press
226 North Street
Bedminster
Bristol BS3 1JD

AENEID
BOOK SIX

FOREWORD

THIS edition of Vergil's Aeneid VI has been prepared
on the same principles as previous volumes in the
Modern School Classics. That is to say, the editors,
believing that the annotated classical texts of the past
generation give too little practical help in translation,
and yet at the same time have their commentaries
overloaded with unnecessary information on points
only remotely connected with the text, have sought
to write notes that will make it possible for the school
boy or girl of today, who is quite likely to begin the
preparation of the School Certificate set books without
having previously read any continuous Latin texts at
all, to produce, in reasonable time, and without the
discouragement of being baffled by difficulties, a
correct translation of passages set by their teachers
for preparation.

In these times such pupils will need a great deal of
help which in the spacious days of classical teaching
fifty years ago they were considered not to require,
and they will need moreover that such help should at
first be given repeatedly, until each difficulty of
construction becomes familiar.

The editors, bearing in mind, as they have tried to
do throughout, the difficulties experienced by present-
day pupils in the study of a subject which once received

a much more generous share of the time table, hope that they have done something, in the present edition, to smooth their path.

H. E. G.

J. L. W.

LONDON, 1945.

CONTENTS

LIST OF ILLUSTRATIONS

INTRODUCTION

Publius Vergilius Maro

VERGIL was born on October 15th, 70 B.C. at Andes, near Mantua in Cisalpine Gaul—the Lombardy plain. Andes is usually identified with the present Pietole, three miles from Mantua ; this identification, however, has been rejected by some modern scholars, who favour a site close to the existing towns of Carpendolo and Calvisano.

The poet's family seems to have been of some local importance, and his father, who owned and worked a farm, was able to give his son the ancient equivalent of a university education. Vergil studied at Cremona and Milan, and later went to Rome to complete his course in rhetoric and philosophy.

No doubt his father wished Vergil to make his way, as Cicero had done, by his eloquence, first in the law courts as a pleader, or barrister, and then in politics by standing as a candidate for the various magistracies which led ultimately to the consulship and a seat in the senate. Vergil's temperament, however, for he was shy, nervous and awkward in society, was quite unsuited to such a career, and after a single appearance before a jury, he decided to devote his life to philosophy and poetry.

Vergil returned to his native district, where he began

to write his first important work, the Eclogues, or Bucolics, ten poems, in semi-dramatic form, in which the persons are imaginary shepherds and their loves.

VERGIL, AND THE MUSES OF HISTORY AND TRAGEDY

The illustration is taken from a mosaic found in North Africa. Clio, the Muse of History, stands on the poet's right, reading from a scroll. The figure on his left is Melpomene, the Muse of Tragedy, bearing in her left hand a tragic mask.

This fashion of poetry, called ' pastoral ', was developed by the Sicilian Greek Theocritus. The Eclogues made Vergil's reputation as a poet and gained the attention

of Maecenas, who at that time was the most trusted
adviser in home affairs of Octavian, heir and successor
of Julius Caesar, and destined shortly to become master
of the Greco-Roman world as the first Roman Emperor,
Augustus.

During this period of his life, in 41 B.C., Vergil was
one of the many landed proprietors who saw their
farms ruthlessly confiscated and allotted to demobilized
soldiers—a common event during those troubled years
of civil war which preceded the collapse of the Roman
Republic. Fortunately for the poet, however, the
fame of the Eclogues and his friendship with Maecenas
made Vergil's position secure under the new régime,
and enabled him to devote the rest of his life to poetical
composition, free from all economic anxiety, at Naples
and Nola in Campania.

Thus, in or about 37 B.C., Vergil began his second
great work, the Georgics, a long poem, in four books,
which describes the Roman methods of farming, the
production of crops, of the vine and the olive, the
breeding of stock and the keeping of bees. As we
know from Vergil himself that he was asked to write
on this subject by Maecenas, we may safely assume
that his poem was designed as propaganda for Augustus'
' new order ' in Italy, and to reinforce that emperor's
attempts to revive Roman religion, Roman Agriculture,
and the simple but hardy virtues which had made
Rome great.

The two thousand odd lines of the poem were written

very slowly, the years 37–30 B.C. being devoted to their composition, and reveal the highest standard of pure craftsmanship yet reached in Latin poetry. Moreover, though his subject in this poem might seem unlikely to produce great poetry, Vergil found the theme so congenial to his nature that he overcame the many difficulties, and not only produced a valuable text book for farmers, but also wrote some of the noblest poetry in the Latin language.

Soon after the completion of the Georgics, Vergil, now 40 years of age, embarked, again no doubt at the instigation of his political patrons, upon his greatest and most ambitious work, the writing of an epic, i.e. heroic narrative poem, the Aeneid, which should rival Homer's Iliad and Odyssey, and honour the imperial achievements of the Roman race, glorify the Roman character and focus Roman national sentiment on Augustus as the man sent by destiny to bring peace, stability and prosperity to the Greco-Roman world, racked for so many years by civil war, fear and uncertainty.

The Aeneid occupied Vergil's whole attention for the remaining years of his life. In 19 B.C., after a journey to the East, he fell ill on his return to Italy at Brundisium. His health had never been robust, and realizing that his end was near he gave instructions that the great epic, for which he had planned a three years' revision, and of whose imperfections, as an intensely self-critical artist, he was very conscious, should be destroyed. This instruction, fortunately for literature, was disregarded by the poet's literary executors.

The Aeneid is an epic poem in twelve books, and tells how a Trojan prince, Aeneas, a survivor from the sack of Troy by the Greeks, is directed by the gods to seek a new home in Italy. In that land, after many vicissitudes, he settles with his Trojan companions, and it is from these colonists that the Romans liked to believe that they were sprung. Into this legend Vergil weaves a glorification of the family of Augustus, connecting the Julian clan, to which it belonged, with Iulus, the son of Aeneas.

Criticism of the poem has always recognized its superlative artistry, despite Vergil's own dissatisfaction with its lack of final polish, and is unanimous in detecting in Vergil's mind, and reflected by the poem, a profound sensitivity and sympathy with human troubles, hardly paralleled in Latin literature. In so far as judgment has been adverse, it has fastened on the character of the hero, Aeneas himself, in whom the virtue of *pietas*, ' dutifulness ', whether towards father, country or gods, is allowed prominence at the expense of warmer and more human feelings.

The story of the epic, book by book, is as follows.

Book I. Aeneas and his companions are driven by a storm aroused by Juno, implacable enemy of the Trojan race, towards the North African coast, where, thanks to the intervention of Neptune, most of the ships find shelter, their crews landing safely and making their way to Carthage. In this city, which has just been founded by Dido, a young widowed princess from Tyre, they are hospitably received by the queen, who, at a banquet, invites Aeneas to relate the story of his wanderings.

BOOK II. The Trojan hero begins his narrative with the story of the final siege, capture and sack of Troy. We hear of the treacherous Sinon, who feigns to be a deserter, persecuted by his Greek fellows, in order to gain entrance to the city, of the trick of the Wooden Horse, the cruel death of Laocoon and his sons, who sought to warn the Trojans of their approaching doom, the entry of the Greeks, their murder of King Priam, and the escape of Aeneas from the burning city with his aged father, Anchises, his young son Iulus, known also as Ascanius, and the household gods. In the confusion his wife Creusa is lost, but later Aeneas meets her ghost and is told that he is destined to found a new kingdom in Italy.

BOOK III. The narrative continues with the escape of Aeneas and his Trojan comrades from the mainland, and their voyage to various places in search of the ' promised land '—to Thrace, Delos, Crete, and finally to the West, by way of the Strophades Islands, and the coast of Epirus (Albania), where Aeneas is advised by Helenus to sail round Sicily, to make for the west coast of Italy, and there to consult a prophetess, the Sibyl, at Cumae, and to appease Juno. Aeneas does as

Helenus suggests, and thus, after seven years' wandering over the Eastern Mediterranean, he arrives at the western end of Sicily, where he spends the winter. Aeneas concludes his narrative to the queen, his hostess, by recording the death in Sicily of his father, Anchises.

BOOK IV. Meanwhile Dido, who has been greatly attracted to Aeneas from the first owing to the influence of Venus, his mother, now falls more and more deeply in love with him. Shortly after his arrival at Carthage, by the power of Juno and Venus, who from quite different motives favour such a development, Dido and Aeneas become lovers. Jupiter, however, now intervenes, and warns Aeneas, through Mercury, that he must leave Africa at once and fulfil his destined task of founding a new realm in Italy. Realizing the strength of Dido's passion for him, he tries to depart secretly, but his intentions become known to her. Yet he remains unmoved by her entreaties, which turn in the end to words of scorn and hatred. As he sails away, Dido destroys herself.

BOOK V. Aeneas returns to western Sicily and there celebrates the anniversary of his father's death with funeral games.[1] During the latter, Juno, pursuing her relentless hostility to their race, persuades the Trojan women, weary as they are of their wanderings, to set

---

[1] The elaborate account of these games, which occupies most of Book V, is no doubt due to the influence of Homer, who in the Iliad describes at great length the funeral games of the hero Patroclus.

fire to the ships, but a sudden rain-storm subdues the flames and only four are destroyed. The Trojans sail away from Sicily. On the voyage Palinurus, the helmsman, is overcome by sleep, and falling overboard, is drowned.

Book VI. In this, to many readers the finest book of the poem, Aeneas, having at last set foot on the coast of Western Italy, visits the Sibyl of Cumae and receives from her directions for the visit he longs to pay to the underworld. Armed with the ' golden bough ', which alone can procure him access to the nether regions of Hades, he traverses the various quarters of that kingdom and meets the spirit of his father, who parades for Aeneas the souls of all great Romans that are awaiting incarnation.[1] In this way Vergil is able to give his readers a kind of national cavalcade of all the great figures in Roman history from the earliest times down to his own day. Thus the pageant closes with the greatest figure of them all, the emperor Augustus.

The sixth book contains the famous lines (851–3), which epitomize the Roman's pride in the city's greatness as an imperial power :

Tu regere imperio populos, Romane, memento ;
Hae tibi erunt artes ; pacisque imponere morem,
Parcere subiectis, et debellare superbos.

[1] Note again Vergil's indebtedness to Homer. Odysseus, too, in Book XI of the Odyssey, is made to visit the underworld.

' Thou, O Roman, remember to rule the nations 'neath thy
sway.
These shall be thine arts, to impose the laws of peace,
To spare the conquered and to chasten the proud in war.'

BOOK VII. Aeneas at last enters his promised land
by the mouth of the river Tiber, the natural frontier
between the districts of Latium, lying south of the
river, and Etruria to the north. He is welcomed by
Latinus, king of Latium, who sees in Aeneas the
bridegroom for his daughter Lavinia, for whom he
has been advised by an oracle to find a foreign
husband.

Turnus, however, chieftain of the neighbouring
Rutuli, and worthiest of Lavinia's suitors, is enraged
at the proposal of Latinus, and supported by Amata,
the latter's queen, arouses the Latins against the
Trojans. The book closes with a magnificent catalogue
of the Italian forces—another epic convention, originat-
ing in Homer's catalogue of the Greek ships in the
Iliad, Book II.

BOOK VIII. The river god Tiberinus sends Aeneas
to seek aid from a Greek, Evander, who has settled on
the Palatine Hill in what is destined to be the future
Rome. Evander promises help and conducts Aeneas
through the city, explaining the origin of various Roman
sites and names. Venus persuades Vulcan, her husband, to make Aeneas a suit of armour, and a shield [1]

---

[1] Homer, too, in the Iliad, Book XVIII, describes at length
a shield, that of the Greek hero, Achilles.

on which are depicted in relief various events in the future history of Rome, down to the battle of Actium, 31 B.C., by which Vergil's patron Augustus gained undisputed sovereignty over the ancient world.

Book IX. While Aeneas is absent, Turnus makes an attempt, barely frustrated, to storm the Trojan camp by the Tiber, and is successful in setting fire to their ships. Nisus and Euryalus, two Trojans, endeavour to slip through the enemy lines in order to inform Aeneas of the critical situation. They slay some of the foe, but are eventually discovered and killed. The next day, when Turnus renews his assault, he succeeds in entering the camp, but is cut off, and only effects his escape by plunging into the Tiber.

Book X. A council of the gods is held in Olympus and Jupiter decides to leave the issue of the war to fate. Aeneas now wins the support of an Etruscan army which has revolted against the cruelties of the king Mezentius, and joined by reinforcements from Evander under the leadership of the latter's son, Pallas. he returns to aid the hard-pressed Trojans. In the furious fighting, Mezentius and his son Lausus are slain, but Turnus kills Pallas.

Book XI. A truce is arranged for the burial of the dead. On the arrival of an embassy from the Latins, Aeneas offers to settle the issue by a single combat between himself and Turnus. The Latins hold a council of war and determine to continue the struggle, but they are defeated a second time by the Trojans and their allies in spite of many deeds of valour, especially on the part of Camilla, a warrior maiden who is killed in the fighting.

BOOK XII. Another truce is arranged, and Turnus agrees to accept Aeneas' challenge, despite the opposition of the queen Amata and his sister, Juturna. The latter provokes the Latins to violate the truce. In the ensuing struggle Aeneas is wounded, but is miraculously healed by his mother, the goddess Venus. He returns to the fray, routs the Latins and Rutulians and eventually meets Turnus in single combat. The Rutulian chieftain is wounded and rendered helpless. Aeneas is minded to spare him until he notices that he is wearing the belt of the dead Pallas, whereupon he slays him.

THE JOURNEY OF AENEAS AND THE SIBYL THROUGH THE LOWER WORLD

After making their entry into the underworld, by a cave near Lake Avernus,[1] Aeneas and the Sibyl first come to a place described as ' right before the entrance and in the very corridor of Orcus ' (l. 273), where are found the personifications Grief, Care, Disease, . . . War, and the Eumenides, in the middle an elm tree, the abode of dreams, and hard by, many monsters of mythology, Centaurs, Scylla, Chimaera, Gorgons, and

[1] Homer's home of the dead was above ground, in the far north-west.

Harpies. Then they reach the banks of the first under-world river, Acheron, with Charon and his ferry-boat, and the ghosts of those who have recently died, begging to be ferried across. All have the right to cross the stream except the unburied dead, who must, as the Sibyl explains, wander a hundred years along the bank unless their bodies meanwhile receive burial. Here they en-counter Palinurus, the helmsman of Aeneas, who, over-come by sleep, had fallen over-board, been cast ashore, murdered by the natives, and left unburied on the coast. The Sibyl promises him burial. Only the sight of the Golden Bough persuades Charon to allow Aeneas to take his seat in the boat and to be ferried across the Acheron.

When he lands on the opposite shore with his com-panion, they are still not yet within the underworld proper, but only on the outskirts. Here they meet with Cerberus, the triple-headed Dog, guardian of the ap-proach to the citadel, and send him to sleep with a drugged cake. In this part of the underworld there are two regions, one, Limbo, inhabited by those who have died in infancy, and the other where dwell all those who have met a violent death.[1] The last group includes the falsely condemned, suicides, victims of love (among them Dido), and, finally, those who have fallen in war.

---

[1] The German scholar Norden has tried to prove with some probability that the victims of violent death could enter Tartarus only when they had completed what would have been normally the full span of their natural life.

Among the latter, Aeneas meets and talks with Deiphobus and hears the frightful story of his murder on
the night of the fall of Troy.

Over one group of these victims, the falsely condemned, Minos is said, in language reminiscent of the
procedure of the Roman law-court, to sit in judgment,
but what he is doing is not quite clear. Scholars differ,
but the most natural interpretation would seem to be
as follows : After hearing of their life and the charge
brought against them, Minos, if he thinks them guilty,
destines them for Tartarus, where they will go when
they have fulfilled their normal life ; if he thinks them
innocent, they have the chance along with the other
dead of eventually reaching the Elysian Fields.

Aeneas and the Sibyl are now at the double-road, the
parting of the ways ; the road on the right leads
beneath the walls of Tartarus to Elysium, where dwell
the righteous souls ; that on the left to Tartarus
itself, where the sinners meet with punishment. The
citadel is girt by the river Phlegethon, protected by a
gate of adamant and an iron tower with Tisiphone on
guard. The Sibyl explains to Aeneas (for as he is a
holy person he may not enter) that, within, Rhadamanthus tries the wrong-doers,—hears their con-
fessions, and pronounces their punishment, which is
entrusted to Tisiphone and her sisters, the Furies. The
Sibyl mentions some of the great sinners within,
Tityos, Ixion, the Titans, all of whom belong to Greek
legend ; then follows a catalogue of the ordinary

sinners, a list which seems to modern readers very arbitrarily composed.[1]

Passing the walls of the citadel, Aeneas fixes the Golden Bough to the portal as Proserpina's gift, and then continues his journey to the Elysian Fields.

Of these Vergil gives a beautiful description, and includes among the inhabitants ordinary men, as well as mythical figures. Finally, Aeneas encounters his father, who leads him to another division of the underworld, the banks of the river Lethe, whose waters are drunk by those destined to return for another life in the world above. In answer to his son's enquiries, Anchises gives his account of life in the underworld and unfolds for him the pageant of the heroes of Rome from the first kings, right through Republican times to Julius Caesar, Augustus, and Marcellus.

After this, Aeneas returns to the upper world through the ivory gate, the portal by which false dreams come to men.

THE GOLDEN BOUGH

Vergil describes the Golden Bough as *Iunoni infernae dictus sacer* (138), and as a gift dear to Proserpina (142), and he compares, without actually identifying, it with the mistletoe (205). As there is no other reference in Greek or Roman literature to the Golden Bough, its identity and meaning are very obscure.

[1] The impious, the fraudulent, the avaricious, the adulterers, rebels, traitors, corrupt politicians, the incestuous.

There are two views. Some authorities think the Bough is actually of gold, and belongs to the region of myth. On the other hand, many believe that it is the branch of a real tree or plant. In that case it must be identified with the mistletoe. Although we have said above there is no evidence for its meaning in Greek or Roman folk-lore,[1] we do know that in European folk-lore the mistletoe is famous for its magical qualities, and for its mysterious growth and winter fruiting. Thus Mr. A. B. Cook is led by its use in modern folk-lore as a divining rod to unlock the secrets of the earth, to infer that the mistletoe may have been regarded as a key to gain admission to the lower world.

Again, the mistletoe may have symbolised life in the midst of death and thus have been the suitable gift for one coming from the earth above to take to Proserpina in the lower world.

Norden has tried to show that the mistletoe was not only a symbol of life and death, but also an apotropaic [2] against demons.

The Eschatology[3] of Vergil and its Sources

A great deal has been written about the picture of the underworld which Vergil gives his readers in the Sixth Book of the Aeneid, and varying emphasis is laid by

[1] Pliny (N. H. 13, 119), quoting another authority, says the mistletoe was indestructible by fire or water.

[2] Something that serves to turn away or keep off.

[3] Beliefs as to the life after death.

commentators on its sources, its topography, its many inconsistencies and difficulties. In these brief remarks an attempt will be made to summarise the sources of Vergil's picture ; and the inconsistencies and difficulties, some of which are undoubtedly due to lack of revision, will be ignored. In any case, we may point out that we should not expect Vergil to give us a coherent account of the underworld and its inhabitants, for it is not his purpose to provide a Guide Book for future visitors.

On two points the commentators agree ; first that the sources of Vergil's eschatology are entirely Greek, and secondly, that he has succeeded in welding his sources skilfully together to provide a matchless poetic and artistic vision in which we may see some of his deepest thoughts on life, destiny, and death.

Those who are familiar with the home of the dead in Homer, Odyssey Book IX, will notice a big difference between his world, situated above ground, and in the far north-west, inhabited by shadowy, almost witless forms, and Vergil's organised underworld, which has ' shades ' with a full personality, the idea of rewards and punishment, metempsychosis, and rebirth. The date and origin of such beliefs is uncertain, but it is known that traces of them appear in the sixth century B.C., and were probably found in popular Greek folk-lore. Norden has suspected the existence of popular ' theologies ' which no doubt included details of underworld topography. Then, it is believed, these popular beliefs developed in the teaching of the Pythagorean philo-

sophy and the doctrines of the mystic cult known as
Orphism, two systems which were popular in South
Italy and had poetic accounts of descents to the lower
world. According to H. E. Butler, they both included
belief in purgatory, hell, paradise, metempsychosis, and
rebirth. Some of these ideas occur in the odes of Pindar
and the works of Plato, but, it is important to notice
that we cannot get behind the evidence of these Greek
authors to the original source. Obvious evidence of
popular beliefs in Vergil can be found in the personified
abstractions and the monsters that either haunt or
guard the gate of the lower world.

Finally, we have to examine the influence on Vergil
of the Stoic doctrine of the Anima Mundi, that world
spirit, God, which is the supporting principle of the
universe, and in man becomes corrupted in association
with his body and his bodily desires, but may be
purified or refined again. This doctrine is developed
in fuller detail in the famous speech of Anchises.

It is interesting to note that the vision of a future life
which Cicero gives in the sixth book of his De Republica,
the Dream of Scipio, is strongly patriotic in tone, with
emphasis on the rewards that await great historical figures
and those who have saved their country, and may have
suggested to Vergil the idea of his cavalcade of heroes,[1]
which to many is one of the finest passages in the Aeneid.

---

[1] This may, however, have developed naturally out of the
idea of metempsychosis and rebirth, which, as we have shown,
was an integral part of the underworld tradition.

The Metre of the Poem

Most English verse consists of lines in which stressed syllables alternate with unstressed, as for example in the lines :

'The ploughman homeward plods his weary way,

And leaves the world to darkness and to me.

Such verse is called *accentual*.

The principle of Greek and Latin verse is different. It is based on the rhythmical arrangement of long and short syllables, the long syllables taking twice as long to pronounce as the short. This system may be compared with music, long syllables corresponding to *crotchets* and short to *quavers*, one *crotchet* being equal to two *quavers*. This type of verse is called *quantitative*.

Just as, to appreciate the rhythm of English verse, you are taught to *scan*, i.e. to divide the lines into *feet* and mark the stress in each foot, so you must learn to scan Latin verse by a similar division into feet and by marking the syllables long (–) or short (◡). Not only is it necessary to do this in order to understand the construction of the verse and the musical qualities of the poetry, but the ability to do so is a great help in translation, by making it possible to distinguish words alike in spelling but different in quantity, for example, *pŏpŭlŭs*, 'people', from *pōpŭlŭs*, 'poplar tree'.

The verses of the Aeneid are called heroic hexa-

meters. In this verse two kinds of feet, or bars, are
found. One is the *dactyl*, a long syllable followed by
two short syllables, the other, the *spondee*, two long
syllables. Each line, or hexameter, contains six feet,
the first four of which may be either dactyls or spon-
dees, the fifth being almost always a dactyl and the
sixth a spondee. In place of this sixth-foot spondee a
trochee (– ◡) is allowable.

Thus the scheme of the hexameter is as follows :

	1	2	3	4	5	6
	– ◡ ◡	– ◡ ◡	– ◡ ◡	– ◡ ◡	– ◡ ◡	– –
or	– –	– –	– –	– –		– ◡

In the scansion of these lines, no account is taken
of syllables at the close of words *ending* in a vowel
or an *m*, if they are followed immediately by a word
commencing with a vowel or an *h*. Such a final syllable is said to be *elided*, ' struck out ', though it was
more probably slurred in pronunciation. Thus in
l. 2 of the present book,

> *et tandem Euboicis Cumarum adlabitur oris,*

the -*em* of *tandem* and the final -*um* of *Cumarum* are
ignored in scanning.

*   *   *

A long syllable is one that contains a vowel long *by
nature*, or a diphthong ; or a vowel, naturally short,
that is long *by position*, i.e., is followed by two consonants.

A short syllable is one that contains a vowel short *by*

nature and ends either with no consonant, or with only one.

The two consonants which have been mentioned as having the effect of lengthening a syllable need not both occur in the same word. Thus, in l. 2, the first syllable is long, though the *e* in *et* is naturally short, because that *e* is followed by *t* and the *t* of *tandem*.

PROSODY

The following information about the quantity of Latin syllables will be found useful.

A. Relating to all syllables.

All diphthongs are long, except before another vowel.

B. Relating to final syllables.
  1. Final *a* is usually short.
  Except
     (*a*) in the abl. sg. of 1st decl. nouns, e.g. *mensā* ;
     (*b*) in the 2nd sg. imperative active of 1st conjugation verbs, e.g. *amā* ;
     (*c*) in indeclinable words such as *intereā, frustrā*.
  2. Final *e* is usually short.
  Except
     (*a*) in the abl. sg. of 5th decl. nouns, e.g. *aciē* ;
     (*b*) in the 2nd sg. imperative active of 2nd conjugation verbs, e.g. *monē* ;
     (*c*) in adverbs formed from adjectives of the 1st and 2nd declensions, e.g. *pulchrē*, from *pulcher, -chra, -chrum*. (Note, however, *benĕ, malĕ*.)

3. Final *i* is usually long.

Except in *mihi, tibi, sibi, ubi, ibi*, in which it may be long or short, and in *quasi, nisi*.

4. Final *o* is usually long.

Except in *modo, duo, ego*.

C. Final syllables of words of more than one syllable, ending in any single consonant other than *s*, are short.

Except

(*a*) *dispār* ;

(*b*) in the perfects *iīt* and *petiīt*.

D. 1. Final *as, os, es*, are long.

Except

(*a*) *compŏs, penĕs* ;

(*b*) in nominatives singular in *es* of 3rd declension nouns (consonant stems) having genitive singular in *-ĕtis, -ĭtis, -idis* : e.g. *segĕs, milĕs, obsĕs*. (But note *pariēs, abiēs, Cerēs*.)

(*c*) in compounds of *es* (from *sum*), e.g. *abĕs, prodĕs*.

2. Final *us* and *is* are short.

Except *ūs*

(*a*) in gen. sg., nom., voc. and acc. pl. of 4th decl. nouns, e.g. *gradūs* ;

(*b*) in the nom. sg. of consonant stem 3rd decl. nouns having gen. sg. with a long syllable before the last, e.g. *tellūs* (*-ūris*), *palūs* (*-ūdis*), *virtūs* (*-ūtis*).

And except *īs*

    (*c*) in dat. and abl. pl., e.g. *mensīs, dominīs, vinīs* ;

    (*d*) in acc. pl. of 3rd decl. -*i* stems, e.g. *navīs, omnīs*;

    (*e*) in the 2nd pers. sg. of 4th conjugation verbs, e.g. *audīs* ; and in *sīs*, and compounds of *sīs*, as *possīs* ; and in *velīs, nolīs, malīs*, and *īs* (from *eo*).

E. Quantity of syllables determined by position in the same word.

1. A syllable ending with a vowel or diphthong, immediately followed by a syllable beginning with a vowel, or with *h* and a vowel, is short : e.g. *vĭa, prae-ustus, trăhit.*

Except

    (*a*) in the case of genitives in -*ius*, e.g. *alīus, solīus, utrīus.* (But note *illĭus*.)

    (*b*) *e* preceding *i* in 5th decl. nouns, e.g. *diēi*, and in *ēi* (from *is*).

    (*c*) the syllable *fī* in *fīo*. (But note *fĭeri, fĭerem*, the *ĭ* being short before *er*.)

2. A syllable containing a vowel immediately followed by two consonants, or by *x* or *z*, which are really double consonants (*cs* and *ds*) is long ; e.g. the second syllable in *regent, auspex.*

Except if the two consonants are a combination of one of the following, *b, c, d, f, g, p, t*, with (following) *l* or *r*.

If a short vowel precedes such a combination the syllable is not necessarily long.

Finally it must be remembered that these rules apply to Latin words only, and not to many Greek proper names which will be encountered in this book.

*   *   *

Let us now see if, with the information given above, we can scan one of the hexameters of this poem.

Looking at line 32, for example,

> *bis conatus erat casus effingere in auro,*

(i) see first whether any syllable requires to be elided, i.e. not taken into account. In this line the final *e* of *effingere* will be disregarded before the vowel *i* of *in*.

(ii) Mark long (–) all syllables where long quantity can be determined by the rules given above.

bis, rat, ef, fin

are all long syllables (by Rule E 2).

au is a long syllable, because it is a diphthong (Rule A), as is the *ro* of *auro* (by Rule B 4).

This now gives us

bīs conatus erāt casus ēffinger' in auro

(iii) Mark short (⌣) all syllables whose short quantity can be determined by rule.

The *us* of *conatus* is a short syllable, (Rule D 2), giving us now :

bīs conatŭs erāt casus ēffinger' in auro.

Generally speaking it will be found that such an application of the rules of prosody will give enough syllables of known quantity to make it possible to scan the line completely.

To do this, work backwards from the end of the line, because the pattern of the last two feet ($-\cup\cup\mid--$ or $-\cup$) is constant.[1] This gives us, for these feet,

$$5 \qquad 6$$
$$\mid \bar{fi}ng\breve{e}r' \; \breve{i}n \mid \bar{au}r\bar{o}$$

Working backwards again, the fourth foot is obviously a spondee :

$$4$$
$$\mid \bar{u}s \; \bar{e}f \mid$$

and so must be the third :

$$3$$
$$\mid r\bar{a}t \; c\bar{a}s \mid$$

This leaves us with five syllables to be got into the remaining two feet, which must be spondee, dactyl, since the quantity of the penultimate syllable of the second foot is short :

$$1 \qquad 2$$
$$\mid b\bar{i}s \; c\bar{o} \mid n\bar{a}t\breve{u}s \; \breve{e} \mid$$

And the whole line, divided into feet and with the quantities marked, is :

[1] Very occasionally a spondee is found in the 5th foot.

1   2   3   4   5   6

bīs cō | nātŭs ĕ | rāt cās | ūs ēf | fīngĕr' ĭn | aūrō

One thing remains to be done before the scansion is complete. It is a rule that, usually in the 3rd foot, more rarely in the 4th, one word must end and another begin. This is called the *caesura* or ' cutting '. If this break occurs after the first syllable of the foot, the caesura is said to be strong ; if after the second, weak. In this line we obviously have a strong caesura in the 3rd foot. The caesura is regularly marked in scansion by a pair of vertical lines.

Thus the scansion of the line, as completed, is

1   2   3   4   5   6

bīs cō | nātŭs ĕ | rāt || cās | ūs ēf | fīngĕr' ĭn | aūrō

You will find that, with careful attention to the pronunciation of Latin words, you will gradually learn to scan by ear, without the necessity of applying for help to the rules of prosody. You should try to develop this power as early as possible.

Note that the scheme of the hexameter makes it elastic, and gives it a variable length, as long as 17 or as short as 13 syllables. This makes possible such onomatopoeic lines as

quādrŭpĕ- | dāntĕ pŭ- | trem sŏnĭ- | tū quătĭt | ūngŭlă |

cāmpŭm

(where the poet, describing the galloping of horses, imitates the sound of them), and as

$$\bar{ill}(i)\ \bar{in}\text{-}\ |\ \bar{ter}\ \bar{se}\text{-}\ |\ \bar{se}\ \bar{mag}\text{-}\ |\ \bar{na}\ \bar{vi}\ |\ \bar{bracchi}\breve{a}\ |\ \bar{toll}\breve{u}nt,$$

(where again sound is matched to sense, for the line describes the alternate blows upon an anvil delivered by two smiths.)

VERGIL

AENEID VI.

*Aeneas, with his Trojan fleet, comes to Cumae and seeks the
Sibyl, a prophetess inspired by Apollo, near whose temple,
with its elaborately carved doors, she dwells.*

Sic fatur lacrimans, classique immittit habenas,
et tandem Euboicis Cumarum adlabitur oris.
obvertunt pelago proras ; tum dente tenaci
ancora fundabat navis, et litora curvae
praetexunt puppes. iuvenum manus emicat ardens 5
litus in Hesperium ; quaerit pars semina flammae
abstrusa in venis silicis ; pars densa ferarum
tecta rapit silvas, inventaque flumina monstrat.
at pius Aeneas arces, quibus altus Apollo
praesidet, horrendaeque procul secreta Sibyllae, 10
antrum immane, petit, magnam cui mentem animumque
Delius inspirat vates, aperitque futura.
iam subeunt Triviae lucos atque aurea tecta.

Daedalus, ut fama est, fugiens Minoia regna,
praepetibus pennis ausus se credere caelo, 15
insuetum per iter gelidas enavit ad Arctos,
Chalcidicaque levis tandem super astitit arce.
redditus his primum terris tibi, Phoebe, sacravit
remigium alarum, posuitque immania templa.
in foribus letum Androgeo ; tum pendere poenas 20
Cecropidae iussi—miserum !—septena quotannis
corpora natorum ; stat ductis sortibus urna.

I

contra elata mari respondet Gnosia tellus :
hic crudelis amor tauri, suppostaque furto
Pasiphae, mixtumque genus prolesque biformis 25
Minotaurus inest, Veneris monimenta nefandae ;
hic labor ille domus, et inextricabilis error ;
magnum reginae sed enim miseratus amorem
Daedalus ipse dolos tecti ambagesque resolvit,
caeca regens filo vestigia. tu quoque magnam 30
partem opere in tanto, sineret dolor, Icare, haberes.
bis conatus erat casus effingere in auro,
bis patriae cecidere manus. quin protinus omnia
perlegerent oculis, ni iam praemissus Achates
adforet, atque una Phoebi Triviaeque sacerdos, 35
Deiphobe Glauci, fatur quae talia regi :
'non hoc ista sibi tempus spectacula poscit ;
nunc grege de intacto septem mactare iuvencos
praestiterit, totidem lectas de more bidentis.'
talibus adfata Aenean—nec sacra morantur 40
iussa viri—Teucros vocat alta in templa sacerdos.

*At the Sibyl's bidding, Aeneas prays to Apollo that the promise of
a new kingdom in Italy may be fulfilled, and vows to build
there a temple to the god.*

Excisum Euboicae latus ingens rupis in antrum,
quo lati ducunt aditus centum, ostia centum,
unde ruunt totidem voces, responsa Sibyllae.
ventum erat ad limen, cum virgo, ' poscere fata 45
tempus,' ait ; ' deus, ecce, deus ! ' cui talia fanti
ante fores subito non vultus, non color unus,

non comptae mansere comae ; sed pectus anhelum,
et rabie fera corda tument, maiorque videri
nec mortale sonans, adflata est numine quando   50
iam propiore dei. ' cessas in vota precesque,
Tros,' ait, ' Aenea? cessas? neque enim ante dehiscent
attonitae magna ora domus.' et talia fata
conticuit. gelidus Teucris per dura cucurrit
ossa tremor, funditque preces rex pectore ab imo :   55
' Phoebe, gravis Troiae semper miserate labores,
Dardana qui Paridis derexti tela manusque
corpus in Aeacidae, magnas obeuntia terras
tot maria intravi duce te penitusque repostas
Massylum gentis, praetentaque Syrtibus arva,   60
iam tandem Italiae fugientis prendimus oras ;
hac Troiana tenus fuerit fortuna secuta.
vos quoque Pergameae iam fas est parcere genti,
dique deaeque omnes, quibus obstitit Ilium et ingens
gloria Dardaniae. tuque, o sanctissima vates,   65
praescia venturi, da—non indebita posco
regna meis fatis—Latio considere Teucros,
errantisque deos agitataque numina Troiae.
tum Phoebo et Triviae solido de marmore templum
instituam, festosque dies de nomine Phoebi.   70
te quoque magna manent regnis penetralia nostris ;
hic ego namque tuas sortis arcanaque fata,
dicta meae genti, ponam lectosque sacrabo,
alma, viros. foliis tantum ne carmina manda,
ne turbata volent rapidis ludibria ventis :   75
ipsa canas oro.' finem dedit ore loquendi.

The Sibyl, in an oracle, gives Aeneas obscure warning of many troubles yet to be endured. He begs her to aid him in his desire to visit his dead father Anchises in the Underworld.

At, Phoebi nondum patiens, immanis in antro
bacchatur vates, magnum si pectore possit
excussisse deum : tanto magis ille fatigat
os rabidum, fera corda domans, fingitque premendo. 80
ostia iamque domus patuere ingentia centum
sponte sua vatisque ferunt responsa per auras :
' o tandem magnis pelagi defuncte periclis—
sed terrae graviora manent : in regna Lavini   84
Dardanidae venient (mitte hanc de pectore curam),
sed non et venisse volent. bella, horrida bella,
et Thybrim multo spumantem sanguine cerno.
non Simois tibi nec Xanthus nec Dorica castra
defuerint : alius Latio iam partus Achilles,
natus et ipse dea : nec Teucris addita Iuno   90
usquam aberit ; cum tu supplex in rebus egenis
quas gentis Italum aut quas non oraveris urbes !
causa mali tanti coniunx iterum hospita Teucris,
externique iterum thalami.
tu ne cede malis, sed contra audentior ito,   95
qua tua te fortuna sinet. via prima salutis,
quod minime reris, Graia pandetur ab urbe.'
    Talibus ex adyto dictis Cumaea Sibylla
horrendas canit ambages antroque remugit,
obscuris vera involvens ; ea frena furenti   100
concutit et stimulos sub pectore vertit Apollo.
ut primum cessit furor, et rabida ora quierunt,

incipit Aeneas heros : ' non ulla laborum,
o virgo, nova mi facies inopinave surgit ;
omnia praecepi atque animo mecum ante peregi. 105
unum oro : quando hic inferni ianua regis
dicitur et tenebrosa palus Acheronte refuso,
ire ad conspectum cari genitoris et ora
contingat ; doceas iter, et sacra ostia pandas.
illum ego per flammas et mille sequentia tela 110
eripui his umeris, medioque ex hoste recepi ;

' SI POTUIT MANIS ACCERSERE CONIUGIS ORPHEUS. . . . '

This illustration, from a Greek vase painting of the Fourth Century, B.C., shows Orpheus playing the lyre in the Underworld. The other figures are Proserpine, with a cross-headed torch, and Pluto.

ille, meum comitatus iter, maria omnia mecum
atque omnis pelagique minas caelique ferebat,
invalidus, viris ultra sortemque senectae.
quin, ut te supplex peterem et tua limina adirem,   115
idem orans mandata dabat. natique patrisque,
alma, precor, miserere, potes namque omnia, nec te
nequiquam lucis Hecate praefecit Avernis.
si potuit manis accersere coniugis Orpheus,
Threïcia fretus cithara fidibusque canoris ;   120
si fratrem Pollux alterna morte redemit,
itque reditque viam totiens—quid Thesea magnum,
quid memorem Alciden?—et mi genus ab Iove summo.'

The Sibyl tells Aeneas that before he seeks out his father in Hades two things must be done : he must find and pluck the Golden Bough which Proserpine demands as her offering, and lay to rest a dead comrade, whose unburied corpse pollutes the Trojan fleet.

Talibus orabat dictis arasque tenebat ;
cum sic orsa loqui vates : ' sate sanguine divum,   125
Tros Anchisiade, facilis descensus Averno ;
noctes atque dies patet atri ianua Ditis ;
sed revocare gradum superasque evadere ad auras,
hoc opus, hic labor est. pauci, quos aequus amavit
Iuppiter, aut ardens evexit ad aethera virtus,   130
dis geniti potuere. tenent media omnia silvae,
Cocytusque sinu labens circumvenit atro.
quod si tantus amor menti, si tanta cupido est
bis Stygios innare lacus, bis nigra videre

Tartara, et insano iuvat indulgere labori ;   135
accipe, quae peragenda prius. latet arbore opaca
aureus et foliis et lento vimine ramus,
Iunoni infernae dictus sacer : hunc tegit omnis
lucus, et obscuris claudunt convallibus umbrae.
sed non ante datur telluris operta subire,   140
auricomos quam qui decerpserit arbore fetus.
hoc sibi pulchra suum ferri Proserpina munus
instituit. primo avulso non deficit alter
aureus, et simili frondescit virga metallo.
ergo alte vestiga oculis et rite repertum   145
carpe manu ; namque ipse volens facilisque sequetur,
si te fata vocant : aliter non viribus ullis
vincere nec duro poteris convellere ferro.
praeterea iacet exanimum tibi corpus amici,
—heu nescis !—totamque incestat funere classem,   150
dum consulta petis nostroque in limine pendes.
sedibus hunc refer ante suis, et conde sepulcro.
duc nigras pecudes ; ea prima piacula sunto.
sic demum lucos Stygis et regna invia vivis
aspicies.' dixit, pressoque obmutuit ore.   155

*Aeneas learns that the dead man of whom the Sibyl speaks is the
trumpeter Misenus, and preparations are made for his
funeral.*

Aeneas maesto defixus lumina vultu
ingreditur, linquens antrum, caecosque volutat
eventus animo secum : cui fidus Achates
it comes et paribus curis vestigia figit.

multa inter sese vario sermone serebant,   160
quem socium exanimum vates, quod corpus humandum
diceret. atque illi Misenum in litore sicco,
ut venere, vident indigna morte peremptum,
Misenum Aeoliden, quo non praestantior alter
aere ciere viros Martemque accendere cantu.   165
Hectoris hic magni fuerat comes, Hectora circum
et lituo pugnas insignis obibat et hasta.
postquam illum vita victor spoliavit Achilles,
Dardanio Aeneae sese fortissimus heros
addiderat socium, non inferiora secutus.   170
sed tum forte cava dum personat aequora concha,
demens, et cantu vocat in certamina divos,
aemulus exceptum Triton, si credere dignum est,
inter saxa virum spumosa immerserat unda.
ergo omnes magno circum clamore fremebant ;   175
praecipue pius Aeneas. tum iussa Sibyllae,
haud mora, festinant flentes aramque sepulcro
congerere arboribus caeloque educere certant.
itur in antiquam silvam, stabula alta ferarum :
procumbunt piceae ; sonat icta securibus ilex ;   180
fraxineaeque trabes cuneis et fissile robur
scinditur ; advolvunt ingentis montibus ornos.
nec non Aeneas opera inter talia primus
hortatur socios paribusque accingitur armis.

Aeneas is led by two doves to the Golden Bough, which he breaks off.

Atque haec ipse suo tristi cum corde volutat, 185
aspectans silvam immensam, et sic forte precatur :
'si nunc se nobis ille aureus arbore ramus
ostendat nemore in tanto ! quando omnia vere
heu nimium de te vates, Misene, locuta est.'
vix ea fatus erat, geminae cum forte columbae 190
ipsa sub ora viri caelo venere volantes,
et viridi sedere solo. tum maximus heros
maternas agnoscit avis, laetusque precatur :
' este duces, o, si qua via est, cursumque per auras
derigite in lucos, ubi pinguem dives opacat 195
ramus humum. tuque, o, dubiis ne defice rebus,
diva parens.' sic effatus vestigia pressit
observans quae signa ferant, quo tendere pergant.
pascentes illae tantum prodire volando,
quantum acie possent oculi servare sequentum. 200
inde ubi venere ad fauces grave olentis Averni,
tollunt se celeres liquidumque per aëra lapsae
sedibus optatis geminae super arbore sidunt,
discolor unde auri per ramos aura refulsit.
quale solet silvis brumali frigore viscum 205
fronde virere nova, quod non sua seminat arbos,
et croceo fetu teretis circumdare truncos :
talis erat species auri frondentis opaca
ilice, sic leni crepitabat brattea vento.
corripit Aeneas extemplo avidusque refringit 210
cunctantem, et vatis portat sub tecta Sibyllae.

*The body of Misenus is consumed upon a funeral pyre,
and the remains are committed to a tomb.*

Nec minus interea Misenum in litore Teucri
flebant, et cineri ingrato suprema ferebant.
principio pinguem taedis et robore secto
ingentem struxere pyram, cui frondibus atris   215
intexunt latera, et feralis ante cupressos
constituunt, decorantque super fulgentibus armis.
pars calidos latices et aëna undantia flammis
expediunt, corpusque lavant frigentis et unguunt.
fit gemitus. tum membra toro defleta reponunt,   220
purpureasque super vestis, velamina nota,
coniciunt. pars ingenti subiere feretro,
triste ministerium, et subiectam more parentum
aversi tenuere facem. congesta cremantur
turea dona, dapes, fuso crateres olivo.   225
postquam conlapsi cineres et flamma quievit,
reliquias vino et bibulam lavere favillam,
ossaque lecta cado texit Corynaeus aëno.
idem ter socios pura circumtulit unda,
spargens rore levi et ramo felicis olivae,   230
lustravitque viros, dixitque novissima verba.
at pius Aeneas ingenti mole sepulcrum
imponit, suaque arma viro remumque tubamque,
monte sub aërio, qui nunc Misenus ab illo
dicitur, aeternumque tenet per saecula nomen.   235

Aeneas sacrifices to the gods of the underworld, and with the Sibyl enters the mouth of a cavern which leads down to it.

His actis propere exsequitur praecepta Sibyllae.
spelunca alta fuit vastoque immanis hiatu,
scrupea, tuta lacu nigro nemorumque tenebris ;
quam super haud ullae poterant impune volantes
tendere iter pennis : talis sese halitus atris   240
faucibus effundens supera ad convexa ferebat :
[unde locum Grai dixerunt nomine Aornon.]
quattuor hic primum nigrantis terga iuvencos
constituit, frontique invergit vina sacerdos ;
et summas carpens media inter cornua saetas   245
ignibus imponit sacris, libamina prima,
voce vocans Hecaten, caeloque Ereboque potentem.
supponunt alii cultros, tepidumque cruorem
suscipiunt pateris. ipse atri velleris agnam
Aeneas matri Eumenidum magnaeque sorori   250
ense ferit, sterilemque tibi, Proserpina, vaccam.
tum Stygio regi nocturnas incohat aras,
et solida imponit taurorum viscera flammis,
pingue super oleum fundens ardentibus extis.
ecce autem, primi sub lumina solis et ortus,   255
sub pedibus mugire solum, et iuga coepta moveri
silvarum, visaeque canes ululare per umbram,
adventante dea. ' procul o, procul este, profani,'
conclamat vates, ' totoque absistite luco :
tuque invade viam, vaginaque eripe ferrum :   260
nunc animis opus, Aenea, nunc pectore firmo.'

tantum effata, furens antro se immisit aperto :
ille ducem haud timidis vadentem passibus aequat.
  Di, quibus imperium est animarum, umbraeque
    silentes,
et Chaos, et Phlegethon, loca nocte tacentia late,   265
sit mihi fas audita loqui ; sit numine vestro
pandere res alta terra et caligine mersas.

Aeneas and the Sibyl enter Hades, and behold a great array
of monstrous creatures.

  Ibant obscuri sola sub nocte per umbram,
perque domos Ditis vacuas et inania regna :
quale per incertam lunam sub luce maligna   270
est iter in silvis, ubi caelum condidit umbra
Iuppiter, et rebus nox abstulit atra colorem.
vestibulum ante ipsum primisque in faucibus Orci
Luctus et ultrices posuere cubilia Curae,
pallentesque habitant Morbi, tristisque Senectus,   275
et Metus, et malesuada Fames, ac turpis Egestas,
terribiles visu formae, Letumque, Labosque ;
tum consanguineus Leti Sopor, et mala mentis
Gaudia, mortiferumque adverso in limine Bellum,
ferreique Eumenidum thalami, et Discordia demens, 280
vipereum crinem vittis innexa cruentis.
in medio ramos annosaque bracchia pandit
ulmus opaca, ingens, quam sedem Somnia vulgo
vana tenere ferunt, foliisque sub omnibus haerent.
multaque praeterea variarum monstra ferarum   285
Centauri in foribus stabulant, Scyllaeque biformes,

et centumgeminus Briareus, ac belua Lernae
horrendum stridens, flammisque armata Chimaera,
Gorgones, Harpyiaeque, et forma tricorporis umbrae.
corripit hic subita trepidus formidine ferrum
Aeneas, strictamque aciem venientibus offert,
et, ni docta comes tenuis sine corpore vitas
admoneat volitare cava sub imagine formae,
inruat, et frustra ferro diverberet umbras.   294

Aeneas sees a vast throng of spirits on the bank of the Styx,
over which Charon ferries the souls of the buried.

Hinc via Tartarei quae fert Acherontis ad undas.
turbidus hic caeno vastaque voragine gurges
aestuat atque omnem Cocyto eructat harenam.
portitor has horrendus aquas et flumina servat
terribili squalore Charon : cui plurima mento
canities inculta iacet ; stant lumina flamma ;   300
sordidus ex umeris nodo dependet amictus.
ipse ratem conto subigit, velisque ministrat,
et ferruginea subvectat corpora cumba,
iam senior ; sed cruda deo viridisque senectus.
huc omnis turba ad ripas effusa ruebat,   305
matres atque viri, defunctaque corpora vita
magnanimum heroum, pueri innuptaeque puellae,
impositique rogis iuvenes ante ora parentum :
quam multa in silvis autumni frigore primo

lapsa cadunt folia, aut ad terram gurgite ab alto 310
quam multae glomerantur aves, ubi frigidus annus
trans pontum fugat et terris immittit apricis.
stabant orantes primi transmittere cursum,
tendebantque manus ripae ulterioris amore ;
navita sed tristis nunc hos nunc accipit illos, 315
ast alios longe summotos arcet harena.
Aeneas miratus enim motusque tumultu,
' dic,' ait, ' o virgo, quid vult concursus ad amnem?
quidve petunt animae? vel quo discrimine ripas
hae linquunt, illae remis vada livida verrunt? ' 320
olli sic breviter fata est longaeva sacerdos :
' Anchisa generate, deum certissima proles,
Cocyti stagna alta vides Stygiamque paludem,
di cuius iurare timent et fallere numen.
haec omnis, quam cernis, inops inhumataque turba
    est : 325
portitor ille Charon ; hi, quos vehit unda, sepulti.
nec ripas datur horrendas et rauca fluenta
transportare prius quam sedibus ossa quierunt.
centum errant annos volitantque haec litora circum ;
tum demum admissi stagna exoptata revisunt.' 330
constitit Anchisa satus et vestigia pressit,
multa putans, sortemque animo miseratus iniquam.
cernit ibi, maestos et mortis honore carentis,
Leucaspim et Lyciae ductorem classis Oronten,
quos simul a Troia ventosa per aequora vectos 335
obruit Auster, aqua involvens navemque virosque.

Aeneas meets the shade of Palinurus, a murdered shipmate, who is refused passage over the Styx because his corpse is unburied. The Sibyl tells him that his murderers will be driven by portents from heaven to bury his body.

Ecce gubernator sese Palinurus agebat,
qui Libyco nuper cursu, dum sidera servat,
exciderat puppi mediis effusus in undis.
hunc ubi vix multa maestum cognovit in umbra,   340
sic prior adloquitur : ' quis te, Palinure, deorum
eripuit nobis, medioque sub aequore mersit?
dic age. namque mihi, fallax haud ante repertus,
hoc uno responso animum delusit Apollo,
qui fore te ponto incolumem finisque canebat   345
venturum Ausonios. en haec promissa fides est? '
ille autem : ' neque te Phoebi cortina fefellit,
dux Anchisiade, nec me deus aequore mersit.
namque gubernaclum, multa vi forte revulsum,
cui datus haerebam custos cursusque regebam,   350
praecipitans traxi mecum. maria aspera iuro
non ullum pro me tantum cepisse timorem,
quam tua ne, spoliata armis, excussa magistro,
deficeret tantis navis surgentibus undis.
tris Notus hibernas immensa per aequora noctes   355
vexit me violentus aqua ; vix lumine quarto
prospexi Italiam summa sublimis ab unda.
paulatim adnabam terrae : iam tuta tenebam,
ni gens crudelis madida cum veste gravatum
prensantemque uncis manibus capita aspera montis   360
ferro invasisset, praedamque ignara putasset.

nunc me fluctus habet, versantque in litore venti.
quod te per caeli iucundum lumen et auras,
per genitorem oro, per spes surgentis Iuli,
eripe me his, invicte, malis : aut tu mihi terram　　365
inice, namque potes, portusque require Velinos ·
aut tu, si qua via est, si quam tibi diva creatrix
ostendit—neque enim, credo, sine numine divum
flumina tanta paras Stygiamque innare paludem,—
da dextram misero, et tecum me tolle per undas,　　370
sedibus ut saltem placidis in morte quiescam.'
talia fatus erat coepit cum talia vates :
' unde haec, o Palinure, tibi tam dira cupido?
tu Stygias inhumatus aquas amnemque severum
Eumenidum aspicies, ripamve iniussus adibis?　　375
desine fata deum flecti sperare precando.
sed cape dicta memor, duri solacia casus :
nam tua finitimi, longe lateque per urbes
prodigiis acti caelestibus, ossa piabunt,
et statuent tumulum, et tumulo sollemnia mittent,
aeternumque locus Palinuri nomen habebit.'　　381
his dictis curae emotae, pulsusque parumper
corde dolor tristi : gaudet cognomine terra.

*Charon challenges Aeneas at his approach to the bank, but, on being
　　shown the Golden Bough, suffers him to embark and cross the
　　Styx.*

Ergo iter inceptum peragunt fluvioque propinquant.
navita quos iam inde ut Stygia prospexit ab unda　385
per tacitum nemus ire pedemque advertere ripae,

sic prior adgreditur dictis, atque increpat ultro :
' quisquis es, armatus qui nostra ad flumina tendis,
fare age, quid venias, iam istinc, et comprime gres-
    sum.
umbrarum hic locus est, somni noctisque soporae ; 390
corpora viva nefas Stygia vectare carina.
nec vero Alciden me sum laetatus euntem
accepisse lacu, nec Thesea Pirithoumque,
dis quamquam geniti atque invicti viribus essent.
Tartareum ille manu custodem in vincla petivit   395
ipsius a solio regis traxitque trementem :
hi dominam Ditis thalamo deducere adorti.'
quae contra breviter fata est Amphrysia vates :
' nullae hic insidiae tales : absiste moveri ;
nec vim tela ferunt : licet ingens ianitor antro   400
aeternum latrans exsanguis terreat umbras ;
casta licet patrui servet Proserpina limen.
Troius Aeneas, pietate insignis et armis,
ad genitorem imas Erebi descendit ad umbras.
si te nulla movet tantae pietatis imago,   405
at ramum hunc '—aperit ramum, qui veste latebat—
' agnoscas.' tumida ex ira tum corda residunt ;
nec plura his. ille admirans venerabile donum
fatalis virgae, longo post tempore visum,
caeruleam advertit puppim, ripaeque propinquat.   410
inde alias animas, quae per iuga longa sedebant,
deturbat, laxatque foros : simul accipit alveo
ingentem Aenean. gemuit sub pondere cumba
sutilis, et multam accepit rimosa paludem.

tandem trans fluvium incolumis vatemque virum-
que ~~~~~~~~~~~~~~~~~~~~ 415
informi limo glaucaque exponit in ulva.

*Aeneas drugs the monster Cerberus and so contrives to pass him.
He passes those regions of Hades inhabited by the spirits of
babes, of those unjustly put to death, and of those who laid
violent hands upon themselves.*

Cerberus haec ingens latratu regna trifauci
personat, adverso recubans immanis in antro.
cui vates, horrere videns iam colla colubris,
melle soporatam et medicatis frugibus offam   420
obicit. ille fame rabida tria guttura pandens
corripit obiectam, atque immania terga resolvit
fusus humi, totoque ingens extenditur antro.
occupat Aeneas aditum custode sepulto,
evaditque celer ripam inremeabilis undae.   425
continuo auditae voces, vagitus et ingens,
infantumque animae flentes, in limine primo
quos dulcis vitae exsortis et ab ubere raptos
abstulit atra dies et funere mersit acerbo.
hos iuxta falso damnati crimine mortis.   430
nec vero hae sine sorte datae, sine iudice, sedes:
quaesitor Minos urnam movet ; ille silentum
conciliumque vocat vitasque et crimina discit.
proxima deinde tenent maesti loca, qui sibi letum
insontes peperere manu, lucemque perosi   435
proiecere animas. quam vellent aethere in alto
nunc et pauperiem et duros perferre labores !

fas obstat, tristisque palus inamabilis undae
alligat, et novies Styx interfusa coercet.

*Aeneas comes to the Mourning Plains, the abode of unhappy
lovers ; among these he sees Dido, and seeks to justify his
desertion of her, but she removes herself from his presence.*

Nec procul hinc partem fusi monstrantur in om-
    nem   440
Lugentes Campi ; sic illos nomine dicunt.
hic, quos durus amor crudeli tabe peredit,
secreti celant calles et myrtea circum
silva tegit : curae non ipsa in morte relinquunt.
his Phaedram Procrimque locis, maestamque Eri-
    phylen,   445
crudelis nati monstrantem vulnera, cernit,
Euadnenque, et Pasiphaen ; his Laodamia
it comes, et iuvenis quondam, nunc femina, Caeneus,
rursus et in veterem fato revoluta figuram.
inter quas Phoenissa recens a vulnere Dido   450
errabat silva in magna : quam Troius heros,
ut primum iuxta stetit agnovitque per umbras
obscuram, qualem primo qui surgere mense
aut videt aut vidisse putat per nubila lunam,
demisit lacrimas, dulcique adfatus amore est :   455
' infelix Dido, verus mihi nuntius ergo
venerat exstinctam, ferroque extrema secutam?
funeris heu tibi causa fui? per sidera iuro,
per superos, et si qua fides tellure sub ima est,
invitus, regina, tuo de litore cessi.   460

sed me iussa deum, quae nunc has ire per umbras,
per loca senta situ cogunt noctemque profundam,
imperiis egere suis ; nec credere quivi
hunc tantum tibi me discessu ferre dolorem.
siste gradum, teque aspectu ne subtrahe nostro.   465
quem fugis? extremum fato quod te adloquor hoc est.'
talibus Aeneas ardentem et torva tuentem
lenibat dictis animum, lacrimasque ciebat.
illa solo fixos oculos aversa tenebat ;
nec magis incepto vultum sermone movetur,   470
quam si dura silex aut stet Marpesia cautes.
tandem corripuit sese, atque inimica refugit
in nemus umbriferum, coniunx ubi pristinus illi
respondet curis, aequatque Sychaeus amorem.
nec minus Aeneas, casu concussus iniquo,   475
prosequitur lacrimis longe, et miseratur euntem.

*Aeneas comes to that quarter of Hades in which dwell the ghosts of
  famous warriors ; and there the shades of his enemies, the
  Greeks, shrink from him in terror.*

Inde datum molitur iter. iamque arva tenebant
ultima, quae bello clari secreta frequentant.
hic illi occurrit Tydeus, hic inclutus armis
Parthenopaeus et Adrasti pallentis imago ;   480
hic multum fleti ad superos belloque caduci
Dardanidae, quos ille omnis longo ordine cernens
ingemuit, Glaucumque, Medontaque, Thersilochumque,
tres Antenoridas, Cererique sacrum Polyboeten,
Idaeumque, etiam currus, etiam arma tenentem.   485

circumstant animae dextra laevaque frequentes.
nec vidisse semel satis est : iuvat usque morari
et conferre gradum et veniendi discere causas.
at Danaum proceres Agamemnoniaeque phalanges
ut videre virum fulgentiaque arma per umbras,   490
ingenti trepidare metu : pars vertere terga,
ceu quondam petiere rates ; pars tollere vocem
exiguam : inceptus clamor frustratur hiantis.

*Among the warriors Aeneas sees the Trojan Deiphobus, hideously
   mutilated, and is told by him of his treacherous betrayal by
   Helen.*

Atque hic Priamiden laniatum corpore toto
Deiphobum vidit, lacerum crudeliter ora,   495
ora manusque ambas, populataque tempora raptis
auribus, et truncas inhonesto vulnere naris.
vix adeo agnovit pavitantem et dira tegentem
supplicia, et notis compellat vocibus ultro :
' Deiphobe armipotens, genus alto a sanguine Teucri,   500
quis tam crudelis optavit sumere poenas?
cui tantum de te licuit? mihi fama suprema
nocte tulit fessum vasta te caede Pelasgum
procubuisse super confusae stragis acervum.
tunc egomet tumulum Rhoeteo litore inanem   505
constitui, et magna manis ter voce vocavi.
nomen et arma locum servant ; te, amice, nequivi
conspicere et patria decedens ponere terra.'
ad quae Priamides : ' nihil o tibi, amice relictum ;

omnia Deiphobo solvisti et funeris umbris.   510
sed me fata mea et scelus exitiale Lacaenae
his mersere malis : illa haec monimenta reliquit.
namque ut supremam falsa inter gaudia noctem
egerimus, nosti ; et nimium meminisse necesse est.
cum fatalis equus saltu super ardua venit   515
Pergama, et armatum peditem gravis attulit alvo :
illa, chorum simulans, euantis orgia circum
ducebat Phrygias ; flammam media ipsa tenebat
ingentem, et summa Danaos ex arce vocabat.
tum me confectum curis somnoque gravatum   520
infelix habuit thalamus, pressitque iacentem
dulcis et alta quies placidaeque simillima morti.
egregia interea coniunx arma omnia tectis
amovet, et fidum capiti subduxerat ensem :
intra tecta vocat Menelaum, et limina pandit ;   525
scilicet id magnum sperans fore munus amanti,
et famam exstingui veterum sic posse malorum.
quid moror? inrumpunt thalamo ; comes additus una
hortator scelerum Aeolides. di, talia Grais
instaurate, pio si poenas ore reposco.   530
sed te qui vivum casus, age fare vicissim,
attulerint. pelagine venis erroribus actus,
an monitu divum? an quae te fortuna fatigat,
ut tristis sine sole domos, loca turbida, adires? '
hac vice sermonum roseis Aurora quadrigis   535
iam medium aetherio cursu traiecerat axem ;
et fors omne datum traherent per talia tempus ;
sed comes admonuit, breviterque adfata Sibylla est ;

'nox ruit, Aenea ; nos flendo ducimus horas.
hic locus est, partis ubi se via findit in ambas :   540
dextera quae Ditis magni sub moenia tendit,
hac iter Elysium nobis ; at laeva malorum
exercet poenas, et ad impia Tartara mittit.'
Deiphobus contra : ' ne saevi, magna sacerdos ;
discedam, explebo numerum, reddarque tenebris.   545
i decus, i, nostrum ; melioribus utere fatis.'
tantum effatus, et in verbo vestigia torsit.

*Aeneas sees a frowning fortress, the place where the wicked are
tried and punished. He is told by the Sibyl of some of the
victims of this punishment, and of their crimes.*

Respicit Aeneas subito, et sub rupe sinistra
moenia lata videt, triplici circumdata muro ;
quae rapidus flammis ambit torrentibus amnis   550
Tartareus Phlegethon, torquetque sonantia saxa.
porta adversa ingens, solidoque adamante columnae,
vis ut nulla virum, non ipsi exscindere bello
caelicolae valeant ; stat ferrea turris ad auras,
Tisiphoneque sedens, palla succincta cruenta,   555
vestibulum exsomnis servat noctesque diesque.
hinc exaudiri gemitus, et saeva sonare
verbera : tum stridor ferri, tractaeque catenae.
constitit Aeneas strepitumque exterritus hausit :
' quae scelerum facies? o virgo, effare ; quibusve   560
urgentur poenis? quis tantus clangor ad auris? '
tum vates sic orsa loqui : ' dux inclute Teucrum,
nulli fas casto sceleratum insistere limen ;

ΖΕΥΣ

ZEUS HURLING A WINGED THUNDERBOLT AT A GIANT.
(Sixth-Century vase.)

sed me cum lucis Hecate praefecit Avernis,
ipsa deum poenas docuit, perque omnia duxit.   565
Gnosius haec Rhadamanthus habet durissima regna,
castigatque auditque dolos, subigitque fateri,
quae quis apud superos, furto laetatus inani,
distulit in seram commissa piacula mortem.
continuo sontis ultrix accincta flagello   570
Tisiphone quatit insultans, torvosque sinistra
intentans anguis vocat agmina saeva sororum.

FURY.
She is dressed as for the chase, and carries a torch and a serpent.
(From a vase of the Fourth Century B.C.)

tum demum horrisono stridentes cardine sacrae
panduntur portae. cernis custodia qualis
vestibulo sedeat, facies quae limina servet?   575
quinquaginta atris immanis hiatibus Hydra
saevior intus habet sedem. tum Tartarus ipse
bis patet in praeceps tantum tenditque sub umbras,

quantus ad aetherium caeli suspectus Olympum.
hic genus antiquum Terrae, Titania pubes,   580
fulmine deiecti, fundo volvuntur in imo.
hic et Aloidas geminos, immania vidi
corpora, qui manibus magnum rescindere caelum
adgressi, superisque Iovem detrudere regnis.
vidi et crudelis dantem Salmonea poenas,   585
dum flammam Iovis et sonitus imitatur Olympi.
quattuor hic invectus equis et lampada quassans
per Graium populos mediaeque per Elidis urbem
ibat ovans, divumque sibi poscebat honorem,
demens, qui nimbos et non imitabile fulmen   590
aere et cornipedum pulsu simularet equorum.
at pater omnipotens densa inter nubila telum
contorsit, non ille faces, nec fumea taedis
lumina, praecipitemque immani turbine adegit.   594
nec non et Tityon, Terrae omniparentis alumnum,
cernere erat, per tota novem cui iugera corpus
porrigitur ; rostroque immanis vultur obunco
immortale iecur tondens fecundaque poenis
viscera rimaturque epulis habitatque sub alto
pectore, nec fibris requies datur ulla renatis.   600
quid memorem Lapithas, Ixiona Pirithoumque?
quo super atra silex iam iam lapsura cadentique
imminet adsimilis : lucent genialibus altis
aurea fulcra toris, epulaeque ante ora paratae
regifico luxu ; Furiarum maxima iuxta   605
accubat, et manibus prohibet contingere mensas,
exsurgitque facem attollens, atque intonat ore.

hic, quibus invisi fratres, dum vita manebat,
pulsatusve parens, aut fraus innexa clienti,
aut qui divitiis soli incubuere repertis,   **610**

THESEUS AND PIRITHOUS IN HADES.

The illustration, from a vase painting, shows Theseus and
Pirithous (the naked figures) after the failure of their
attempt to carry off Proserpina. One of the two is being
bound by a Fury, while Proserpina stands in the back-
ground and Pluto is seated on the left.

nec partem posuere suis, quae maxima turba est,
quique ob adulterium caesi, quique arma secuti
impia, nec veriti dominorum fallere dextras,
inclusi poenam exspectant. ne quaere doceri

quam poenam, aut quae forma viros fortunave mer-
    sit.   615
saxum ingens volvunt alii, radiisve rotarum
districti pendent : sedet aeternumque sedebit
infelix Theseus ; Phlegyasque miserrimus omnis
admonet, et magna testatur voce per umbras :
' discite iustitiam moniti et non temnere divos.'   620
vendidit hic auro patriam, dominumque potentem
imposuit, fixit leges pretio atque refixit :
hic thalamum invasit natae vetitosque hymenaeos :
ausi omnes immane nefas, ausoque potiti.
non, mihi si linguae centum sint oraque centum, 625
ferrea vox, omnis scelerum comprendere formas,
omnia poenarum percurrere nomina possim.'

*Aeneas is brought by the Sibyl to a gateway, where he leaves the
Golden Bough. Then they enter the Abode of the Blest, where
they seek Anchises, the father of Aeneas.*

  Haec ubi dicta dedit Phoebi longaeva sacerdos :
' sed iam age, carpe viam, et susceptum perfice munus.
acceleremus,' ait. ' Cyclopum educta caminis   630
moenia conspicio, atque adverso fornice portas,
haec ubi nos praecepta iubent deponere dona.'
dixerat, et pariter gressi per opaca viarum
corripiunt spatium medium, foribusque propinquant.
occupat Aeneas aditum, corpusque recenti   635
spargit aqua, ramumque adverso in limine figit.
  his demum exactis, perfecto munere divae,
devenere locos laetos, et amoena virecta

fortunatorum nemorum, sedesque beatas.
largior hic campos aether et lumine vestit   640
purpureo, solemque suum, sua sidera norunt.
pars in gramineis exercent membra palaestris,
contendunt ludo et fulva luctantur harena ;
pars pedibus plaudunt choreas et carmina dicunt.
nec non Threicius longa cum veste sacerdos   645

From a vase painting of the Fifth Century, B.C.   The
player holds in his left hand the lyre with its seven strings
—'septem discrimina vocum'—and in the right the
plectrum or ' quill ' (called pecten in l. 647).

obloquitur numeris septem discrimina vocum,
iamque eadem digitis, iam pectine pulsat eburno.
hic genus antiquum Teucri, pulcherrima proles,
magnanimi heroes, nati melioribus annis,
Ilusque Assaracusque et Troiae Dardanus auctor.   650
arma procul currusque virum miratur inanis.
stant terra defixae hastae, passimque soluti

per campum pascuntur equi. quae gratia currum
armorumque fuit vivis, quae cura nitentis
pascere equos, eadem sequitur tellure repostos.   655
conspicit, ecce, alios dextra laevaque per herbam
vescentis laetumque choro paeana canentis
inter odoratum lauri nemus, unde superne
plurimus Eridani per silvam volvitur amnis.
hic manus ob patriam pugnando vulnera passi,   660
quique sacerdotes casti, dum vita manebat,
quique pii vates et Phoebo digna locuti,
inventas aut qui vitam excoluere per artis,
quique sui memores alios fecere merendo.
omnibus his nivea cinguntur tempora vitta.   665
quos circumfusos sic est adfata Sibylla,
Musaeum ante omnis : medium nam plurima turba
hunc habet, atque umeris exstantem suspicit altis :
' dicite, felices animae, tuque, optime vates :
quae regio Anchisen, quis habet locus? illius ergo   670
venimus, et magnos Erebi tranavimus amnis.'
atque huic responsum paucis ita reddidit heros :
' nulli certa domus ; lucis habitamus opacis,
riparumque toros et prata recentia rivis
incolimus. sed vos, si fert ita corde voluntas,   675
hoc superate iugum ; et facili iam tramite sistam.
dixit, et ante tulit gressum, camposque nitentis
desuper ostentat ; dehinc summa cacumina linquunt.

Anchises is found in a green valley, meditating as he surveys the
spirits of heroes yet unborn. Father and son exchange
greetings.

At pater Anchises penitus convalle virenti
inclusas animas superumque ad lumen ituras   680
lustrabat studio recolens, omnemque suorum
forte recensebat numerum carosque nepotes,
fataque fortunasque virum moresque manusque.
isque ubi tendentem adversum per gramina vidit
Aenean, alacris palmas utrasque tetendit,   685
effusaeque genis lacrimae, et vox excidit ore :
' venisti tandem, tuaque exspectata parenti
vicit iter durum pietas? datur ora tueri,
nate, tua, et notas audire et reddere voces?
sic equidem ducebam animo rebarque futurum   690
tempora dinumerans, nec me mea cura fefellit.
quas ego te terras et quanta per aequora vectum
accipio ! quantis iactatum, nate, periclis !
quam metui, ne quid Libyae tibi regna nocerent ! '
ille autem : ' tua me, genitor, tua tristis imago,   695
saepius occurrens, haec limina tendere adegit.
stant sale Tyrrheno classes. da iungere dextram,
da, genitor ; teque amplexu ne subtrahe nostro.'
sic memorans largo fletu simul ora rigabat.
ter conatus ibi collo dare bracchia circum :   700
ter frustra comprensa manus effugit imago,
par levibus ventis volucrique simillima somno.

Aeneas learns from Anchises that a great host of spirits before him are awaiting re-birth.

Interea videt Aeneas in valle reducta
seclusum nemus et virgulta sonantia silvae,   704
Lethaeumque domos placidas qui praenatat amnem.
hunc circum innumerae gentes populique volabant ;
ac velut in pratis ubi apes aestate serena
floribus insidunt variis, et candida circum
lilia funduntur ; strepit omnis murmure campus.
horrescit visu subito causasque requirit   710
inscius Aeneas, quae sint ea flumina porro,
quive viri tanto complerint agmine ripas.
tum pater Anchises : ' animae, quibus altera fato
corpora debentur, Lethaei ad fluminis undam
securos latices et longa oblivia potant.   715
has equidem memorare tibi atque ostendere coram
iampridem hanc prolem cupio enumerare meorum,
quo magis Italia mecum laetere reperta.'
' o pater, anne aliquas ad caelum hinc ire putandum est
sublimis animas, iterumque in tarda reverti   720
corpora? quae lucis miseris tam dira cupido? '
' dicam equidem, nec te suspensum, nate, tenebo,'
suscipit Anchises, atque ordine singula pandit.

*Anchises explains how the divine in men is ever at war with their
earthy bodies ; how spirits are purified in Hades, and
oblivious of former life, return again to the world of the living.*

' Principio caelum ac terram camposque liquentis
lucentemque globum lunae Titaniaque astra   725

spiritus intus alit : totamque infusa per artus
mens agitat molem, et magno se corpore miscet.
inde hominum pecudumque genus vitaeque volantum
et quae marmoreo fert monstra sub aequore pontus.
igneus est ollis vigor et caelestis origo   730
seminibus, quantum non noxia corpora tardant
terrenique hebetant artus moribundaque membra.
hinc metuunt cupiuntque, dolent gaudentque, neque
        auras
dispiciunt clausae tenebris et carcere caeco.
quin et supremo cum lumine vita reliquit,   735
non tamen omne malum miseris nec funditus omnes
corporeae excedunt pestes, penitusque necesse est
multa diu concreta modis inolescere miris.
ergo exercentur poenis, veterumque malorum
supplicia expendunt. aliae panduntur inanes   740
suspensae ad ventos ; aliis sub gurgite vasto
infectum eluitur scelus, aut exuritur igni.
quisque suos patimur manis ; exinde per amplum
mittimur Elysium, et pauci laeta arva tenemus,
donec longa dies, perfecto temporis orbe,   745
concretam exemit labem, purumque reliquit
aetherium sensum, atque aurai simplicis ignem.
has omnis, ubi mille rotam volvere per annos,
Lethaeum ad fluvium deus evocat agmine magno :
scilicet immemores supera ut convexa revisant   750
rursus et incipiant in corpora velle reverti.'

*Anchises shows Aeneas the spirits of famous Romans yet unborn,
and declares that the genius of the Roman people will express
itself in the arts of government.*

Dixerat Anchises : natumque unaque Sibyllam
conventus trahit in medios, turbamque sonantem :
et tumulum capit, unde omnis longo ordine posset
adversos legere, et venientum discere vultus.   755
' nunc age, Dardaniam prolem quae deinde sequatur
gloria, qui maneant Itala de gente nepotes,
inlustris animas nostrumque in nomen ituras,
expediam dictis, et te tua fata docebo.
ille, vides, pura iuvenis qui nititur hasta,   760
proxima sorte tenet lucis loca, primus ad auras
aetherias Italo commixtus sanguine surget,
Silvius, Albanum nomen, tua postuma proles ;
quem tibi longaevo serum Lavinia coniunx
educet silvis regem regumque parentem ;   765
unde genus Longa nostrum dominabitur Alba.
proximus ille Procas, Troianae gloria gentis,
et Capys, et Numitor, et qui te nomine reddet
Silvius Aeneas, pariter pietate vel armis
egregius, si unquam regnandam acceperit Albam.   770
qui iuvenes ! quantas ostentant, aspice, viris,
atque umbrata gerunt civili tempora quercu !
hi tibi Nomentum, et Gabios, urbemque Fidenam,
hi Collatinas imponent montibus arces,
Pometios, Castrumque Inui, Bolamque, Coramque.   775
haec tum nomina erunt, nunc sunt sine nomine terrae.
quin et avo comitem sese Mavortius addet

Romulus, Assaraci quem sanguinis Ilia mater
educet. viden ut geminae stant vertice cristae,
et pater ipse suo superum iam signat honore?   780
en huius, nate, auspiciis illa incluta Roma
imperium terris, animos aequabit Olympo,

Roman founded
753 BC

'BERECYNTIA MATER . . . TURRITA.'
This statue of Cybele, goddess of earth and its cities,
shows her wearing the crown, in the likeness of a city's
walls and towers, with which she is commonly represented.

septemque una sibi muro circumdabit arces,
felix prole virum : qualis Berecyntia mater
invehitur curru Phrygias turrita per urbes,   785
laeta deum partu, centum complexa nepotes,
omnis caelicolas, omnis supera alta tenentis.

huc geminas nunc flecte acies, hanc aspice gentem
Romanosque tuos. hic Caesar, et omnis Iuli
progenies, magnum caeli ventura sub axem.   790
hic vir, hic est, tibi quem promitti saepius audis,

' HIC VIR, HIC EST, TIBI QUEM PROMITTI SAEPIUS AUDIS,
AUGUSTUS CAESAR, DIVI GENUS.'

From a gold coin struck in Gaul. The reverse shows
the corona civica, a garland of oak-leaves awarded to one
who had saved the life of a fellow-citizen and worn by
Augustus as having delivered the Romans from civil war.
The inscription means : ' For having saved his fellow-
citizens.'

Augustus Caesar, Divi genus, aurea condet
saecula qui rursus Latio, regnata per arva
Saturno quondam ; super et Garamantas et Indos
proferet imperium ; iacet extra sidera tellus,   795
extra anni solisque vias, ubi caelifer Atlas
axem umero torquet stellis ardentibus aptum.
huius in adventum iam nunc et Caspia regna
responsis horrent divum et Maeotia tellus,
et septemgemini turbant trepida ostia Nili.   800
nec vero Alcides tantum telluris obivit,
fixerit aeripedem cervam licet, aut Erymanthi
pacarit nemora, et Lernam tremefecerit arcu :
nec, qui pampineis victor iuga flectit habenis,

Liber, agens celso Nysae de vertice tigris.   805
et dubitamus adhuc virtutem extendere factis?
aut metus Ausonia prohibet consistere terra?
quis procul ille autem ramis insignis olivae
sacra ferens? nosco crinis incanaque menta
regis Romani, primam qui legibus urbem   810
fundabit, Curibus parvis et paupere terra
missus in imperium magnum. cui deinde subibit,
otia qui rumpet patriae residesque movebit
Tullus in arma viros et iam desueta triumphis
agmina. quem iuxta sequitur iactantior Ancus,   815
nunc quoque iam nimium gaudens popularibus auris.
vis et Tarquinios reges animamque superbam
ultoris Bruti fascisque videre receptos?
consulis imperium hic primus saevasque securis
accipiet, natosque pater, nova bella moventis,   820
ad poenam pulchra pro libertate vocabit,
infelix ! utcumque ferent ea facta minores :
vincet amor patriae laudumque immensa cupido.
quin Decios Drusosque procul, saevumque securi
aspice Torquatum, et referentem signa Camillum.   825
illae autem, paribus quas fulgere cernis in armis,
concordes animae nunc, et dum nocte premuntur,
heu quantum inter se bellum, si lumina vitae
attigerint, quantas acies stragemque ciebunt,
aggeribus socer Alpinis atque arce Monoeci   830
descendens, gener adversis instructus Eois !
ne, pueri, ne tanta animis adsuescite bella,
neu patriae validas in viscera vertite viris :

tuque prior, tu parce, genus qui ducis Olympo ;
proice tela manu, sanguis meus !   835
ille triumphata Capitolia ad alta Corintho
victor aget currum, caesis insignis Achivis.
eruet ille Argos Agamemnoniasque Mycenas,
ipsumque Aeaciden, genus armipotentis Achilli,
ultus avos Troiae, templa et temerata Minervae.   840
quis te, magne Cato, tacitum, aut te, Cosse, relinquat?
quis Gracchi genus, aut geminos, duo fulmina belli,
Scipiadas, cladem Libyae, parvoque potentem
Fabricium, vel te sulco, Serrane, serentem?
quo fessum rapitis, Fabii? tu Maximus ille es,   845
unus qui nobis cunctando restituis rem.
excudent alii spirantia mollius aera,
(credo equidem), vivos ducent de marmore vultus,
orabunt causas melius, caelique meatus
describent radio, et surgentia sidera dicent :   850
tu regere imperio populos, Romane, memento,—
hae tibi erunt artes,—pacisque imponere morem,
parcere subiectis, et debellare superbos.'

*Last among the pageant of Romans yet unborn is Marcellus, a
youth of great promise, doomed to an untimely death. Anchises, having thus fired Aeneas with the greatness of his
destiny, and warned him of trials that lie ahead, guides him
and the Sibyl back to the world above.*

Sic pater Anchises, atque haec mirantibus addit :
aspice, ut insignis spoliis Marcellus opimis   855
ingreditur, victorque viros supereminet omnis !

hic rem Romanam, magno turbante tumultu,
sistet, eques sternet Poenos Gallumque rebellem,
tertiaque arma patri suspendet capta Quirino.'
atque hic Aeneas, una namque ire videbat   860
egregium forma iuvenem et fulgentibus armis,
sed frons laeta parum, et deiecto lumina vultu :
' quis, pater, ille, virum qui sic comitatur euntem?
filius, anne aliquis magna de stirpe nepotum?
qui strepitus circa comitum ! quantum instar in
    ipso !   865
sed nox atra caput tristi circumvolat umbra.'
tum pater Anchises, lacrimis ingressus obortis :
' o nate, ingentem luctum ne quaere tuorum.
ostendent terris hunc tantum fata, neque ultra
esse sinent. nimium vobis Romana propago   870
visa potens, superi, propria haec si dona fuissent.
quantos ille virum magnam Mavortis ad urbem
Campus aget gemitus ! vel quae, Tiberine, videbis
funera, cum tumulum praeterlabere recentem !
nec puer Iliaca quisquam de gente Latinos   875
in tantum spe tollet avos ; nec Romula quondam
ullo se tantum tellus iactabit alumno.
heu pietas, heu prisca fides, invictaque bello
dextera ! non illi se quisquam impune tulisset
obvius armato, seu cum pedes iret in hostem,   880
seu spumantis equi foderet calcaribus armos.
heu, miserande puer, si qua fata aspera rumpas !
tu Marcellus eris. manibus date lilia plenis
purpureos spargam flores, animamque nepotis

his saltem accumulem donis, et fungar inani 885
munere.' sic tota passim regione vagantur
aëris in campis latis, atque omnia lustrant.
quae postquam Anchises natum per singula duxit,
incenditque animum famae venientis amore,
exim bella viro memorat, quae deinde gerenda, 890
Laurentisque docet populos urbemque Latini,
et quo quemque modo fugiatque feratque laborem.
  sunt geminae Somni portae, quarum altera fertur
cornea, qua veris facilis datur exitus umbris,
altera candenti perfecta nitens elephanto, 895
sed falsa ad caelum mittunt insomnia manes.
his ibi tum natum Anchises unaque Sibyllam
prosequitur dictis, portaque emittit eburna :
ille viam secat ad navis, sociosque revisit ;
tum se ad Caietae recto fert litore portum. 900
ancora de prora iacitur ; stant litore puppes.

NOTES

Line 1. **fatur lacrimans.** The subject is Aeneas. He is weeping because he has just lost his pilot, Palinurus, who has fallen asleep and been swept overboard. His fate is further described in this book, when Aeneas meets his shade in the Underworld.

immittit, ' gives '.

l. 2. **tandem,** ' at last ', i.e. after his seven years' wanderings over the Mediterranean.

Euboicis . . . oris. Cumae, situated on a promontory in the bay of Naples, possesses ' Euboean shores ', because the original settlers in this Greek colony had come from the island of Euboea. In translating, make **Euboicis** agree with **Cumarum.**

Finally note that in poetry, the dative is often used to denote *place whither.* Cf. **pelago** in the next line.

l. 3. **obvertunt.** The Trojan sailors turned their ships round, prows seaward, dropped anchor from the prow, made them fast by backing water, and then attached their ship to the shore by stern cables. Such a manoeuvre made it possible to leave quickly, should the need arise.

l. 4. **ancora,** nominative, as can be seen if the line is scanned.

navis. Note carefully this form of the acc. pl. of 3rd decl. I-stems. Cf. **bidentis,** l. 39, etc.

litora, plural for singular.

l. 5. **puppes. pupp**is, literally ' poop ', ' stern ', is very often used in poetry for ' ship ', just as in English we have such expressions as ' a fleet of twenty sail '. This figure of speech, the use of a word denoting part of a thing to express the thing itself, is called *synecdoche.*

ardens, ' in hot haste ' ; *lit.,* ' burning ', ' glowing '.

l. 6. **Hesperium. Hesperius,**[1] ' western ' is often used in Latin poetry for ' Italian '. For the Trojans, sailing from Asia Minor, Italy, their promised land, was, of course, in the west.

[1] A Greek word. To the Greeks Italy was ' the land of the evening ', i.e. of the setting sun.

41

ll. 6–7, pars . . . pars, ' some . . . others '.

l. 6. semina flammae, ' seeds of flame ' refer to the sparks which were supposed to be hidden in the flint until struck out of it.

l. 8. tecta . . . silvas are in apposition. Translate silvas first, then take densa ferarum tecta next. Rapit, either ' scour ' for game, or ' pillage ' for firewood.

l. 9. pius Aeneas. Aeneas is often given the epithet pius, ' good ' or ' dutiful ', by Vergil because of his loyalty to his father Anchises and of his devotion to the mission which the gods had given him, to found a new and greater Troy in Western Lands.

ll. 9–11. at . . . petit. Order for translation, at pius Aeneas petit arces quibus . . . praesidet, -que immane antrum procul, secreta (in apposition with antrum) horrendae Sibyllae.

l. 9. altus Apollo praesidet, ' Apollo sits enthroned '. The god is identified with his temple.

Cumae was on high ground, crowned by two peaks. On one of these was the temple of Apollo. The town has been recently excavated.

l. 10. procul, ' hard by '.

l. 11. mentem animumque, ' insight and inspiration '.

l. 12. Delius vates, ' the Delian seer ' is Apollo. He is called Delian because Delos, a small island in the Aegean, was, according to myth, his birthplace, and in historic times contained an important oracle of the god.

One of Apollo's most important ' spheres of influence ' was ' prophecy '.

l. 13. Triviae lucos. The temple of Apollo (aurea tecta in this line) is surrounded by a grove sacred to Trivia.

Trivia and Hecate are often used in Latin poetry for Diana, the sister of Apollo, especially in her rôle as the goddess of incantations and of the Underworld. In this rôle Diana was often worshipped at cross-roads.[1]

---

[1] Trivium = cross-road.

l. 14. **Daedalus** was, according to Greek mythology, an Athenian architect and sculptor of great skill[1] who murdered his nephew in a fit of jealousy (he had discovered the use of the saw, the compass, and potter's wheel) and, being condemned to death, fled to Crete where Minos reigned with his wife Pasiphae.

Daedalus is described in this line as fleeing from the realm of Minos. He had been imprisoned by Minos in the labyrinth which he had made for the Minotaur, and, to escape, he constructed wings of feathers for himself and his son Icarus, and flew first northwards from Crete towards Samos, where Icarus, forgetting that his wings were fastened on with wax, flew too near the sun, with the result that his wings fell into the sea and he was drowned. Daedalus continued his journey safely and landed first at Cumae in Italy.

ut fama est, ' as the story goes, (*lit.*, is) '. Note that Vergil assumes that his readers are very familiar with the story of Daedalus. In this case, he introduces him mainly to give an account of the wonderful carvings he had wrought on the double gates which led into the temple of Apollo. The subjects of these carvings were all taken from the craftsman's life and experiences in Crete.

For a good account of the Daedalus and Icarus story, see Ovid, Metamorphoses VIII, ll. 183–235.

l. 16. **gelidas ad Arctos,** ' to the icy Bears ' = ' to the icy North '. **Arctos** is the double constellation, the Great and the Lesser Bear.

l. 17. **Chalcidica . . . arce,** ' in the Chalcidian summit ', i.e. at Cumae. Chalcis was a town in Euboea, whence came many of the original settlers of Cumae. See the note on l. 2.

levis, ' lightly '. Latin often uses adjectives where English prefers adverbs.

l. 19. **remigium alarum,** ' the oarage of his wings '. This dedication had a double significance, as a thanksgiving for a safe journey, and as an indication that Daedalus would no longer use his wings. In the ancient world, it was usual on

---

[1] The name Daedalus = ' cunning workman '.

retirement to dedicate the tools or instruments of one's calling or profession to the god or goddess of that calling.

posuit, ' built '.

l. 20. Androgeo, genitive, Greek form, ' of Androgeos '.

l. 21. **Cecropidae,** ' the children of Cecrops ' = ' the Athenians ', for Cecrops was the legendary founder of Athens.

According to the legend, the Athenians had murdered Androgeos, a son of Minos, and after being defeated by the Cretan king, were condemned to pay him a yearly tribute of seven youths and seven maidens. The victims were chosen by lot and offered as a sacrifice to the monstrous Minotaur, who lived in the labyrinth constructed by Daedalus.

miserum, ' alas ! ' the word is parenthetical, i.e. it is outside the grammatical structure of the sentence.

l. 23. **contra,** adverb, ' opposite ', i.e. on the opposite half of the folding doors.

elata mari, ' rising from the sea ' ; **elata** from **effero.**

Gnosia tellus, ' the Cretan land ', since Gnosus or Gnossus was the capital city of Minos, king of Crete. This is a good example of those allusive or literary epithets in which Latin poetry abounds. Cf. l. 17, and l. 2.

ll. 24–26. **hic crudelis amor,** etc. Because she had aroused the anger of Venus, Pasiphae, the wife of Minos, was inspired with ' a cruel passion for a bull '. She was assisted by Daedalus to gratify her passion (**furto** l. 24), and the result of her union with the animal was the monster, half-man, half-bull, the Minotaur which Minos had enclosed in the famous labyrinth, specially constructed for the purpose by Daedalus.

l. 24. **suppostaque ... Pasiphae,** ' and Pasiphae mated by stealth '.

l. 25. **mixtumque ... Minotaurus,** *lit.,* ' the mongrel breed. and the two-shaped offspring, the Minotaur '.

l. 26. **monimenta,** in apposition with **Minotaurus, proles** and **genus.**

l. 27. **hic,** adverb ' here '. **labor ille domus,** ' that toil of the

house ', = ' the house of toil ', i.e. the labyrinth constructed by
Daedalus in the shape of a maze.

l. 28. **sed enim,** ' but indeed '. **reginae,** ' of the princess ',
i.e. of Ariadne, daughter of Minos, who fell in love with Theseus,
the Athenian prince who had voluntarily offered to accompany
the youths and maidens sent as tribute from Athens to Crete.
On the advice of Daedalus, she gave Theseus a sword, and a ball
of thread by which he could retrace his steps through the
labyrinth.

miseratus, *lit.*, ' having pitied ', but translate by present
participle, ' pitying '. Perfect participles of deponent verbs
are often used with the meaning of the present.

l. 29. **dolos tecti ambagesque,** ' the deception and windings
of the palace ', =' the deceptive windings of the palace '.

Note the hendiadys,[1] the expression where two words co-
ordinated (here **dolos, ambages**) are used instead of an expression where one qualifies the other grammatically (here ' deceptive ' qualifies ' windings ').

Hendiadys is common in Greek and Latin, not so in English.

l. 30. **vestigia,** i.e. of Theseus.

tu. Note the dramatic effect of the change to direct address.

l. 31. **partem ... haberes.** With **sineret dolor,** supply **si.**
' You too, O Icarus, would have ... did grief permit ',—a good
example of a conditional clause, unreal in present time, imperfect subjunctive in protasis and apodosis.

l. 32. **conatus erat.** The subject is Daedalus ; **casus,** accusative plural, and plural for singular.

l. 33. **cecidere** =**ceciderunt.** **-ere** for **-erunt** is common in
poetry as the ending of the 3rd plural perfect indicative active.

quin protinus, ' nay more '. **omnia ;** scan as two syllables.

l. 34. **praemissus Achates.** Achates, the faithful comrade of
Aeneas, had been sent on ahead to announce the approach of
the Trojan hero to the prophetess. He has now returned with
her.

[1] Greek =' one thing by means of two '.

l. 35. **adforet** = **adesset.** Note once again the conditional clause, unreal in present time, imperfect subjunctive, and compare l. 31. ' And they would be scanning . . . had not Achates appeared.'

una, adverb, ' together (with him) '.

l. 36. **Deiphobe Glauci,** ' Deiphobe, (daughter) of Glaucus '.

l. 37. **non ista** . . . **spectacula,** ' not sights such as these '. **iste** is the demonstrative of the 2nd person : here it might almost be rendered ' not sights such as you are looking at '.

l. 38. **grege de intacto,** ' from the unbroken herd ', i.e. from a herd which has not been used for work.

l. 39. **praestiterit,** perfect subjunctive, ' it were better '. This kind of subjunctive is known as *potential* and it may be explained as the apodosis of a conditional clause for which a protasis can easily be supplied, (here, ' if you wish to pursue your task '). On the other hand, the present and perfect subjunctives are often used to express a speaker's opinion merely as an opinion.

l. 39. **lectas de more,** ' duly chosen '. **de more,** *lit.,* ' according to custom ', i.e. with proper observance of religious ceremonial.

l. 40. **Aenean,** accusative (a Greek form) of **Aeneas.**

ll. 40–41. **nec sacra** . . . **viri,** ' the heroes do not delay (to obey) her sacred commands '.

l. 41. **Teucros,** ' Trojans '. Teucer was a legendary king of Troy.

l. 42. **excisum,** etc., order for translation, **ingens latus Euboicae rupis (est) excisum in antrum.**

For **Euboicae rupis,** see the note on l. 2.

It seems that behind or just below the temple of Apollo lay the cave or grotto of the Sibyl, hewn out of the face of the rock. The volcanic hills of Cumae are perforated with many grottos.

ll. 43–44. **quo lati,** etc., ' whither lead a 100 wide gateways, a

100 mouths, whence rush as many voices, the answers of the Sibyl '.

In the oracle of Apollo, the supplicant communicates his petition and receives the god's reply from the Sibyl who is within the cave, through the perforations in the volcanic rock.

l. 45. **ventum erat,** ' they had come '. Intransitive verbs in Latin are often used impersonally in the passive. Cf. **pugnatum est,** ' there was fighting ', ' men, *or* they, fought '.

limen, ' threshold (of the cave) ', **cum,** ' when ', **poscere fata tempus (est),** ' (it is) time to ask the oracles '.

ll. 46–47. **cui talia fanti,** ' to her speaking such things before the doors, suddenly nor face nor colour (was) the same **(unus)** '. Translate ' As she thus spake ', etc.

l. 48. **mansere = manserunt.** See note on l. 33.

l. 49. **rabie fera corda.** It is important to determine the length of the final syllable of **fera** by scanning. Why? To see whether the adjective agrees with **rabie** (fem. sg.) in which case we shall find **ferā**, or with **corda** (neut. pl.), in which case we shall expect **feră**. If you scan, you will find it is the latter.

ll. 49–50. **maiorque videri . . . sonans,** *lit.*, ' and she (is) taller to be seen (= to behold) nor uttering mortal (sound) '.

videri, explanatory or epexegetic infinitive ; i.e. it explains in what sense she is greater, *viz.* ' in the being seen '. In this and similar uses of the infinitive, one can see its original dative nature.

mortale sonans, ' mortal sounding '. Neuter pronouns and adjectives are often used in the accusative to modify a verb *from within* (internal or adverbial accusative). Cf. **eadem peccare,** ' to make the same mistake ' and the cognate accusative, so called when the dependent word is of the same origin or of kindred meaning with the verb, e.g. **vitam vivere.**

l. 50. **quando,** ' since '; **adflata est,** *lit.*, ' she has been breathed upon ', = ' she has been filled with '.

l. 51. **cessas in vota precesque,** ' are you slow for vows and prayers ', = ' are you slow to vow and to pray '.

l. 52. Aenea, voc. of **Aeneas,** with which **Tros** agrees.

ll. 52–53. neque enim ante, etc., ' for neither, until you pray **(ante),** will the mighty mouths of the . . . gape open '.

The ' mighty mouths ' are the perforations in the rock to which reference has been made in the note on l. 43.

attonitae domus ; the house is awestruck because it too feels the presence of the god.

l. 54. Teucris, dative, where English prefers a genitive.

l. 56. miserate, voc. masc. sg. of the perfect participle of **miseror (1),** ' having pitied ', =' who hast pitied '.

ll. 57–58. Dardana qui . . . Aeacidae. Paris, son of Priam and Hecuba, carried off Helen, wife of Menelaus, and so was the cause of the Greek expedition against Troy. Towards the end of the 10 years' siege, he killed Achilles, the foremost Greek hero. It was Apollo who guided the dart into Achilles' heel, the only vulnerable part of his body, for it was by the heel that his mother Thetis held him as she plunged him into the river that made him invulnerable.

derexti = derexisti. **Aeacidae,** ' of the grandson of Aeacus ' = Achilles.

ll. 58–59. magnas . . . duce te. Order for translation : **te duce, intravi tot maria obeuntia magnas terras,** etc.

ll. 59–60. penitusque . . . arva, ' and the far distant tribes of the Massylians and the fields that fringe the Syrtes '.

repostas = repositas (from **repono**). **Massylum,** gen. plur. ; **-um,** the original ending of the genitive plural, 2nd declension, is often found in verse. The Massylians were a North African race.

The Syrtes were two wide gulfs on the N. African coast which the ancients considered dangerous to shipping. They are off the coasts of Tripoli and Tunis.

l. 62. hac, etc., ' thus far only may the fortune of Troy have followed us.'

Note : (i) **hactenus,** separated here **hac . . . tenus,**[1] ' thus far.'

---

[1] This separation is known as tmesis, ' cutting '.

(ii), **fuerit secuta**, optative (i.e. expressing a wish) subjunctive. **fuerit secuta** = secuta sit (pf. subj.)

l. 63. **vos.** Juno, Minerva, Neptune were the most bitter enemies of Troy among the gods.

Pergameae. Pergama (neut. pl.) or Pergamum was a poetical name for Troy : hence Pergameus means ' of Troy '.

l. 64. **quibus . . . Dardaniae**, ' to whom Troy and Dardania's great glory were a stumbling block '.

Note these three poetical names for Troy, **Pergamum (or a)**, **Ilium, Dardania.** The latter is derived from Dardanus,[1] ancestor of the royal house of Troy : hence **Dardanidae**, ' Trojans ', and **Dardanus, Dardanius,** ' Trojan '.

l. 66. **praescia venturi.** Adjectives denoting *fullness, power, knowledge* are followed by the genitive in Latin. ' Foreknowing of what is to come ' = ' that foreknows the future '.

da, ' grant ' ; followed by accusative and infinitive, **Teucros considere Latio**, etc.

l. 67. **regna**, pl. for sg. **meis fatis**, ' to my destiny '. Aeneas had been promised by the gods a new kingdom in Italy.

Latio, ' in Latium ' ; ablative of *place where*, very common in poetry without the preposition *in* which accompanies it in prose. Latium was a district in Central Italy enclosed within the boundaries of the Tyrrhenian sea, River Tiber and the Apennines.

l. 68. **agitata**, ' storm-tossed '. Aeneas brought with him from Troy the images of his native gods.

l. 69. **Triviae**, see the note on l. 13.

ll. 69–70. **templum instituam festosque dies.** With **templum**, **instituam** means ' build ' ; with **festos dies**, ' establish '. Perhaps ' set up ' will do for both objects.

Vergil is referring, first to the famous temple of Apollo, built in 28 B.C. by Augustus on the Palatine Hill, in memory of his victory over Antony and Cleopatra at the battle of **Actium** (31 B.C.) ; secondly to the *Ludi Apollinares*, ' Games of Apollo ',

---

[1] Dardanelles is also derived from it.

established in 212 B.C. during a crisis in the second Punic War. These games were held annually, lasted 9 days, and consisted chiefly of performances on the stage.

l. 70. de nomine, ' in the name '.

l. 71. regnis nostris, ablative of place where without a preposition. See the note on l. 67. magna penetralia, ' a great sanctuary '. Vergil is again referring to his own times, for the Sibylline books were placed by Augustus in the temple of Apollo which he had erected on the Palatine.

The Sibylline books, a collection of oracular sayings in Greek hexameters, were said to have been sold by the Sibyl of Cumae to the last of the Roman kings, Tarquinius Superbus.[1] They were kept in the temple of Jupiter Capitolinus, and always consulted in times of crisis by officers of high rank. In 83 B.C., when the books were destroyed by fire, envoys were sent to various places to assemble a similar collection of oracular utterances.

l. 72. hic, adverb, ' here '. namque, translate this first in the line. sortis, ' oracular sayings '; arcana fata, ' secret utterances '.

l. 73. lectos . . . viris, ' chosen men '. The officers appointed to attend to and consult the Sibylline books, were originally two in number, and then later increased to ten and finally fifteen.

l. 74. alma, voc., addressed to the Sibyl. foliis . . . manda. Note : (i) tantum, adv., ' only '. (ii) ne manda, a poetic construction, which in prose would be noli mandare. (iii) carmina, ' oracles ', because they were given in hexameter verse. See also ipsa canas oro of l. 76.

In book III[2] of the Aeneid, we read that Aeneas had been warned that the Sibyl's oracles were traced on leaves and arranged in order, but that when the doors of the cave were

---

[1] Superbus decided to buy the remaining three books (the other six having been burnt by the Sibyl) at the same price as that which was asked for the complete collection.

[2] ll. 445–452

opened, they were stirred and scattered by the wind, so that: those who had come for advice **inconsulti abeunt sedemque odere Sibyllae,** ' depart unadvised and loathe the Sibyl's seat '.

l. 75. **rapidis ludibria ventis,** ' a sport for the rushing winds '.

l. 76. **ipsa canas oro,** =**oro ut ipsa canas,** ' I pray that you utter (them) yourself ', i.e. ' with your own lips '.

dedit, ' made '.

l. 77. **Phoebi nondum patiens,** ' not yet enduring (the sway) of Phoebus '. Vergil describes the Sibyl as resisting the inspiration of Apollo, who gradually tames her and brings her under his control.

immanis, ' wildly ', adjective for adverb.

l. 78. **si,** ' in the hope that '. **pectore,** ' from her breast ', ablative of separation.

l. 79. **excussisse.** Note the perfect infinitive, ' to have shaken off ', i.e. ' to be rid of '.

tanto magis, etc., the sense is ' (the more she raves), the more he tires her foaming mouth ', etc.

l. 80. **fingitque premendo,** ' and moulds (her) by controlling ', =' and moulds her with (strong) control '.

l. 81. **patuere** =**patuerunt.** This form of the 3rd pl. perf. indic. active will not be noticed again.

ostia ingentia centum, ' the hundred mighty mouths ' are again the perforations in the volcanic rock leading into and from the Sybil's cave. While Aeneas was making his prayer and vow to Apollo, the Sibyl must have passed into her cave, where, now mastered by the inspiration of the god, she delivers the god's reply.

l. 83. **defuncte,** voc. sg. masc. of the perfect participle of **defungor,** which is followed by the ablative case. ' O thou, that hast fulfilled.'

l. 84. **terrae,** probably locative case, ' by land ' ; **graviora,** supply **pericula** as subject and **te** as the object of **manent.**

in regna Lavini, ' into the realm of Lavinium '. The latter was a town in Latium, not far from the coast, said to have been founded by Aeneas, in honour of his wife Lavinia, daughter of the Latin king, Latinus.

l. 85. **Dardanidae.** See the note on l. 64.

l. 86. **non ... venisse ;** take the **non** closely with **venisse. et,** ' also '.

l. 87–90. **Thybrim,** acc. of **Thybris,** ' the Tiber '. Apollo promises Aeneas his new realm in Latium, but not without a grim struggle which will be reminiscent of the fighting of Greeks and Trojans around Troy. The Trojan rivers Simois and Xanthus will have their counterparts in the Numicus[1] and Tiber of Latium. Instead of the Greek camp there will be the camp of the hostile Latins, and in Turnus, champion of the natives against the invading Trojans, Aeneas will find a new Achilles, (**alius Latio iam partus Achilles**).

l. 89. **non Simois ... defuerint,** ' no Simois, no Xanthus, no Greek camp will have been lacking to you ', =' you will not lack a Simois ', etc.

Note that it is difficult to bring out the full meaning of the Latin future-perfect, ' will have been lacking ', =' will prove to be lacking '. The use of that tense is suitable for an oracular utterance.

Latio, ablative of place where without a preposition, ' in L.'. **partus** from **pario, -ere,** ' beget ', ' obtain ', ' win ', ' acquire '.

l. 90. **natus et ipse dea,** ' he too born of a goddess '. **dea,** ablative of origin, a development of the ablative of separation.

Most of the heroes of the old epic stories claimed divine origin. Thus Thetis, a sea divinity, was the mother of Achilles, Venus the mother of Aeneas, and Venilia, a nymph, the mother of Turnus. The latter was king of the Rutuli, and leader of the native opposition to Aeneas and his Trojans. The last six books of the Aeneid (VII–XII) deal with the struggle between the two champions and their opposing forces, while the whole epic is closed by the single combat between the two heroes in which Turnus is killed. Most readers of the Aeneid agree that

---

[1] Not mentioned by Vergil here.

Turnus appears as a much more spirited figure than the rather shadowy Aeneas.

nec Teucris . . . aberit, ' nor will Juno anywhere be absent, added to the Trojans ', = ' nor will Juno fail anywhere to dog the T.'.

In Book **I,** ll. 23 ff., Vergil gives the following reasons for Juno's hatred of Troy, (i) the prophecy that from Trojan blood would arise a race destined to overthrow her beloved Carthage ; (ii) the slight she received from the Trojan, Paris, in the contest of the three goddesses ; (iii) jealousy, because Dardanus, the ancestor of the Trojans, was the son of her divine husband Jupiter and Electra, her rival.

l. 91. **cum,** ' when ', or ' and then '.

l. 92. **quas . . . urbes.** Note (i) the sudden change to a question (a rhetorical one) ; (ii) the future-perfect **oraveris,** which can be rendered as a future simple (see note on l. 89) ; (iii) **Italum** = Italorum (see note on l. 59).

quas gentis . . . urbes, ' what tribes . . . what cities '.

l. 93. **coniunx hospita,** ' an alien bride ', complement to **est,** (to be supplied.)

Helen, wife of the Greek king Menelaus, eloped with the Trojan prince Paris, and so was the cause of the Greek expedition against Troy. In Italy, the ' new Helen ' was to be Lavinia, daughter of the native king Latinus, who, though betrothed to Turnus, is given by her father in marriage to Aeneas.

l. 94. This unfinished line is an indication of the unrevised nature of the whole work.

l. 95. **ne cede** = noli cedere of prose.

ll. 95–96. **sed contra . . . sinet,** ' but advance to meet it (contra) more boldly, by such road as (**qua** = qua via) your Destiny shall allow '.

Note **ito,** 2nd sg. second or future imperative of **eo.** This form of the imperative ending in **-to,** is found chiefly in laws, legal documents, proverbs, and maxims.

l. 97. **reris,** 2nd sg. present indic. of **reor. Graia ab urbe,**

' from a Grecian city ', i.e. Pallanteum, a town established by
the Greek Evander on the site of the future Rome. He gave
Aeneas much assistance in his struggle with Turnus.

l. 99. **antroque remugit,** ' and echoes from the cave '.

l. 100. **ea frena . . . Apollo,** ' such reins does Apollo shake to-
her-raging (**furenti**) and plies the goad beneath her breast ', =
' as she rages so does Apollo shake the reins ', etc. The meta-
phor is taken from driving a horse.

l. 102. **ut primum,** ' as soon as '.   **quierunt,** = quieverunt.
Note that in verbal forms containing the letter ' v ', that and
the following vowel often disappear. The resulting word is
said to be a *syncopated* form.

ll. 103–104. **non ulla . . . surgit.** Order for translation :
non ulla (= nulla) **facies laborum nova** (= strange) **-ve** (or)
inopina surgit mihi (= before me).

l. 105. **praecepi,** ' I have anticipated ' *or* ' forecast ' ;
animo mecum, ' in my inmost thoughts ' ;   **ante,** *adv.,* ' ere
this '.

l. 106. **quando,** ' since ' ;   **hic,** *adv.,* ' here '.   **inferni regis,** i.e.
Pluto.

l. 107. **tenebrosa . . . refuso,** ' the gloomy marsh, Acheron
having overflowed ' ; = ' the gloomy marsh from Acheron's
overflow '.   Note that in Latin many verbs in the passive are
equivalent to an English intransitive verb, e.g. **refundo,** ' I
cause to overflow ' ;   **refundor,** ' I am caused to overflow ' =
' I overflow '.

The gloomy marsh is the lake Avernus near Cumae, which
was supposed to be caused by the overflow from Acheron, one
of the rivers of Hades.   Sometimes Avernus is used for the
underworld itself, as in l. 126.

l. 109. **contingat,** ' may it be my fortune ' ;   *lit.,* ' may it
happen '.

doceas . . . pandas, subjunctive in indirect command, dependent on **oro** l. 106.   But translate as imperatives.

l. 111. **recepi,** ' I recovered safely '.

l. 112. comitatus, 'accompanying'; *lit.*, 'having accompanied'. Cf. note on miseratus l. 28.

Anchises, the father of Aeneas, accompanied his son's wandering in search of the 'promised land' through the Eastern Mediterranean to Thrace, Crete, Epirus (modern Albania) and Sicily, where he died. The story of his travels is narrated by Aeneas in Book III of the Aeneid. On his return to Sicily from Carthage, a year later, Aeneas celebrated funeral games in his father's honour (beginning of Book V).

l. 113. pelagique . . . caelique. The first **-que** (meaning 'both') can be ignored in translation.

ferebat, 'endured'.

l. 114. invalidus. Note the emphatic position of this word, 'weak (though he was)'.

viris ultra . . . senectae. ultra governs **viris** as well as **sortem.** This phrase goes closely with **ferebat,** not with **invalidus.** The normal 'lot' of old age is rest and repose.

l. 115. quin, 'nay more'. Cf. l. 33.

l. 115–116. ut te supplex . . . dabat ; *lit.*, 'that I should a suppliant seek thee and visit thy threshold, the same man praying gave instructions'.

Note : (i) **supplex,** adj. for adv. Translate, 'humbly'. (ii) **idem,** translate, 'he too'. (iii) **orans . . . mandabat,** make two finite verbs of this, 'prayed and urged me'.

l. 116. natique patrisque, genitive depending on **miserere, l. 117.** The latter is the imperative of **misereor.**

l. 117. omnia, internal (adverbial) accusative, explained in the note on ll. 49–50.

l. 118. lucis Avernis, dative, but we say 'of the Groves of Avernus'. For Avernus, see the note on l. 107.

ll. 119–120. Order for translation : **si Orpheus fretus Threïcia cithara fidibusque canoris potuit accersere manis coniugis.**

Note : (i) **fretus** + abl., 'relying on'. (ii) **fides, -is, f.,** 'string' (of an instrument).

l. 119. Orpheus. Orpheus, the Thracian musician, of such power that he could hold the wild beasts spellbound, went to the Underworld and by the aid of his music persuaded Proserpine to release his wife Eurydice. There was, however, one condition (**namque hanc dederat Proserpina legem**) ; he was not to look back on his wife as she followed him to the upper air. He forgot and broke this condition and his wife was lost to him for ever.

One of the most beautiful versions of this legend is to be found in Vergil's Georgic IV, ll. 457–529.

l. 121. **si fratrem . . . redemit**, ' if Pollux ransomed his brother by alternate death ', =' by dying in his turn '.

Of the twin brothers Castor and Pollux, brothers of Helen, Pollux was immortal, and, on his brother's death, asked to go with him to Hades. Zeus (Jupiter) allowed them to spend alternate days in Hades and in the upper world.

Another version says that they took it in turns to stay in Hades.

ll. 122–123. **quid Thesea . . . Alciden,** ' why should I mention mighty Theseus, why Hercules '.

Note : (i) **memorem**, deliberative subjunctive. (ii) **Alciden,** *lit.*, ' descendant of Alcaeus ', the latter being Hercules' grandfather. (iii) This common method of bringing to an end a long list.

Theseus descended to the Underworld to help his friend Pirithous carry off Persephone, queen of that region. They were captured and imprisoned by Pluto, and remained there, until Hercules arrived to carry out his twelfth labour, the seizure of Cerberus, the triple-headed dog that guarded the entrance to Hades.

l. 123. **mi**=**mihi**. Aeneas was the grandson of Jupiter, for his mother Venus was the daughter of the king of the gods.

l. 125. **cum,** ' when '. **orsa**=**orsa est** (from **ordior**).

sate sanguine divum. sate, voc. of **satus,** *lit.*, ' sown ', perfect partic. pass. of **sero,** but often used in poetry for ' sprung from '. **sanguine,** abl. of origin (cf. note on l. 90). **divum**=**divorum.** This genitive plural of the 2nd declension will not be noticed again.

l. 126. Anchisiade, voc. of **Anchisiades,** ' son of Anchises '.

facilis . . . Averno. Supply **est** between **facilis** and **descensus. Averno,** dat. for **in Avernum** of prose. Note that **Avernus** is used here as a name for the Underworld. See note on l. 107.

l. 127. noctes atque dies, accusative of duration of time. Translate the plural by the singular.

l. 129. pauci, ' a few '. **aequus,** ' favourable '.

l. 131. dis (=deis) **geniti,** ' born from the gods ', =' sons of the gods '.

The phrase is in apposition with the nom. pl., subject, **pauci.** For the abl. **dis,** see the note on l. 90. **geniti** is from **gigno.**

tenent . . . silvae. silvae is nom. pl. **media omnia,** ' all the mid-space ', i.e. between where Aeneas and the Sibyl are now and the Underworld. However, there is no mention of these woods later.

l. 132. Cocytus means literally, ' river of wailing '. Cf. Milton's *Paradise Lost,* II, 579, ' Cocytus, named of lamentation loud.'

l. 133. quod si, ' but if '. **menti,** ' to thy heart ' =' in thy heart '.

l. 134. Stygios lacus, ' the Stygian lake '. The Styx was the principal river of the nether world, round which it was believed to flow seven times.

l. 135. Tartara, neuter pl. **Tartarus,** m. sg., or **Tartara,** neut. pl., is another name for the nether world.

iuvat, ' and if it delights (thee) '. Note the impersonal use of **iuvare.**

l. 136. accipe . . . prius, ' hear what (is) to-be-done first '.

arbore opaca, ' in a shady tree ', abl. of place where without a preposition.

l. 137. aureus . . . ramus, ' a bough golden both in leaves and pliant stem '. For the golden bough, see the introduction, p. xxii.

l. 138. **Iunoni infernae,** ' to Juno of the underworld ', i.e. Proserpine.

l. 139. **umbrae,** nom. pl.

ll. 140–141. **sed non . . . fetus,** ' but it is not granted to enter the hidden parts of the earth until a man (**qui**) has plucked the golden-foliaged fruit from the tree '.

Note (i) **ante . . . quam** by tmesis for **antequam.** (See footnote to l. 62.) (ii) **decerpserit,** future-perfect. Latin is much more precise than English in the use of tenses, specially in subordinate clauses. (iii) The use of **qui** (adj.) for the more usual **quis,** ' anyone '.

l. 142. **suum . . . munus,** ' (as) her own gift.' **ferri,** present infin. passive.

l. 143. **primo avulso,** abl. absol., ' when the first has been torn away '. **alter,** ' a second (bough) '.

l. 144. **virga,** ' the branch ', nominative.

l. 145. **alte,** adv., ' aloft '. **rite** : take closely with **carpe.**

l. 146. **repertum** ' (it when) found ', object of **carpe.** **rite,** ' duly ', shows that the only way of plucking the bough sanctioned by a proper observance of religious ceremonial was by the hand.

l. 147. **non viribus ullis,** by no force '.

l. 149. **exanimum tibi corpus amici,** ' the lifeless body of thy friend '.

Note that the dative of the personal pronoun **tibi** is translated into English by the corresponding possessive adjective.

This kind of dative, very common in Latin, is known as the dative *of the person interested.*

The dead friend is Misenus, of whose death Aeneas learns in l. 162. Aeneas cannot enter Hades until he has buried with due ceremony the body of his friend.

l. 151. **consulta,** acc. plural of **consultum,** ' the responses (of the gods) '. **pendes,** ' thou tarriest '.

l. 152. **sedibus . . . suis,** ' restore him to his proper resting-place first '.

Note : (i) **ante,** adverb, ' first ' ; (ii) the translation of **suis,** ' proper '.

l. 153. **nigras.** Black victims, because they were offered to the gods of the Underworld.

ea . . . sunto, ' let these be the first propitiatory offerings '. For the 3rd person future imperative, **sunto,** see the note on l. 96.

l. 154. **sic demum,** ' only so '. **regna invia vivis,** ' realms pathless to the living ' = ' realms the living may not traverse '.

l. 155. **presso ore,** ' with closed lips '.

l. 156. **defixus lumina,** *lit.,* ' having cast his eyes down ' = ' with downcast eyes '.

Note that the Latin poets occasionally give the *passive* voice, especially in the perfect participle, an *active* sense, with an accusative directly dependent on it.

This use is very similar to the Greek middle voice, which, while having most of its forms identical with those of the passive, expresses active action done *to* or *for* oneself.

l. 157. **caecos,** this word, properly ' blind ', ' unseeing ', often means ' unseen ', ' hidden '. Here it agrees with **eventus,** ' issues '.

l. 158. **animo secum.** See l. 105.

l. 158–159. **cui . . . comes,** ' to whom . . . as comrade ', = ' as his comrade '.

For the dative, see the note on l. 149. **figit** = **ponit.**

l. 159. **paribus curis,** ' (weighed down) by similar anxieties '.

l. 160. **inter sese,** ' with one another '. **multa serebant,** *lit.,* ' they joined many (words) '.

ll. 161, 162. **quem . . . diceret.** This indirect question depends on some understood participle, such as ' demanding ', implicit in the **multa serebant,** ' spoke at length '. **quem** and **quod** should both be translated ' what ', and **diceret,** l. 162, is ' meant'.

l. 162. **illi,** i.e. Aeneas and Achates. Misenus, a fellow Trojan, and Aeneas' trumpeter.

l. 163. **venere** = **venerunt.**

l. 164. **Aeoliden, acc.** sg., according to the Greek form.

quo, abl. of comparison, ' than whom '.

The verb to the nominative **alter** is **erat** understood. **non alter** go together, meaning ' no other '.

l. 165. *Lit.*, ' to summon the heroes with the brass and set the battle aflame with music '. The infinitives (called by grammarians epexegetic, i.e. explanatory) limit **praestantior** and explain the matter in which no other was ' more excellent ' than Misenus. Say, ' at summoning the heroes with (trumpet of) brass, and kindling the war-spirit with his music '. Notice how the name of the god, Mars, is used for the thing with which he is associated.

l. 166. **hic, i.e.** Misenus. **Hectora, acc.** sg. governed by **circum.**

l. 167. **insignis,** ' marked out ' from others ; **lituo** and **hasta** tell *what by.*

l. 168. **illum** is Hector.

vita, abl., the thing of which Achilles despoiled him.

ll. 169, 170. **sese addiderat socium,** ' had added himself (as) comrade ', i.e. ' had become the comrade (of) '. Notice the omission of any word for ' as ' in this expression. It is a common Latin usage.

l. 170. **non inferiora secutus,** ' following (things) not lower ', i.e. ' following no meaner destiny '. Vergil jealously claims that the service of his own hero, Aeneas, was as high a calling as the service of Hector.

secutus. Observe that the perf. participles of deponent verbs may be used in a present sense. Cf. **miseratus,** l. 28.

l. 171. **concha.** A large sea-shell is a natural trumpet and was the usual instrument of the sea-god, Triton. To have challenged him upon his own instrument adds to the folly of Misenus. **cava concha.** abl., as the scansion shows.

personat, and **vocat,** l. 172. Render these by past tenses and remember that **dum** is constantly used with the present, whatever the tense demanded by the context.

l. 173. **exceptum.** Translate this as **exceperat et,** ' had caught the hero up ... and ... '. It is the regular Latin way, when a subject performs two actions, thus to turn the first of the two into a passive participle. Thus, ' he wrote and sealed the letter ' is **litteras scriptas obsignavit,** *lit.,* ' he sealed the having-been-written letter.'

si credere dignum est, *lit.,* ' if it is worthy to believe ', i.e. ' if the tale can be believed '.

l. 176. **iussa,** acc. pl.

l. 177. **haud mora,** ' (there is) not delay ', i.e. ' without delay '.

l. 178. **certant** is ' vie (with one another) ' and the infinitives **congerere** and **educere** tell *what in,* i.e. they are epexegetic, cf. l. 165.

caelo, dat., instead of the prose construction, **ad caelum.**

l. 179. **itur,** *lit.,* ' it is gone ', i.e. ' they go '—the impersonal passive construction ; cf. **ventum erat,** l. 45.

l. 182. **scinditur** agrees with the nearer of its two subjects, **robur,** only. This is common in Latin, but we must translate by a plural verb.

advolvunt. The subject is ' they ', the Trojans.

montibus is abl., and would have a preposition, **de,** in good prose.

l. 183. **nec non Aeneas,** ' Aeneas, too '. The negatives in **nec** and **non** cancel each other, leaving only the equivalent of **et,** the conjunctional part of **nec.**

primus is ' foremost ', and goes closely with **opera inter talia.**

l. 184. **accingitur** ' is girt with ' = ' equips himself with '. In Latin the passive is often equal to the active + reflexive pronoun object. Thus **accingitur** here means just the same as **sese accingit.**

armis. These ' arms ' or ' tools ' are axe, wedge, and mallet.

l. 185. **haec,** acc. pl., ' these (thoughts) '.

cum. We say not ' with ', but ' in '.

ll. 187, 188. **si ... ostendat,** ' if only ... would show ', expressing a wish.

l. 188. **quando,** conjunction here, ' since '.

l. 189. **vates,** i.e., the Sibyl.

l. 190. **forte.** ' By chance ' is strangely put here, because the doves are sent by divine agency on purpose to lead Aeneas to the golden bough.

l. 191. **caelo,** abl.—a caelo in prose.

venere, i.e. **venerunt.** The past tenses of the indicative are used, instead of the subjunctive, after **cum,** if the conjunction introduces a clause which is only nominally subordinate but is, in meaning, principal. Compare the present case with such an English sentence as ' It was striking nine when my father returned '. The important part of this sentence is the fact that ' my father returned ', and yet grammatically, it is subordinate. Such clauses are called ' Inverse **cum** clauses '.

l. 192. **sedere,** cf. **venere** above. **solo,** ' local ' ablative—in solo in prose.

l. 193. **maternas.** The dove was sacred to Venus, the mother of Aeneas.

l. 194. Begin with **o.**

este, 2nd pl. imperative of **sum.**

qua, nom. sg. feminine of the *indefinite* adjective **qui.**

cursum, ' (your) course '.

l. 196. **ne defice,** poetic for **noli deficere. defice** has, as object, **me** understood.

(in) dubiis rebus, ' in my perplexity '. The expression is similar to **res adversae,** ' adversity ' and **res prosperae,** ' prosperity '.

l. 198. **ferant** and **pergant** are subjunctives in indirect questions. **quo** is the adverb, ' whither ' or ' where '.

l. 199. **illae,** the doves.

pascentes, render by a clause, ' as they fed '.

prodire. The ' historic ' infinitive, which is frequently used instead of, and with the same meaning as, an imperfect indicative.

volando, abl. of the gerund, ' by flying '. Say ' in flight '. Vergil means that the doves constantly took wing for short flights and then settled anew.

ll. 199, 200. **tantum** and **quantum** are acc. sgs. neut., and the accusative is one of extent : ' advanced just so far as . . . '

l. 200. The doves took care to keep within view of those following. Hence the final (i.e. purpose) subjunctive.

acie. The word means ' gaze ' here.

sequentum. -ium is the more usual ending of the genitive pl. of present participles.

l. 201. **venere,** alternative form of the 3rd pl. perf. indic. act.

grave, acc. sg. neut, of the adjective **gravis.** The accusative is called internal or adverbial. Cf. note on **mortale sonans,** ll. 49, 50. **grave** goes closely with **olentis,** ' evil-smelling '.

l. 202. **tollunt se,** ' raise themselves ', i.e. ' rise '.

celeres, ' swiftly '. The adjective is used where English prefers an adverb. This is quite common in Latin.

aëra, acc. sg., Greek form.

lapsae. Translate this as a present participle. The perfect participles of deponent verbs are very frequently used with present meaning.

l. 203. **sedibus optatis,** abl. of place where, common in poetry without the preposition **in** which is obligatory in prose. Translate ' on the desired spot '. **sedibus,** pl., is put for the singular. The substitution of pl. for sg. is very common in Latin poetry. The reverse is also found, but less frequently.

geminae, ' both '.

l. 204. **aura,** ' gleam ', an unusual meaning.

ll. 205–207 consist of a simile, in which the poet compares the contrasting hues of the gold and the green foliage with those of mistletoe berries and bare tree trunks in winter.

l. 205. **quale**, ' even as '. Actually **quale** is acc. sg. neut. of **qualis**, and the accusative is adverbial, of the same type as **grave**, l. 201.

silvis, ' upon the forest trees ', abl. of place where, similar to **sedibus** in l. 203.

brumali frigore, ' in the cold of winter ', abl. of time when, regularly found, even in prose, without a preposition.

viscum is nom., subject to **solet** and the relative clause **quod** . . . **arbos**, l. 206, must be translated immediately after it.

l. 206. **sua arbos**. There are various ways of taking this. The simplest is ' its own tree ', meaning the tree on which, though, of course, as a parasite, the mistletoe grows.

l. 209. **ilice**. ' Local ' ablative without preposition. Cf. note on **sedibus**, l. 203.

leni vento is an ablative of cause, but looking at it differently we should say in English ' in the light breeze '.

l. 210. The object of **corripit** and **refringit** is **eum** (=ramum) understood, with which **cunctantem**, l. 211, agrees.

avidus, adj. for adv. See note on **celeres**, l. 202.

l. 211. **cunctantem**. Render by a clause, ' though it resists '.

l. 213. **cineri**. Vergil seems to forget that Misenus is not yet cremated. See l. 226. **ingrato**, ' thankless ', because Misenus, being dead, was not capable of gratitude.

suprema, acc. pl. neut., ' the last dues '. It was customary to take leave of the dead with certain funeral offerings to the ashes.

l. 214. **pinguem**, ' resinous ', because of the abundance of that substance in the **taedae**, ' pine-wood faggots '.

l. 215. **struxere**. See note on **venere**, l. 201.

cui. The dative is frequently used in Latin where in English we should have a possessive genitive. Render ' whose ', depending on **latera**.

frondibus atris, ' with dark foliage '. This was naturally selected as indicative of mourning.

l. 216. **cupressos.** In England, too, the cypress is a graveyard tree.

super, adv.

armis, those of Misenus, of course.

l. 218. **pars,** and also l. 222. **pars** is often used as an alternative for **alii.** Hence the translation is ' some ' . . . ' others ' . . . and the verbs are plural.

flammis, ' over flames ', local abl. See note on **sedibus,** l. 203.

l. 219. **corpus frigentis,** *lit.,* ' the body of the cold one ' = ' his corpse, cold in death '.

l. 220. **fit,** ' there rises ', *lit.,* ' there is made '.

toro. Again the local ablative, ' on the bier '.

defleta, ' lamented ', grammatically in agreement with **membra.** But translate ' after the lament was over '.

l. 221. **super,** adv.

l. 222. **pars.** See note, l. 218.

subiere. Cf. **venere** and note, l. 201. **subiere,** ' went under ' = ' lifted high '.

feretro, ' bier ', the same thing as **torus,** l. 220.

l. 223. **triste ministerium,** ' a pitiful service ' is a phrase in apposition to the three preceding words. This is an instance of the ' accusative in apposition to the sentence '. Shakespeare, *King Lear,* has this example :

' Half-way down hangs one that gathers samphire, *dreadful trade* '.

subiectam, ' down-thrust '. The torch was applied to the base of the pyre.

more, ' after the fashion ', an example of the ablative of manner. Translate the phrase **more parentum** last in the sentence, immediately after **aversi.**

l. 224. **aversi,** ' turned away ', i.e. ' with eyes averted '.

l. 225. **dapes,** ' the flesh ' (*lit.,* ' banquet '), no doubt of victims sacrificed, which, with the other offerings, were given to the shade of Misenus.

fuso crateres olivo, ' bowls of (*lit.*, with) out-poured oil '. Vergil has a fondness for avoiding the obvious which he betrays here by a rather strained use of the abl. case where the genitive was required.

l. 226. **postquam** is often best translated ' when '. **conlapsi** is for **conlapsi sunt.**

l. 228. **ossa lecta texit,** ' and Corynaeus gathered up the bones, and placed them in a brazen urn '. The literal rendering is ' hid the gathered-up bones with a brazen urn '. Notice how, instead of using two finite verbs, **legit** and **texit,** the first is expressed by the perfect participle passive in agreement with the object. Compare with this **litteras scriptas obsignavit,** normal Latin for ' he wrote and sealed the letter '.

l. 229. **idem circumtulit,** ' the same man purified ', i.e. ' he, too, it was who purified '. It is obvious that **circumferre** originally meant ' carry round ' and had for its object the purifying water.

l. 230. **spargens.** The object is **eos** (=**socios**) understood.

rore . . . olivae, ' with a gentle dew from (*lit.*, and) a sprig of fruitful olive '. For the hendiadys see note on l. 29. The sprig, dipped in water, was shaken in the direction of the participants, as in Catholic churches the priest sprinkles the congregation.

l. 231. **lustravit viros** repeats **socios circumtulit** of l. 229.

novissima verba. These ' last words ' would be **ave atque vale,** ' hail and farewell ', the regular formula at parting from the dead.

l. 232. **ingenti mole,** ' of vast bulk ', adjectival phrase qualifying **sepulcrum.** The construction is called the ablative of description, and, as here, always consists of noun and adjective.

l. 233. **imponit,** ' erects upon (the ashes) '.

viro. Translate as if **viri,** and for the unexpected case (abl.) cf. **olivo** and note, l. 225.

remumque tubamque. Drop the first -que in translation. The words should be in apposition with **arma,** for ' the hero's personal (**sua**) arms' *were* ' his oar and his trumpet '. His armour is spoken of, l. 217, as having been laid on the pyre before it was fired.

ll. 234, 235. **Misenus ab illo dicitur,** ' is called M. after him '. There is still a Punta di Miseno (Cape Misenus) forming the northern limit of the Bay of Naples.

aeternum. The adjective is used as an adverb, ' for ever '. Cf. note on **celeres,** l. 202.

l. 236. **his actis,** ' these (things) having been done ', the ablative of attendant circumstances or ablative absolute. The literal translation is rarely suitable. Often as here, the best method is to turn by an active participle, ' having completed this '

l. 237. **-que** joins **alta** and **immanis :** ' there was a cavern, deep and vast, with a great yawning mouth '

l. 238. **nemorum tenebris,** ' gloomy woods ', *lit.,* ' gloom of woods '.

l. 239. **super** governs **quam.**

haud ullae. Take this as a single expression, equal to **nullae.**

volantes, ' fliers ', poetic diction for ' birds '.

l. 240. **tendere iter pennis,** ' make their way with wings ', i.e. ' wing their way '.

talis, ' so foul ', *lit.,* ' such '.

ll. 240, 241. **sese ferebat,** ' there rose ', *lit.,* ' wafted itself '.

l. 241. **atris faucibus,** ' from ', etc. The ablative expressing place whence without a preposition is common in poetry.

effundens, ' streaming out '. **effundo** is not usually an intransitive verb. Probably **se** as object is to be understood.

l. 242. This line is probably what is called an interpolation, i.e. a marginal note, metrical in form, which was incorporated in error by copyists into the text. The line suggests that the Latin name of the place—**Avernus**—is derived from the Greek Aornos, ' birdless '.

dixerunt nomine = **nominaverunt,** ' named '.

l. 243. **hic,** adverb. **nigrantis terga,** ' black of hide ', the phrase qualifying **iuvencos.** The literal rendering is ' black as to their hides ', and **terga** is an example of the accusative of respect, or part concerned. For this construction cf. **os umerosque deo similis,** ' like to a god in face and shoulders '.

l. 244. **fronti,** ' upon their brows ', sg. for pl. See note on **sedibus,** l. 203.

invergit vina. This outpouring of wine, called libation, was part of the ancient ritual of sacrifice.

l. 245. **media inter cornua,** ' (growing) midway between the horns '.

l. 246. **libamina prima,** ' first fruits ', is in apposition to **saetas.**

l. 247. **voce,** ' with the voice ', i.e., ' aloud '.

Hecaten caeloque Ereboque potentem, ' Hecate powerful in heaven and in hell '. The goddess Hecate was identified with Luna (the Moon) in heaven, and with Proserpina in Hades.

l. 248. **supponunt alii cultros,** i.e. they cut the throats of the victims.

l. 250. **matri Eumenidum magnaeque sorori.** The datives, and **tibi,** l. 251, express ' in honour of '. ' The mother of the Furies ' is Night ; ' her great sister ', Earth.

l. 252. **Stygio regi,** i.e. Dis, or Pluto, king of the Underworld.

nocturnas, adj. for adv., ' by night '. Sacrifices to the underworld gods were made at night.

l. 253. **flammis,** ' on the flames ' ; probably dative, as this case is frequently found in association with verbs compounded with a preposition.

l. 254. **super** is part of **superfundens,** and detached from it by what is called tmesis, ' cutting '.

The -**er** of **super** is counted long here.

l. 255. **primi solis,** ' the first sun ', i.e. ' the new day '.

sub, ' just before '.

ortus, acc. pl., and pl. for sg

lumina et ortus, ' beams and rising ' : say ' rising beams '.

l. 256. The verb to the nominative **solum** is **coeptum est,** understood from **coepta (sunt)** following.

ll. 256, 257. **iuga silvarum,** ' ridges of forests ', Vergilian for ' wooded heights '.

l. 256. **moveri,** ' to quake '. The passive of **moveo** is used where English uses the active voice intransitively.

l. 257. **visae,** understand **sunt.** The auxiliary is frequently omitted from the compound tenses. Cf. **coepta** for **coepta sunt** in the previous line.

l. 258. **adventante dea,** ' as the goddess approached ', abl. abs. The goddess is Hecate, and it is her hell-hounds who ' seemed to howl '.

procul este, ' stand (*lit.,* be) aloof '.

profani, ' ye unhallowed ones ', vocative, addressed to the companions of Aeneas.

l. 260. **tu** is addressed to Aeneas.

l. 261. **opus,** supply **est.** The phrase **opus est** means ' there is need of ', and the thing needed is put in the abl. case (**animis, pectore firmo**). The phrase is often accompanied, though not here, by a dative, expressing the person affected, e.g. **opus est tibi auxilio,** ' you need help '.

l. 262. **effata.** The participle agrees with the understood subject of **immisit,** ' she ', the prophetess.

tantum, ' so much ' is the object of **effata.**

furens, because the frenzy of the divine presence is upon her.

antro aperto, dative, for the **in antrum apertum** of prose.

l. 263. **ducem,** i.e. the prophetess. **haud timidis,** ' not fearful ', i.e. ' bold ', ' confident ', by an idiom, quite common in English too, called litotes, ' understatement '.

ll. 264–267. Vergil in these lines entreats the powers of darkness for leave to tell of their mysteries.

l. 264. **Di** is vocative, as are **umbrae, Chaos, Phlegethon** and loca. quibus . . . animarum, ' to whom there is command of souls ', i.e. ' who have dominion over souls '.

l. 265. loca nocte tacentia late, ' regions extending silent in the darkness '. ' Extending ' stands for late, literally an adverb, ' far and wide '.

l. 266. sit fas, ' let it be lawful '. The subjunctive sit expresses a wish. This use is called ' optative '. fas is to be repeated with the second sit.

audita, acc. pl. neuter, ' heard things ', i.e. ' what I have heard '.

ll. 270, 271. quale est iter in silvis, ' it was like a journey through woods '. The expression is condensed for tale erat iter quale est iter : ' the way was such as is the road '.

l. 270. per incertam lunam sub luce maligna, ' by the uncertain moon, under its grudging light ', or, more naturally, ' under a hidden moon's grudging light '. Vergil suggests that the approach to the Underworld was through a gloom almost unrelieved.

l. 272. rebus, ' from things ', a dative, such as is frequently found with compound verbs meaning ' to take away '.

l. 273. Orci. Orcus was one of the names for the Underworld, and also for its king.

l. 274. Luctus, Curae. These nouns, and all the nouns beginning with capital letters down to l. 280 (except Eumenidum) are personifications, and should thus have capitals in English, too. ' Avenging Cares ' are stings of conscience.

l. 275. habitant. Supply illic, ' there '.

l. 277. terribiles visu, ' fearful to behold '. visu is the supine in -u, properly the ablative case of a verbal noun, so that the literal meaning is ' terrible in the seeing ', and the ablative is one of respect. formae is in apposition with the preceding nominative nouns.

l 278. Homer, Vergil's Greek model, also makes Death and Sleep brothers.

l. 279. adverso in limine, ' full on the threshold '.

mala mentis gaudia, i.e. the evil passions.

l. 280. **ferrei** is scanned as two syllables, the **e** being slurred into the **i** in pronunciation. This is called synizesis. Vergil imagines ' the chambers of the Furies ' to be made of iron, as being compatible with the hard and pitiless character of those avenging goddesses, of whom there were three, named Tisiphone, Megaera and Alecto.

l. 281. ' her snaky locks bound with a bloodstained fillet.' Discord is imagined as a female figure on whose head, instead of hair, grow vipers, suggesting her treacherous nature. The **vitta,** ' fillet ', was a ribbon used to bind the hair. It is bloodstained in consequence of Discord's association with quarrelling and resultant bloodshed.

The grammar of **innexa crinem** needs explaining. The literal meaning is ' having bound her locks '. The Roman poets not infrequently use the passive voice, and particularly the participle, with the active meaning of *doing something to or for oneself*. This they do in imitation, conscious or not, of the Greek, which has a third voice, called the middle, with the same active and indirectly reflexive sense, and having for the most part the same forms as the passive.

ll. 283, 284. **quam sedem . . . ferunt,** ' which dwelling-place they say (**ferunt**) vain Dreams do throng ' (**vulgo tenere,** *lit.,* ' occupy with a multitude ').

l. 284. **haerent.** The Dreams clinging to the underside of every leaf seem to be compared to bats.

l. 285. Supply **sunt** to the nominative **monstra.** Translate **monstra** ' monstrous shapes '.

l. 286. **Centauri.** The Centaurs were mythical creatures, half man, half horse, the Scylla half woman, half fish.

l. 287. **Briareus** was a giant.

belua Lernae. This creature was the Hydra, a monster of many heads, destroyed by Hercules.

l. 288. **horrendum,** the accusative sg. neut. of the adjective used as an adverb : ' dreadfully '.

Chimaera. This was a fire-breathing monster part lion, part goat, and part serpent.

l. 289. **Gorgones.** The Gorgons were three fabulous sisters, so horrible in appearance as to turn all beholders to stone.

Harpyiae. The Harpies were creatures with the bodies of vultures and the faces of women.

forma tricorporis umbrae. This is Geryon, a monster supposed to live in Spain, and to have been slain by Hercules.

l. 290. **hic,** adverb, not pronoun.

l. 291. **venientibus,** dat., dependent on **offert,** ' at the comers ', i.e. ' at these creatures as they approach '.

ll. 292–294. The present subjunctives **admoneat,** etc., are used for graphic effect in place of the normal pluperfect employed in unfulfilled conditions relating to past time. **ni** is for **nisi.** Translate ' and did not his experienced companion (i.e. the Sybil) warn him that . . . he would rush in,' etc. **admoneat** is followed by the accusative and infinitive **tenuis vitas volitare,** ' that they were (only) substanceless, disembodied lives, flitting about under the hollow semblance of form '.

l. 295. **hinc via,** supply **est,** ' hence lies the way '.

Tartarei Acherontis. Acheron was one of the rivers of Hades, for which Tartarus is another name. Vergil's arrangement of the rivers of Hades is so confused as to admit of no satisfactory explanation. We must not expect the poet to worry himself over the exact topography of Hades.

l. 296. **voragine,** sg. for pl.

gurges, i.e. **Acheron.**

l. 297. **Cocyto,** dat., would be **in Cocytum** in prose. **Cocytus,** which means ' wailing ', is another river of Hades.

l. 298. **portitor.** It is over the Styx, not the Acheron, that Charon is usually represented as ferrying the souls of the dead.

l. 299. **terribili squalore** is another example of the ablative of description, explained in the note on **ingenti mole,** l. 232. Here, however, the literal translation, ' the dreadful ferryman,

Charon, of terrible filth ' is unacceptable. Say rather ' terrible
in his self-neglect '.

cui. Translate as if it were **cuius** (dependent on **mento**). It
is not uncommon in Latin to have a dative where we should
expect a possessive genitive.

mento, local ablative, would be **in mento** in prose.

ll. 299–300. **plurima canities inculta,** *lit.,* ' very much unkempt grey hair '. For **plurima** say ' a mass of '.

l. 300. **iacet,** ' lies ', but say ' there is ', or ' there grows '.

stant lumina flammā, ' his eyes stand in flame ', i.e. ' his eyes
are set in a blazing stare '. **lumen,** ' light ', is very common in
poetry for ' eye '.

l. 301. **nodo,** ' by a knot '. The **amictus,** which we render
' cloak ', was actually an unshaped piece of cloth thrown round
the shoulders—thrown round is the meaning of **amictus**—and
as such had to be held in position by the knotting of two of its
corners. Generally they were pinned together with a brooch.

l. 302. Charon uses the pole in shallow, the sails in deep,
water.

l. 303. **ferruginea,** abl., as the scansion shows.

l. 304. **deo.** Translate as if **dei** (gen.) and cf. **cui,** l. 299, and
note.

senectus, supply **est.**

l. 305. **effusa,** ' out-poured ', i.e. ' streaming '. Take **ad
ripas** with this participle, and **huc** with **ruebat.**

l. 306. **defuncta** qualifies **corpora. vita** is abl., dependent on
defuncta : ' done with life ', ' whose life is ended '.

l. 307. **magnanimum,** gen. pl. See note on l. 59.

l. 308. **ora** =' eyes ' here.

ll. 309–311 are difficult because condensed. In logical order,
and with understood words supplied, they would read, **(tam)
multa quam folia (quae) lapsa cadunt in silvis primo frigore
autumni, aut quam aves (quae) glomerantur ad terram ab alto
gurgite.** Translate this, beginning ' as numerous as '. **lapsa
cadunt** is ' glide and fall ', *lit.,* ' gliding, fall '.

l. 311. **annus,** ' season '.

l. 312. **fugat,** supply **eas** (=the birds) as object.

terris apricis, dat. for the prose construction **in terras.**

l. 313. **transmittere cursum,** an unusual phrase for ' to make the crossing '. **transmittere,** dependent on **orantes,** would be **ut transmitterent** in prose.

l. 314. **ripae** is a good example of the objective genitive. In this use of the case the genitive bears a similar relation to the noun on which it depends (here **amore**) as does an object to its verb.

amore, ' in longing (for) '.

l. 315. **navita,** an alternative form of **nauta,** stands here for Charon.

l. 316. **longe summotos arcet,** ' sends far away and keeps at a distance ', as if the Latin were **longe summovet et arcet.** For an example of this use of a participle and a finite verb in preference to two coordinate verbs see the note on l. 228.

harena, local ablative again, ' upon the strand '.

l. 317. **miratus,** translate as present, and cf. note on **lapsae,** l. 202.

enim, ' indeed ', not ' for '.

l. 318. **vult,** ' means '.

l. 319. **quidve.** **-ve** is an enclitic, i.e. a word attached to the end of another. Look it out in the vocabulary.

quo discrimine, ' by what distinction '. Aeneas asks why some (**hae**) are repulsed, others (**illae**) accepted by the ferryman.

l. 321. **olli** =**illi** (dat.).

l. 322. **Anchisa generate,** *lit.,* ' o-thou-begotten from Anchises ', i.e. ' son of Anchises '. **Anchisa** is abl. of origin. Similarly Aeneas is sometimes addressed **nate dea,** ' son of a goddess '.

deum, gen. pl., as often.

proles. Aeneas was the son of Venus by Anchises.

l. 324. ' by whose divinity (numen) the gods fear to swear and to deceive ', i.e. ' to swear falsely '. The oath upon the Styx was of such solemnity, says the Sybil, that the gods themselves dared not use it with intent to perjure themselves. numen: iurare can take an accusative of the thing sworn by.

l. 325. It was, in the view of the ancients, a great tragedy to lack the rites of burial. The story of Palinurus, ll. 337–383, well illustrates this.

l. 326. portitor ille Charon. Supply est.

unda, nominative.

sepulti is complement, and hi the subject, of sunt understood.

l. 327. nec datur, ' nor is it given (to them) ', i.e. ' nor are they permitted '.

l. 328. transportare, unusual Latin for ' to pass '. The normal meaning is ' carry across '.

sedibus, local ablative, ' in their resting-place ', i.e. the grave.

l. 329. annos, acc. of duration of time, ' for . . . '.

circum (preposition) governs the preceding haec litora.

l. 330. admissi revisunt, ' are admitted and revisit ', with the first of the two predicates expressed, in the Latin manner, by the participle. Cf. lapsa cadunt, l. 310, and lecta texit, l. 228.

l. 331. Anchisa satus, ' the son of Anchises '. satus is nom. sg. masc. perf. partic. passive of sero, ' I sow, beget.' Cf. Anchisa generate, l. 322.

l. 332. multa, acc. pl. neut., object of putans.

sortem, i.e. of the unburied.

animo, local abl. without prep., ' in his heart '.

miseratus. The perfect participles of deponent verbs are frequently used, as here, with a present meaning.

l. 333. The plural accs. maestos and carentis agree with the two singular objects Leucaspim and Oronten. honore. The verb careo governs the ablative case. By mortis honos, ' death's due ', Vergil means the ceremony of burial.

l. 334. **Leucaspim, Oronten.** Both men were companions of Aeneas. The case ending **-en** (acc.) is a Greek form.

Lyciae. Lycia was part of Asia Minor.

l. 335. Take **simul** with **vectos.**

vectos, ' sailing '. The passive of **veho, I** carry, is very often used almost as a deponent verb with such meanings as ' go ', ' ride ', ' sail '. For the present meaning of the perfect participle see note on **miseratus,** l. 332.

a Troia. The use of the preposition with the name of a town is not a prose construction.

l. 337. **sese agebat,** ' impelled himself ' (towards them), i.e. ' was approaching '.

l. 338. **Libyco cursu,** ' on the voyage from Libya ', (*lit.*, ' Libyan voyage '). The ablative can be regarded as one of time.

servat. Make a past tense of this. The conjunction **dum,** in the meaning ' while ', has a preference for the present, whatever tense is demanded by the context.

Palinurus watches the stars, of course, in order to steer by them.

l. 339. **puppi. e puppi** in prose. **mediis in undis,** ' in mid ocean '. Mind the case : ' in ', not ' into ', which would require acc.

effusus, ' having been flung overboard ', *lit.,* ' spilled out '.

l. 340. **multa,** abl., with **umbra,** as the scansion shows.

cognovit. The subject of this verb, and of **adloquitur,** is ' he ' (=Aeneas).

l. 341. **prior.** See note on **celeres,** l. 202.

l. 342. **nobis,** ' from us ', but the case is dative. Compound verbs with the general meaning of ' take away ' are often constructed with this case, and the use is termed the ' dative of disadvantage '.

l. 343. **age.** The imperative of **ago** is often used with the imperatives of other verbs, as in English we use ' come ' similarly.

mihi. Translate this as if it were **meum,** qualifying **animum,** l. 344. The use of the dative is similar to that explained in the note on **cui,** l. 215.

fallax haud ante repertus, ' not found false before '. The phrase qualifies the subject **Apollo.** Aeneas means that Apollo, the god of prophecy, had always before given him truthful oracles.

l. 345. **qui.** As it is difficult in translating to get the relative immediately after its antecedent **Apollo,** render ' for he '.

fore, future infinitive of **sum.** The construction is **te fore,** etc., acc. and infin., depending on **canebat.**

ponto, ' on the sea ', local abl. without preposition.

finisque Ausonios. This is the acc. of the goal of motion and would be **ad finis Ausonios** in prose.

canebat. The verb **cano** means ' prophecy ' as well as ' sing '.

l. 346. **Ausonios.** Ausonia was a name for Italy.

l. 347. **ille autem.** Supply **respondet.**

Phoebi. Phoebus was another name for Apollo.

cortina, *lit.,* ' cauldron '. At Delphi, in Greece, a crack in the earth emitted sulphurous fumes, and it was believed that persons inhaling these became inspired, and uttered words of prophecy. Hence a temple of Apollo was built here, and a priestess, called the Pythia, gave oracular answers to those who sought from the god of prophecy foreknowledge of the future. She placed herself upon a cauldron (**cortina**), set on a tripod erected over the steaming cleft in the ground, and waited for inspiration to visit her.

l. 348. **aequore,** local ablative.

ll. 349–351. Begin with **namque** and then take the last three words of this sentence. ' For in my headlong fall (**praecipitans**) I dragged with me the rudder (**gubernaclum**), wrenched away by hazard with great force, to which (as) its appointed (**datus**) guard I clung, and (with which) I was steering our course.'

namque shows the connection in thought, which is : Apollo did not deceive you, nor was I drowned, for I took the rudder with me in my fall, and it buoyed me up.

custos. The omission of any word for ' as ' in such cases as these is usual.

cursus is pl. for sg.

[In the previous book of the Aeneid, l. 855, Vergil has told how the god Sleep (Somnus) stupefied Palinurus and flung him into the sea.]

l. 351. maria aspera, ' by the rough seas ', acc. of the thing sworn by, as in l. 324 (numen).

l. 352 + quam ne from l. 353, ' that I felt (cepisse) no fear for myself so great as lest . . . '. The construction is iuro me cepisse, the me having to be supplied.

l. 353. tua, spoliata, excussa all qualify navis, subject of deficeret, l. 354.

armis, abl. of separation, goes with spoliata : ' robbed of its gear '. By armis Vergil is referring to the rudder.

excussa magistro, ' with its helmsman flung overboard ', as if the construction were excusso magistro, abl. abs. The Latin as it stands is not grammatical, and yet the sense is clear, being helped by the apparently parallel phrase spoliata armis, preceding.

l. 354. deficeret, ' should founder ', the subjunctive being used, as always, in a ne clause expressing a fear.

tantis surgentibus undis, abl. of attendant circumstances, usually known as abl. abs. Render by a ' when ' clause here.

l. 355. tris hibernas noctes, acc. of duration of time, ' for . . .'.

l. 356. violentus aquā, ' blustering over the water '. aqua is local ablative.

lumine quarto, abl. of time when. lumen here =' dawn '.

l. 357. ' did I, uplifted, see Italy from a wave-top '.

l. 358. tuta. The neuter pl. of the adjective is here equal to an abstract noun. Thus tuta tenebam, lit., ' I held safe things ', is ' safety was within my grasp '.

ll. 359, 361. **ni gens crudelis invasisset,** ' had not a savage tribe attacked (me) '. There is an irregularity in the form of the conditional sentence. Suppositions contrary to fact in past time, i.e. sentences of the type ' I would have come if you had called ', have both verbs in the pluperfect subjunctive. Here Vergil puts **tenebam** for **tenuissem** with the artistic purpose of emphasizing how near to fulfilment the unfulfilled condition was.

ll. 359, 360. **gravatum** and **prensantem** agree with **me** understood, object of **invasisset.**

l. 360. **capita,** pl. for sg., and object of **prensantem.**

montis. ' Cliff ' would suit, and yet he speaks, in l. 362, of his body being on the shore. Perhaps ' jagged summit of a rock '.

l. 361. **ferro. ferrum,** ' iron ', is frequently used in poetry with the meaning ' sword '.

praedamque . . . putasset. Supply **me esse. ignara,** adj. for adv. again. Say ' in their ignorance '. ' Their ignorance ' was presumably of the fact that Palinurus was destitute.

l. 362. **versantque in litore venti. verso,** ' turn over and over ', seems rather strong for the action of winds, however boisterous, on a prone corpse.

l. 363. **quod** = ' wherefore '. Properly acc. sg. neut. of the relative, ' as to which ', the construction being acc. of respect

te is the object of **oro,** l. 364.

l. 364. **surgentis,** ' growing ', ' youthful '.

Iuli. Iulus was a boy, the young son of Aeneas.

l. 365. **his malis,** abl. of separation, ' from these miseries '.

ll. 365, 366. **mihi terram inice,** ' throw earth upon me '. Many verbs compounded with prepositions take a dative of the further object.

The sprinkling of earth thrice over a dead body was sufficient to constitute ritual burial.

l. 366. **portusque require Velinos. portus** is pl. for sg. Aeneas is asked by Palinurus to seek this harbour because it is there that his body lies unburied.

l. 367. **qua.** This is the nom. sg. fem. of the *indefinite* adjective **qui**, and means ' any '. **quam** is the acc. sg. fem. of it, and agrees with **viam** understood.

creatrix, i.e. Venus.

l. 368. **neque** is no more than **non** here.

divum, gen. pl.

l. 369. **flumina tanta**, i.e. the various rivers of Hades.

l. 370. **misero** agrees with **mihi** understood.

l. 371. **sedibus placidis**, local abl. ; it would be **in sedibus placidis** in prose.

l. 372. Reverse **coepit cum** before translating. **coepit: cum,** ' when ', which usually takes subjunctive if the accompanying tense is historic, is regularly followed by the indicative if the ' when ' clause, though technically subordinate, is in sense principal. This occurs in such sentences as, ' I was just going out when the doctor called '. ' Inverse cum ' is the usual name given to the conjunction when used in this way.

talia. This is actually the object of **coepit**, but say, ' thus ', or ' as follows '.

l. 373. ' Whence to you, Palinurus, this so dreadful desire ', i.e. ' whence hast thou conceived so dreadful a desire as this '. The ' dreadful desire ', as the next two lines make plain, is to pass over the Styx without being buried.

l. 374. **tu** is emphatic, as are **inhumatus** and **iniussus**.

severum, in grammar agrees with **amnem**, in sense goes with **Eumenidum**. This is an instance of hypallage, ' transferred epithet '.

l. 375. **Eumenidum.** The Eumenides, *lit.*, ' the Kindly Ones ', is a name for the three goddesses of vengeance, Tisiphone, Megaera and Alecto.

l. 376. The order for translation is **desine sperare fata deum flecti precando**. **deum** is gen. pl. and **flecti** = **posse flecti**.

l. 377. **memor**, adjective for adverb, ' heedfully ', **solacia**, consolation ' is acc., in apposition to **dicta**, but say ' in consolation ' and render the genitive **duri casus** by ' for thy hard lot '.

ll. 378-381. The general sense is : those who slew you have been punished for their crime by heaven-sent plagues, and will make the only possible atonement by burying your corpse and erecting a tomb over it.

l. 378. **tua** goes with **ossa**.

finitimi, ' the neighbouring ones ', i.e. ' the people of those parts ', (meaning the region in which Palinurus met his death).

l. 380. **sollemnia**, adj. for noun, ' customary (offerings) '.

l. 381. **aeternum**, adj. for adv., ' for ever '.

l. 382. **emotae** and **pulsus** are for **emotae sunt** and **pulsus est.** This omission of the auxiliary is common.

l. 383. **corde tristi**, for a **corde tristi** in prose. This is abl. of place whence without preposition, common in poetry.

cognomine, unusual (-e instead of -i), abl. sg. fem. of the adj. **cognominis** : ' that bears the same name as he '.

terra. The abl. is the usual case after **gaudeo** : ' in the land '.

l. 384. **inceptum** = **quod inceperant.**

l. 385. Begin with **ut** (= ' when ' here).

navita, i.e. Charon, subject of **prospexit**.

quos. The Romans were fond of beginning sentences with relative pronouns referring to antecedents in previous sentences. This is contrary to English usage, and we must render **quos,** ' them '. **iam inde**, *lit.*, ' already from thence '. The phrase modifies **adgreditur**, l. 387, not **prospexit**, and the sense is that Charon hailed them while still in mid-stream, without waiting for the distance between them to shorten. Render ' forthwith '.

l. 386. **ripae**. See note in **mihi**, l. 365.

l. 387. **adgreditur dictis**, *lit.*, ' assails with words ' ; say ' challenges '.

ultro, *lit.*, ' beyond ', is often used with verbs to denote that an action goes beyond what is expected. Here the sense is that Charon chides them without, *as might have been expected*, first demanding an explanation. Say ' unprovoked '.

l. 389. **fare**, 2nd sg. imperative of the deponent verb **for**.

age. See note on this word, l. 343.

quid, ' why ', a not uncommon meaning. Here it introduces an indirect question, with its verb, **venias**, in the subjunctive, as regularly. **iam istinc** is exactly parallel to **iam inde**, l. 385 ; it means literally ' already from where you are ', and should be rendered ' at once '. It is to be taken with **fare**.

l. 391. The order for translation is **nefas (est) vectare viva corpora Stygiā carinā**. The last two words, abl. of the instrument in the Latin, should be rendered, ' in the Stygian bark '.

l. 392, 393. The order is **nec vero laetatus sum me accepisse lacu Alciden euntem.**

me accepisse is acc. and infin., dependent on **laetatus sum.**

Alciden, acc. sg. Greek form. Alcides was a name for Hercules. He visited the Underworld in the course of the last of his ' twelve labours ', his task being to bring up the dog Cerberus. For allowing his entry Charon was punished, which accounts for his use of the expression **neque sum laetatus. euntem,** *lit.,* ' going '. Say ' when he passed this way '.

lacu. An abl. rather similar to **carina**, l. 391. According to Roman ideas you were carried ' with a ship ', and could even be welcomed or received ' with a lake '. We must say ' in a ship ' and ' on the lake '. Notice how the Styx is variously called by Vergil ' river ', ' marsh ' (369) and ' lake '. These expressions result either from metrical difficulties or from that avoidance of the obvious word which is characteristic of much poetry.

l. 393. **Thesea**, acc. sg., Greek form. **Thesea** and **Pirithoum** are, like **Alciden**, objects of **accepisse.** Theseus and Pirithous, one of the great pairs of friends in mythology, visited the Underworld in an attempt to carry off Proserpine, its queen.

l. 394. The order is **quamquam essert geniti dis atque invicti viribus.**

dis is abl. of origin, ' begotten of gods ', and **viribus**, abl. of respect, ' indomitable in strength '.

essent. quamquam usually takes indicative. A subjunctive could perhaps be justified here on the ground that the clause is technically subordinate to the indirect statement **me accepisse**.

l. 395. **ille** =Hercules.

manu, ' by hand ', =' by force ' here.

Tartareum custodem is the dog Cerberus.

in vincla petivit, *lit.,* ' sought for bonds ' =' sought to bind '.

l. 396. Begin with **traxitque.** The object of this verb is **eum,** understood, with which **trementem** agrees.

regis. ' The king ' is Pluto.

l. 397. **hi** =Theseus and Pirithous, **dominam** Proserpine, **Dis** is another name for Pluto.

thalamo. See note on **corde,** l. 383.

adorti is for **adorti sunt,** and **adorior** has here the meaning ' attempt '.

l. 398. **quae** is acc., governed by the preposition **contra.** For the use of a relative after a full stop see the note on **quos,** l. 385.

Amphrysia =' of Apollo ', because the god once served as a herdsman by the river Amphrysus in Thessaly.

l. 399. **insidiae** is subject to **sunt** understood : ' there is no such treachery here '.

l. 400. **tela.** Aeneas is described as bearing arms in ll. 294, 388.

ferunt, ' offer '.

ll. 400, 401. The construction is **licet (ut) ianitor terreat, licet (ut) Proserpina servet,** ' it is permitted that the doorkeeper should affright, that Proserpine should keep '. Say ' the doorkeeper may ', etc.

ianitor =Cerberus.

antro, ' in his cave ', local abl. without preposition.

aeternum, acc. sg. neut. of the adj. used as an adverb : ' for ever '.

exsanguis, acc. pl., with **umbras.**

l. 402. **patrui.** Pluto bore this relationship to Proserpine.

limen. When Vergil makes the Sybil say ' P. may keep the threshold ', the meaning is: will not be forced by us to stir beyond it.

casta, adj. for adv., ' chastely ', i.e. like the ideal Roman matron.

l. 403. **pietate** and **armis** are ablatives of respect. See note on **visu,** l. 277. For **armis** say ' in war '.

l. 404. The English way of looking at this is a little different. We should say ' is descending to his father in (not ' to ') the lowest shades of Erebus '.

l. 405. **nulla,** in grammar an adjective qualifying **imago,** ' vision ', must be taken in an adverbial sense with **movet:** ' moves thee not '.

l. 406. **at** =' yet '.

ramum hunc, object of **agnoscas,** l. 407.

veste, local ablative, ' beneath her vesture '.

l. 407. **agnoscas.** The 2nd person of the present subjunctive is sometimes used with the same meaning as the imperative. In this use, very common in the 1st and 3rd persons, the subjunctive is called jussive.

tumida, etc. *Lit.,* ' then his heart subsides from swelling wrath '—Vergilian for, ' then the swelling wrath subsides in his heart '.

l. 408. **nec plura his,** supply **dicta sunt. his** is abl. of comparison, ' than these (words) ', ' than this '.

l. 409. **virgae. virga** =**ramus. longo post tempore visum,** ' so long unseen ', *lit.,* ' seen a long time after '.

l. 410. **advertit,** i.e. ' turns . . . (towards them) '.

l. 412. **accipit alveo,** ' admits to the hull '. But **alveo is** really instrumental ablative, and must be compared with **accepisse lacu,** l. 393. Consult the note thereon.

l. 414. **sutilis.** The construction of Charon's bark plainly resembled that of an ancient British coracle. Designed for the transport of disembodied and therefore weightless spirits, it naturally protested at taking aboard a man of flesh and blood, more especially as Aeneas was of heroic proportions (**ingentem**).

rimosa gives the reason : ' (being) leaky '.

paludem, ' marshy water '.

l. 415. **incolumis,** acc. pl.   The plural adjective qualifies both **vatem** and **virum.**

l. 416. **in** governs both **limo** and **ulva** : ' upon the. . .mud and amid the . . . sedge '.

l. 417. **trifauci.** Cerberus, the watch-dog of Hades, had three heads.

l. 419. **cui** is indirect object of **obicit,** l. 421, the direct object being **offam** : ' in his way the priestess . . ., threw a cake. . .'

iam, ' already ', goes with **horrere,** which we should render by a participle.   **colubris.** Cerberus had serpents growing from his body in place of hair.

l. 422. **obiectam** agrees with **eam** (=offam) understood : ' (the morsel) thrown in his path '.

terga is pl. for sg. Cerberus had one back but three necks (l. 419) and three throats (l. 421).

l. 423. **fusus,** ' sprawling ', actually perfect participle passive of **fundo** and therefore meaning literally ' poured '.

humi, locative.

toto antro. It is usual, even in prose, to omit the preposition **in** from place-phrases that include the word **totus.**

ingens. Render as adverb, ' hugely ', with **extenditur,** ' lies extended '.

l. 424. **custode sepulto.** Turn this ablative absolute by a ' when ' clause. **sepulto,** ' buried (in sleep) '.

l. 425. **celer,** adj. for adv.

l. 426. **auditae** =**auditae sunt.**

vagitus et. Reverse these words before translating.

l. 427. **infantum.** Take the **quos** of l. 427 immediately after this word, which depends on **animae flentes.** Then the order is in primo limine, exsortis (acc. pl., agrees with **quos**) **dulcis vitae et raptos ab ubere, atra dies abstulit et mersit acerbo funere.**

in limine primo. Tradition placed all those who suffered an untimely death at the portals of Hades, and held that they had to remain there until they had fulfilled what would have been their normal life. See the Introduction, and Butler's edition, pp. 172 and 174, for a full discussion of this view and the difficulties involved.

l. 429. **atra dies.** The ' black day ' is the day of death.

funere. In prose in funere. **funus,** ' funeral ', is here, and often, used for ' death '.

l. 430. The verb of this line is **sunt** understood. **hos** is governed by the preposition **iuxta.** **damnati,** ' those condemned '. **mortis,** ' to death ', but the idiom of Latin is to put the penalty in the genitive case.

falso crimine, ' upon a false charge '.

l. 431. **datae,** for **datae sunt,** = ' are assigned '.

sine sorte. sors = ' (drawing of) lots '. It was by this means that the panel of judges was selected for a Roman trial.

l. 432. **quaesitor,** ' *is* president of the court *and* '. The language of these three lines is that of the Roman law courts.

Minos, a famous king of Crete renowned for his justice, and according to the myths appointed after his death to be the judge of *all* the dead, not, as here, merely of a group or groups of the dead.

urnam. This is the urn from which the lots were shaken, until one leapt out. Hence **movet.**

silentum, gen. pl. ' The silent ones ' are the dead.

l. 433. The first **-que** = ' both ' and is to be taken with **vocat.**

crimina, ' the accusations *laid against them* '.

l. 434. **maesti** is used as a noun, like **damnati** in l. 430 : those sad ones ', suicides, as the next two lines make clear.

loca, acc. pl. **locus** has two plurals. **loci** means ' (particular) places '.

l. 435. **insontes** is used concessively, ' (though) innocent '.

peperere, 3rd pl. perf. ind. act. of **pario.**

manu, ' by their own hands '.

perosi, from **perodi.** The participle has an active and present meaning.

l. 436. **quam vellent,** ' how much they would wish '—if it were any use wishing, the imperfect subjunctive being em-ployed, as always, in an ' unfulfilled ' condition relating to present time.

aethere in alto. We should say ' under high heaven '. Vergil means in the world of the living.

l. 438 Take **tristis** as nom., **inamabilis** as gen. **undae,** ' water '.

l. 439. The object of **alligat** and **coercet** is eos understood, = the **maesti** of l. 434.

novies interfusa, *lit.,* ' poured between nine times ' i.e. ' with its ninefold windings '. The sense is that the Styx has so meandering a course that nine of its reaches impede souls desirous of returning to the world above.

l. 440. **partem fusi in omnem,** ' extending (fusi, *lit.,* "poured") in every direction '. The extensiveness of the **lugentes campi,** which we may render ' the Plains of Mourning ', is due perhaps to the desire of the mourners for solitude.

monstrantur, i.e. to Aeneas by the Sibyl.

l. 441. **nomine dicunt** is Vergilian for **nominant,** ' they name '.

l. 442. **hic,** adverb, ' here '. **quos.** The antecedent of this is eos understood, which is the object of **celant** and **tegit.**

l. 443. **myrtea.** The myrtle was the tree of Venus, goddess of love.

l. 444. **relinquunt.** The object is **eos** understood.

l. 445. **his locis,** local abl. without preposition.

Phaedram. All the names are those of women who were

unhappy in love. Phaedra, the wife of Theseus, fell in love
with his son Hippolytus and hanged herself. Procris, jealous
of her husband Cephalus, followed him on a hunting expedition
and was accidentally killed by his spear. Eriphyle, when her
husband Amphiaraus concealed himself to avoid a campaign in
which, being gifted with prophecy, he knew he was fated to die,
betrayed his hiding-place for a golden necklace and was in
consequence slain by her own son Alcmaeon. Evadne flung
herself upon the funeral pyre of her husband, Capaneus.
Pasiphaë was the unfaithful wife of Minos, king of Crete, and
became the mother of the monstrous Minotaur. Laodamia
was devoted to her husband, Protesilaus, and when he fell in
the Trojan War was granted his restoration to life for three
hours, after which she accompanied him to Hades. Caeneus
was born a woman, but was changed by Poseidon into a youth.
After death Caeneus again became a woman.

l. 446. **crudelis nati.** The genitive depends on **vulnera,** but
we should say ' dealt by her cruel son '.

ll. 447, 448. **his it comes,** *lit.,* ' goes (as) comrade for these ',
i.e. ' accompanies these '.

l. 448. Take **Caeneus** immediately after **et.**

l. 449. Take the words **rursus et** in reverse order.

l. 450. **quas,** ' these ', with the relative used, as often, even
after a full-stop, instead of a demonstrative. Similarly **quam,**
l. 451 =' her '.

For the story of Dido, who had slain herself for love of Aeneas,
see the Introduction, summary of Bk. IV.

l. 451. **quam,** etc. Begin this sentence with **ut primum,** (*lit.,*
' when first ', i.e. ' as soon as ') from l. 452. **quam** is governed
by **iuxta.**

l. 453. **obscuram** agrees with **quam,** which should be taken a
second time, as the object of **agnovit :** ' recognized her, dim
amid the shadows '.

ll. 454, 455. **qualem ... lunam :** ' like the moon which a
man sees or thinks he has seen rise through clouds, at the
month's beginning.' More literally ' (such) as (he) who in the

early month either sees or considers (himself) to have seen the
moon through clouds.' **talem, is,** and **se** have to be supplied.

l. 456, 457. **verus . . . venerat,** *lit.,* ' came then to me true
news? ' But the emphatic word is **verus,** and we must render,
' was the news then true that came to me? '

venerat. The pluperfect seems to be used sometimes as a
metrical alternative for the perfect.

l. 457. **extinctam, etc.** The full construction is **te exstinctam
esse ferroque extrema secutam esse**—all accusative and infinitive in apposition to **nuntius** : ' that thou wast dead and hadst
sought thine end (*lit.,* last things) with the sword '.

l. 459. **et si, etc.,** ' and by whatever sacred thing (**fides**) there
is in the bowels of the earth ', literally, ' and if there is any
sacred thing under deepest earth '.

l. 461. **deum,** gen. pl.

quae is subject to **cogunt,** the object of which is **me** understood : ' which now compel me to go ', etc.

l. 462. **senta situ.** These words go closely together, ' rough ',
or ' overgrown, with neglect '.

l. 463. **imperiis suis,** ' by their authority '.

quivi is from **queo.**

l. 464. **hunc tantum,** ' this so great ', regular Latin for ' so
great as this '.

me ferre is acc. and infin. depending on **credere** : ' that I was
bringing '.

l. 465. **ne subtrahe.** Negative commands may be expressed
in prose either by **noli (nolite)** +infinitive, or by **ne** +perf. subjunctive. **ne** +imperative, common in Vergil, is poetic.

l. 466. **extremum, etc.** ' This is the last (address) that, by
fate, I address thee ', i.e. ' By fate's decree, I speak to thee now
for the last time '. **quod** is not an object of **adloquor,** but what
is called an adverbial accusative, constructed similarly to such
English expressions as ' he ran a good *race* '.

l. 467. **ardentem et torva tuentem.** The words qualify
animum, ' her burning and grimly staring anger '. Actually it

is Dido, not Dido's wrath, that stares. But the figure of speech is not out of place in poetry.

torva tuentem. The acc. neut. of adjectives, singular and plural, may be used to limit verbs in an adverbial manner. A familiar example is **dulce ridens,** ' sweet(ly) smiling '.

l. 468. **lenibat** is for **leniebat.** It is an old-fashioned form. The imperfect here has what is called its *conative* meaning, ' tried to soothe '.

lacrimasque ciebat, ' and summoned his tears ', **i.e.** ' fell to weeping '.

l. 469. **aversa,** ' averted '.

l. 470. **vultum movetur,** ' changes her countenance '. For the accusative see note on **innexa crinem,** l. 281.

l. 471. **stet** must be translated as if it were **sit** : ' she were '. But the use of **sto** gives additional emphasis to the description of Dido's fixed implacability.

Marpesia. Marpesus was a mountain in the Aegean island of Paros, famous for its marble.

l. 472. **corripuit sese,** ' she started ', a nearly literal equivalent of the colloquial English, ' pulled herself together '.

ll. 473, 474. **illi respondet curis,** ' answers to her with his cares ', i.e. ' matches her woes with his own '. Sychaeus had been murdered by Pygmalion, Dido's brother, and is naturally placed among those who died an untimely death.

amorem, ' (her) love '.

l. 475. **nec minus** goes with **concussus.**

l. 476. **prosequitur lacrimis,** ' escorts her with his tears ', i.e. goes with her, not physically, but in thought and sympathy.

euntem agrees with **eam** (object of **miseratur**) understood : ' her as she goes '.

l. 477. **datum,** ' given ', i.e. ' appointed '.

tenebant, ' they held ', a way of saying ' they had reached '. Cf. **tenebam,** l. 358.

l. 478. **bello clari,** ' those-distinguished in-war '. Remember that adjectives may be used, especially in the plural, as nouns. Thus **boni, bonae, bona** =' good men ', ' good women ', ' good things '.

secreta agrees with **quae**, ' which, (lying) apart '.

l. 479. **hic,** adverb, similarly in l. 481.

occurrit agrees with **Tydeus,** but has four subjects, **Tydeus, Parthenopaeus, imago, Dardanidae.**

Tydeus, Parthenopaeus and Adrastus were three out of a company of heroes who made a famous attack on the Greek city of Thebes. A great Greek play, *Seven Against Thebes,* by the dramatist Aeschylus tells this story.

armis, ' in arms ', i.e. ' in war '.

l. 481. **multum,** etc., ' much bewailed among dwellers-on earth and fallen in war '. **fleti** and **caduci** agree with **Dardanidae. superi,** when the scene is Earth, =' gods ', when it is Hades, ' living men '.

ll. 482, 483. **quos . . . ingemuit.** Take the words in the order **cernens omnis** (*acc.*) **quos longo ordine ille ingemuit** : ' seeing all whom in long array he groaned '. Say ' o'er whom he groaned, seeing them all in long array '.

l. 483. **Glaucumque.** This and the succeeding proper names in the accusative are in apposition to **quos.** They are the names of Trojan warriors. **Medonta, Antenoridas, Polyboeten** are accusatives in the Greek form.

l. 484. **tres,** acc.

Cereri. Ceres was the goddess of corn and the harvest.

l. 485. **currus** is pl. for sg., and acc., object of **tenentem.**

tenentem, ' possessing '.

l. 486. **dextra laevaque,** ' on right and left '. The feminine abl. ending results from the fact that the adjectives agree with **manu** understood.

l. 487. **nec** =**sed . . . non,** the **non** going with **est.**

Supply **eum** as object to **vidisse.**

iuvat with **eos** understood, ' it gives them pleasure '.

l. 488. **conferre gradum,** ' to match their step ' is ' to walk by his side.'

l. 489. **Danaum,** gen. pl.

' Agamemnonian phalanxes ' is Vergilian for ' the hosts of Agamemnon ', shades of dead Greek warriors who fought under King Agamemnon at the siege of Troy.

l. 490. **ut** + indic. = ' as ' or ' when ', here the latter. **vĭdērĕ,** perfect, as the scansion shows. Contrast the infinitive, **vĭdērĕ.**

virum, i.e. Aeneas.

l. 491. **trepidare.** This is a historic infinitive, that is a present infinitive active having approximately the meaning of an imperfect indicative. **vertere,** and **tollere,** l. 492, are similar.

l. 492. **petiere** = **petiverunt.** This is a syncopated (' cut short ') form. The allusion here is to occasions when sorties from Troy drove off the Greek besiegers to the shelter of the fenced camp in which they guarded their beached ships.

l. 493. They try to utter cries of fear at sight of Aeneas, but being ghosts can only produce a faint ghastly wail.

inceptus, *lit.,* ' begun ' : say ' attempted '.

hiantis, acc. pl., ' (them) gaping '. Say ' their parted lips ', from which scarce any sound is heard.

l. 494. **hic,** adv.

Priamiden, Greek acc. sg. It is in apposition to **Deiphobum,** and should follow that word in the translation.

laniatum corpore toto, ' mangled in his whole body ', or, as we should say, ' with his whole body mangled '.

l. 495. **lacerum crudeliter ora,** ' cruelly torn as to the face '. **ora** is acc. of respect, and pl. for sg. **ora manusque ambas,** l. 496, have the same construction. For the accusative cf. **terga,** 243. Translate, ' his face, aye and both his hands, cruelly torn '.

l. 496. **populataque tempora.** The meaning is made clear by the next words, **raptis auribus,** ' with the ears torn away '. **tempora** and **naris,** most simply taken as object of **vidit,** l. 495.

Mutilation of the slain was practised to prevent the ghost from haunting the slayer.

l. 497. **naris**, acc. pl.

l. 498. **agnovit.** The object is **eum**, (understood) with which the participles in -**em** agree.

l. 499. **ultro**, ' ungreeted ', the word **ultro** suggesting as usual that the verb it modifies goes beyond expectation. The expected thing would be that **Deiphobus** should begin the conversation.

l. 500. **genus** is vocative, in apposition to **Deiphobe.** Translate as participle, ' sprung ', (*lit.*, ' offspring '.)

Teucri, Teucer was a king of Troy.

l. 501. **crudelis**, acc. pl.

sumere poenas. Supply de te.

l. 502. **cui tantum de te licuit**, *lit.*, ' to whom was it allowed concerning thee so much? ' i.e. ' to whom was such vengeance upon thee permitted? '

(from **mihi**)–l. 504. The order for translation is **fama tulit mihi te, fessum vasta caede Pelasgum, suprema nocte procubuisse super acervum confusae stragis.** tulit =rettulit, ' reported ', Pelasgum is gen. pl.

suprema nocte. The ' last night ' is the last of Troy's existence. From **te** onwards the construction is acc. and infin.

l. 505. **Rhoeteo litore.** The ' Rhoetean shore ' was the coast in the neighbourhood of Rhoeteum, a cape on the Dardanelles, north of Troy.

inanem. An ' empty tomb ' is a cenotaph.

l. 506. **manis**, acc., understand **tuos.**

vocavi. Aeneas spoke the **novissima verba**, for which see note, l. 231.

l. 507. **nomen**, understand **tuum.**

tĕ, ămīcĕ. The **e** of **te** is shortened, but not elided, before the **a** of amice.

l. 508. **et.** The negative force of **nequivi** persists. Say ' nor '.

patria terra, local ablative without preposition.

ponere, ' bury '. **te** is the object of this infinitive as well as of **conspicere.**

l. 509. **Priamides,** i.e. **Deiphobus.** To this nominative supply some such verb as **respondit.**

tibi relictum (est). ' (was) left (undone) by thee '. **tibi** is dative of the agent, not uncommon in poetry in place of the a + abl. of prose.

l. 510. **omnia solvisti,** ' thou hast discharged all that was due ', *lit.,* ' paid all things '.

funeris, ' of the dead '. **funus** is properly ' funeral '.

l. 511. **fata mea,** pl. for sg.

Lacaenae. The ' Spartan woman ' is Helen, whom Deiphobus married after the death of Paris, who had abducted her from her first husband, the Greek Menelaus. This abduction was the cause of the war between Greeks and Trojans.

l. 512. **his mersere malis,** ' drowned me in these miseries '.

illa, emphatic : ' it was *she* who . . . '.

haec monimenta. Deiphobus points to his scars.

l. 513. **ut** is ' how ', introducing an indirect question depending on **nosti** (=novisti), ' thou knowest '.

falsa gaudia. ' The groundless rejoicings ' resulted from the Trojans' having been tricked, by a pretended deserter, Sinon, into believing that the Greeks had abandoned the siege and sailed home. Actually some of their warriors were introduced into Troy within the wooden horse, which Sinon had persuaded the Trojans to drag into their city in the belief that its possession would ensure the favour of the gods. Meanwhile the rest of the Greeks, in their ships, hidden behind the island of Tenedos, awaited the opening of the city's gates from within by the warriors emerging from the horse. The plot was aided by the fact that the Trojans in their relief at the raising of the siege, celebrated unwisely and kept no guard.

l. 514. **et nimium,** etc., ' and one cannot but remember it too well ', *lit.,* ' it is inevitable to remember (it) too much '.

l. 515. **saltu venit,** ' came with a bound ', i.e. ' came bounding '. Deiphobus, by a flight of imagination, describes the entrance of the Wooden Horse in terms appropriate to a creature of flesh and blood. Actually the walls were breached to allow of its being laboriously dragged in upon rollers.

venit. The indicative shows that **cum** here =' at the moment when '.

l. 516. **armatum peditem,** sg. for pl.

gravis, ' pregnant '. The nom. adjective agrees with the subject.

alvo = in **alvo.**

illa, ' she ' is Helen.

euhantis orgia, ' crying aloud in the rites of Bacchus '.

euhantis is acc. pl., agreeing with **Phrygias. euhans** means literally ' uttering the cry " euhoe " ' (used in the worship of the wine god). It is a stretch of construction for it to be followed by the objective accusative **orgia,** ' rites '.

circum, adverb

l. 518. **media,** nom., ' in the midst ', i.e. of the dancing worshippers.

l. 519. **vocabat,** i.e. by signalling with the torch (**flamma**).

Danaos. These must be the Greeks in the Wooden Horse.

l. 520. **tum,** ' at the time '.

l. 521. Why the **thalamus** is **infelix** is shown by the treacherous conduct of Helen towards him, shortly to be related.

habuit, ' held '.

iacentem agrees with **me** understood. Say ' as I lay '.

l. 523. **egregia** is ironical.

l. 524. **capiti,** ' from beneath my head ' is dative of disadvantage. Cf. **nobis,** l. 341. Deiphobus had grown used, during the ten years of siege, to sleeping with his sword beneath his pillow, ready for sudden night alarms.

l. 525. **vocat.** The subject is ' she ', Helen.

Menelaum. He had been her first husband.

limina. limen, properly ' threshold ', is often used for door ', by a figure of speech called synecdoche, the naming of a part to suggest the whole.

ll. 526, 527. The order is : **sperans scilicet** (plainly) **id fore magnum munus amanti et famam veterum malorum posse sic exstingui.**

id is her betrayal of Deiphobus, **amanti,** ' her lover,' refers to Menelaus. **vetera mala** is a reference to her former desertion of Menelaus for Paris.

l. 528. **quid moror,** ' why do I delay ', i.e. ' what boots it to prolong the tale '.

comes additus una, *lit.,* ' added as companion together (with them) ', i.e. ' and, accompanying them '.

l. 529. **Aeolides.** By ' the son of Aeolus ' Deiphobus means Ulysses. His reputed father was Laertes, but Deiphobus, ' willing to wound, ' hints that his real father was Sisyphus, of the family of Aeolus, a man whose unscrupulous cleverness made him a by-word. There is a further taunt in the words **hortator scelerum** which suggest that Ulysses prompted in others the crimes he lacked the courage to commit himself.

ll. 529, 530. **talia instaurate.** Deiphobus asks the gods to ' renew for the Greeks such treatment ', as he has suffered, i.e. to inflict the like on them.

l. 530. **ore,** ' lips '. Os is often to be so translated.

ll. 531, 532. The order is **sed age, fare vicissim qui casus attulerint te vivum.** **fare** is 2nd sg. imperative of the defective deponent verb **for,** and **attulerint** is subjunctive in an indirect question.

l. 532. **pelagine** = pelagi + ne, interrogative particle.

pelagi erroribus, ' by wanderings of the sea '. Say ' by the wandering currents of ocean '.

l. 534. **tristis,** acc. pl.

adires. adieris, perf. subj., might have been expected after the primary **fatigat.**

ll. 535, 536. It was past mid-day in the world above.

l. 535. **hac vice,** ' during this exchange '. The abl. is that of time.

Aurora, goddess of the dawn.

l. 537. **datum,** ' allotted '.

traherent, ' they would have spent '.

per talia, ' in such (converse) '.

l. 538. **admonuit breviterque adfata est,** *lit.,* ' admonished and briefly addressed (him) ', i.e. ' and briefly addressed him in admonition '.

l. 539. **flendo,** abl. of the gerund of **fleo** : ' in lamentation '.

l. 540. **partis,** acc. pl. Take it at the end of the line, with **ambas** in agreement.

ll. 541, 542. **viā** and **est** must be supplied, and **dextera** (nom.), probably attracted into the case of the relative **quae,** construed as ablative.

' Along this right hand (road), which, etc., lies (est) the way to Elysium for us '. **hac dextera** (**viā**) is abl. of route. **Elysium** is that part of Hades reserved for the good. Notice the acc. **Elysium** expressing, without a preposition, the notion of destination. This, the acc. of the goal of motion, is not uncommon in poetry, though usually it follows upon a verb, rather than as here upon a noun (**iter**), embodying the idea of movement.

l. 542. **laeva** qualifies **via** (nom.) understood : ' but the left-hand way prosecutes the punishment of the evil ', and does so, as the rest of the line makes clear, by leading to Tartarus, the place of punishment. **malorum,** m. pl., ' of wicked men '.

l. 544. **Deiphobus,** supply **inquit.**

ne saevi, for **noli saevire** in prose.

l. 545. By **explebo numerum,** ' I will complete the muster ', Deiphobus means that he will return to the company of ghosts which he has left while following Aeneas.

reddar. Often the passive voice is equivalent to the active
+reflexive pronoun object. Thus it equals here **me reddam,**
' I will take myself back '.

l. 546. **decus nostrum,** ' thou glory of our people '. In
grammar **nostrum** is ' our ', qualifying **decus.**

utere. Parse carefully. **utor** here =' enjoy '.

l. 547. **effatus,** i.e. **effatus est.**

in verbo. We say ' *with* the word '.

l. 548. **respicit subito.** Aeneas looks back after the departing
Deiphobus. In this way he sees, on the left, the citadel of
Tartarus, which Vergil now proceeds to describe. **sinistra,**
with **rupe,** ' on the left '.

l. 549. **moenia,** ' stronghold '.

l. 550. **quae ambit,** ' round it flows '.

flammis torrentibus. The encircling moat is a river of fire.
Say ' of (not " with ") scorching flame '.

l. 551. **torquetque sonantia saxa.** Rocks in the river bed are
swept along by the current of fire, and produce a roaring sound.

l. 552. **adversa,** ' confronting (him) is . . . '—supply **est.**

solido adamante, ' of solid adamant ', abl. of description.
adamas, *lit.,* ' unconquerable ', probably stands for steel, as
the hardest substance known to the ancients.

l. 553. **ut** introduces a consecutive (result) clause : ' so that '.

virum, gen. pl.

l. 554. **valeant,** here equal to **possint,** has two subjects, **vis**
and **caelicolae.**

ad auras. ' (reaching) skywards '.

l. 555. **Tisiphone** was one of the three Furies, goddesses of
vengeance and punishment. Cf. l. 250.

sedens, etc., ' seated, (but) with her blood-stained robe
upgirded '. Her pose is one of rest and yet of readiness for
instant action. The grammar of the last three words is ' girt
with bloody robe '.

exsomnis, adj. for adv.

l. 557. **exaudiri, sonare,** historic infinitives. See note on **trepidare,** l. 491.

l. 558. **tum,** etc. Take **exaudiri** again, with **stridor** and **catenae** as subjects.

tractae catenae, ' the dragging of chains '. Notice how this is done. The literal meaning is ' dragged chains '. The Latin participle expresses what in English it requires a noun to convey. This is common in Latin.

l. 560. **quae scelerum facies.** Supply **est haec. facies,** ' spectacle '.

effare. Cf. the form **utere,** l. 546.

quibusve. **-ve** is an enclitic, i.e. a particle suffixed, like **-que** and **-ne.** It means ' or '.

l. 561. **ad auris** (= **aures,** acc. pl.), ' (that comes) to my ears '.

l. 562. **orsa** = **orsa est** (from **ordior**).

Teucrum, gen. pl.

l. 563. **nulli fas,** supply **est.**

casto, adj. used as noun : ' sinless man '. **nulli,** dative of **nullus,** qualifies it.

l. 564. **me,** object to three verbs, **praefecit, docuit, duxit. lucis,** dative, governed by the verb **praefecit.**

Hecate. See note on l. 247.

praefecit. cum, when it has the meaning ' at the time when ', does not take the subjunctive, as there is then no connection of *cause* between the clauses. Contrast **quae cum audivisset, irascebatur,** ' when (*and* because) he heard this, he grew angry '.

l. 565. **deum poenas,** ' the punishments ordained by (*lit.,* of) the gods '. **deum** is called a *subjective* genitive. In the other possible meaning of the words, ' punishments of (i.e. inflicted on) the gods ' the genitive would be *objective.* The names are given according as the noun in the genitive stands for the doer or the sufferer of the action implied in the noun on which the genitive depends.

omnia, ' all (these scenes) '.

l. 566. **Gnosius** =' Cretan ', Rhadamanthus was a king of that island in his life-time, and brother of Minos.

habet may be rendered ' rules ', and **regna** regarded as pl. for sg.

l. 567. **castigatque auditque dolos,** ' and punishes and learns of their crimes '. Perhaps the sense is that they are chastised in order to extort confession, the ordinary legal practice of Rome, in the case of slaves.

fateri ' (them) to confess '.

ll. 568, 569. The lines are loosely constructed. It is simplest to take **quae** as attracted from its proper case, **quorum,** by being somehow felt as an object to **distulit,** or as in apposition to the real object **piacula.** Translating **quorum,** we get : ' those (crimes) of which a man (**quis**), exulting in his vain deceit, has put off till too late death the atonement incurred (**piacula commissa**) upon earth (**apud superos**) '.

in seram mortem. The opportunity for atonement is lost when death comes.

l. 570. **continuo,** i.e. immediately after they have been sentenced by Rhadamanthus.

sontis, acc. pl.

l. 571. **sinistra,** sc. **manu.**

anguis, acc. pl. You should now be familiar with this acc. in **is,** and it will not always be noticed in future.

l. 572. **agmina,** ' company ', pl. for sg. and even then a poetic exaggeration, as Tisiphone's sisters were only two in number. But perhaps Vergil has in mind another tradition, making the Furies more numerous. Tisiphone calls on her sister Furies to carry away the condemned sinners. She herself cannot leave the gate.

ll. 574, 575. **qualis** and **quae** must precede in translation the nouns **custodia** and **facies** which they respectively qualify.

l. 575. **sedeat, servet,** subjunctives in indirect questions.

l. 577. saevior, fiercer, that is, than the **custodia** in the **vestibulum,** or perhaps than Tisiphone. The Hydra was a monster with fifty heads.

tum, i.e. after one has passed the doors and the vestibulum.

l. 578. in praeceps, ' sheer downwards '.

bis tantum, ' twice as far ', *lit.,* ' twice so much '. Take the words at the end of the line.

sub, ' down to '.

l. 579. quantus (est) suspectus, ' as (is) the upward view '. The sense of this passage is simply : from the top to the bottom of Hades is twice the distance from the earth to the sky.

l. 580. The Titans were giants who fought against Jupiter, were defeated, and imprisoned in Hades.

l. 582. et, ' too '.

vidi. Remember that the Sibyl is still speaking. ' The twin sons of Aloeus ' were named Otus and Ephialtes. They were giants who sought to scale heaven and attack the gods by piling mountains on top of one another, Ossa on Olympus and Pelion on Ossa. All are famous mountains of Greece.

immania corpora, ' monstrous forms ', is in apposition to **Aloidas.**

l. 584. adgressi is for **adgressi sunt,** which means here ' attempted ' and is constructed with the prolative infinitives **rescindere** and **detrudere.**

l. 585. et, as in l. 582.

Salmonea, acc., Greek form. The offence of Salmoneus was, as described in ll. 586–591, that he imitated the thunder and lightning of Jove, and claimed divine honours.

ll. 585–586. Salmoneus is described as ' paying the cruel penalty while he imitated the fire of Jove '. In fact of course the imitating preceded the punishment. The difficulty can be resolved by rendering, ' the penalty (which he incurred) while . . . '

l. 586. sonitus is acc. pl.

l. 587. hic, i.e. Salmoneus.

lampada, acc. sg., Greek form.

l. 588. Graium, gen. pl.

mediae. Translate as if mediam, ' through the midst of the city of Elis '. Elis was the name of a town and a district in the Peloponnese.

l. 589. divum, ' of (i.e. due to) the gods '.

l. 590. demens, qui, ' madman, in that he . . . '.

demens is in apposition to hic. qui + subjunctive is often used with various adverbial meanings such as purpose (very common), consequence, concession and cause. The qui clause here gives the *cause* of his being called demens.

l. 591 refers to the story that Salmoneus mimicked Jove's thunder by driving his chariot over a bridge of brass. For aere say ' with echoing brass '.

l. 593. Leave ille untranslated. Literally it is, ' *he* (threw) not torches ', as Salmoneus had done to imitate the lightning.

ll. 593, 594. nec . . . lumina, ' nor pine-wood's smoky light ', *lit.*, ' lights smoky with pine-wood '.

l. 595. nec non et Tityon, ' and Tityos, too '. The negatives nec and non cancel out, leaving ' and ', (for nec = ' and not '). Thus nec non is merely a spondaic (— —) equivalent for et or atque and had its uses for poets writing in a metre not native to the Latin language.

Tityon is acc., Greek form, object to cernere in l. 596. cernere erat = ' it was possible to see '. Vergil is using sum in the fashion of the Greek equivalent, which sometimes has this meaning.

Tityos was a gigantic son of Earth, punished for offering violence to Latona.

l. 596. cui. Render as if cuius, depending on corpus. Cf. note, l. 215.

l. 598. immortale. The liver of Tityos, which the ' monstrous vulture ' is for ever pecking, is for ever renewed, so that his

agonies are eternal. **iecur** is object of **tondens,** as is **viscera,**
l. 599.

fecunda poenis, *lit.,* ' fruitful in penalties ', i.e. ' ever yielding
fresh punishments '.

l. 599. **rimaturque.** The **-que** =' both ' and may be ignored.

epulis, dat. or abl., ' for ', or ' at, his feast '.

l. 600. **renatis,** ' (ever) re-newed '.

l. 601. **quid memorem,** ' why should I tell of . . . ' deliberative
subjunctive, like the common **quid faciam,** ' what am I to do?'

Lapithas. The Lapithae were a people of Thessaly. Ixion,
and his son Pirithous, were of their number. The first was
punished for offering violence to Juno, the second for aiding
Theseus in an attempt to carry off Proserpine from Hades.

Ixiona, acc., Greek form.

There is apparently a line missing after l. 601, for the description which follows of the rock threatening to fall suits the
story of Tantalus, who has not been mentioned. Ixion is
usually represented as bound to a wheel.

l. 602. **quo** is governed by **super** : ' above whom there hangs
(imminet) a black mass-of-flint, about-to-slip at any moment
iam iam) and apparently falling ' (*lit.,* ' like to a falling (mass) '.

The **e** of **-que** is elided before the **i** of **imminet** in the next
line.

l. 603. **lucent,** etc. Tantalus, if he is the victim referred to,
is represented as having before him a magnificent feast, which
he dares not touch for fear of the Furies. ' The golden feet
gleam upon the high festal couch.'

l. 604. **ora,** pl. for sg., ' before his eyes '. **os,** properly
' mouth ', often stands in poetry for ' face ', ' cheeks ', ' lips ',
or ' eyes '.

paratae =**paratae sunt,** ' is ready ', ' is spread '.

l. 605. **regifico luxu,** abl. of description, ' of regal magnificence '. The phrase qualifies **epulae.**

maxima, i.e. **maxima natu,** ' the eldest '.

iuxta is adv., not prep., here.

l. 606. prohibet, supply **eum** as object.

contingere, ' from touching '. In Latin, with the verb prohibeo, you prevent a person *to do* a thing.

l. 607. **facem.** This is the Fury's weapon.

intonat ore, *lit.,* ' thunders with her mouth ' ; say, ' utters thunderous threats '.

l. 608. After the famous sinners of legend there follows, ll. 608–624, a catalogue of nameless offenders who also suffer eternal punishment. **hic, quibus** = hic (sunt ei) quibus, ' here are those to whom brothers were hateful . . . or (by whom) a father was struck, or treachery was plotted against a dependant '. The active voice is more natural in English. Say ' those who hated their brothers, or struck their father, or plotted treachery against a dependant '. **quibus** in the second case is dative of the agent. Cf. note on **tibi,** l. 519. With **invisi, erant** must be supplied, with **pulsatus** and **innexa, est.**

l. 609. **clienti** is dative of disadvantage. Cf. **nobis,** l. 342. Clientes was the name given to those humbler persons who attached themselves for protection to the men of the great families. Their protectors were called **patroni.** The relationship between **patronus** and **cliens,** and their mutual duties, were recognised by Roman law.

l. 610. **aut qui,** ' or (those) who . . . '.

repertis, ' gained ', i.e. ' which they had gained '.

l. 611. **posuere** = posuerunt, ' set aside '.

suis, dat., ' for their own (kin) '.

quae maxima turba est. This refers to the misers.

l. 612. **quique,** ' and (those) who . . . '.

caesi, i.e. caesi sunt. **secuti,** and **veriti,** l. 613, are similar.

ll. 612, 613. **impia arma,** ' unnatural war ', perhaps war against the fatherland. **sequor** in this connection must mean ' take part in '.

l. 613. **veriti,** ' scrupled '.

fallere dextras, ' to deceive the trust '. **dextras,** properly 'right hands', refers to the handclasp which marked a compact, and so expresses 'trust'.

l. 614. **inclusi**, 'imprisoned'. Say 'in confinement'.

ne quaere. Noli quaerere in prose.

l. 615. **quam poenam (exspectant).** This missing verb, as well as **mersit**, should strictly be subjunctive, as the **quam** and **quae** introduce indirect questions.

forma fortunave, 'form and fortune (of punishment)'.

l. 616. **alii.** This no doubt includes Sisyphus, who was condemned to roll a great rock uphill, whose summit it never attained, but rolled down again to the foot.

radiisque. Elsewhere we learn that Ixion (see note, l. 601) suffered this punishment. **radiis**, abl., goes with **districti**, 'spread-eagled upon the spokes'.

l. 617. **aeternum.** The acc. sg. neut. of the adjective is sometimes used as an adverb : 'eternally'. Theseus was condemned to some form of sedentary punishment.

Phlegyas was the father of Ixion. He was punished for setting fire to the temple of Apollo at Delphi.

omnis, acc. pl.

l. 620. **discite iustitiam moniti.** The use of the participle **moniti** is similar to that noticed on ll. 228, 310, i.e. it replaces a coordinate finite verb. Translate as if **monemini** (2nd pl. imperative).

non temnere is a second object to **discite**.

l. 621. **hic**, 'one'; **hic**, l. 623, 'another'.

auro is abl. of price. But we say 'for gold', just as **pretio**, 'at a price', becomes more naturally 'for bribes'.

l. 622. **fixit atque refixit**, 'made and unmade'. Vergil chooses the word **figo** because in Rome laws were engraved on bronze tablets, which were set up in public.

l. 623. **invasit** is used in two senses, 'entered', (with **thalamum**) and 'contracted' (with **hymenaeos**).

l. 624. **ausi, potiti.** **sunt** must be supplied in each case.

auso is abl. sg. neut. of the participle which, though **audeo is** semi-deponent, is here used with passive meaning : ' the having been dared thing ', ' the thing they dared '. The abl. is the normal case after **potior,** ' achieve '.

l. 625. The **non** belongs to **possim,** l. 627.

mihi si sint, ' if to me there were to be ', i.e. ' if I should have '.

l. 626. **omnis,** acc. pl.

l. 628. **dedit.** In such a case as this English prefers the pluperfect.

l. 630. **acceleremus.** This ' let us ' subjunctive of command is called hortative.

Cyclopum educta caminis, ' produced in the forges of the Cyclopes ' : i.e. the **moenia** were of iron. The Cyclopes, a race of one-eyed giants, were the blacksmiths of mythology and by tradition had their workshops beneath Mt. Etna in Sicily.

l. 631. **adverso fornice,** ' (set) in the archway opposite '.

l. 632. **haec dona,** pl. for sg. The ' prescribed offering ', as l. 636 shows, is the golden bough. Take **praecepta (sc. deorum)** as subject of **iubent.**

l. 633. **dixerat.** As often, this is ' she ceased '.

gressi. Perfect participles of deponent verbs can be used with present meaning.

per opaca viarum. Favourite Vergilian variation for **per opacas vias. Opaca,** of course, is acc. pl. neut. of the adjective used as a noun, *lit.,* ' darknesses of the ways '.

ll. 635, 636. **corpusque.** This ceremony is for purification. It survives in the Roman Catholic custom of crossing oneself with holy water on entering and leaving church.

l. 637. **his,** ' these (rites) or (dues) '. **demum** goes with **devenere,** 3rd pl. perf.

divae refers to Proserpine.

locos laetos et amoena virecta. Ad would precede these words in prose. This is the accusative of the goal of motion.

l. 639. Both **fortunatorum** and **beatas** are 'transferred epithets', i.e. the adjectives do not really relate to **nemora** and **sedes,** but to the souls 'fortunate and blest', who dwell in them. The figure is called hypallage.

l. 640. The order is **largior hic (est) aether et campos vestit lumine purpureo.** hic is an adverb, ' here there is an ampler ether, and it clothes . . '.

l. 641. The ' they ' which is the subject of **norunt** (a syncopated form of **noverunt,** from **nosco**) refers to the souls of the blest.

suum, sua, ' of their own ', i.e. different from the sun and stars familiar to dwellers on earth.

l. 642. The singular noun **pars** is sometimes used with a plural verb in the meaning ' some '.

pars in l. 644 means ' others '.

l. 643. **ludo,** ' in sport '.

l. 644. **pedibus plaudunt choreas,** i.e. they dance.

l. 645. For **nec non** see note on l. 595.

Threicius sacerdos. The ' Thracian priest ' is Orpheus, famous also as a musician and a prophet.

l. 646. ' matches the measures with the seven distinct notes ', literally ' utters in accompaniment (**obloquitur**) to the measures (**numeris**—the dance rhythms performed by the blest) the seven distinctions of sounds '. For **discrimina vocum** cf. **opaca viarum,** l. 633. The seven notes are those of the lyre, of which Orpheus was a legendary master.

l. 647. **eadem,** ' the same (notes) '.

pectine. The **pecten** is the plectrum or quill with which the strings of the lyre were struck. Alternatively they could be plucked with the finger.

l. 648. **hic (erat),** ' here was '.

Teucri. Teucer was the father-in-law of Dardanus. Ilus and Assaracus, (l. 650), were two of the latter's descendants.

l. 649. **melioribus annis,** ' in happier times '.

l. 651. **miratur.** The subject is Aeneas.

virum, gen. pl.

inanis, acc. pl., with **currus,** but to be taken with **arma** too. Their arms and chariots were as ' unsubstantial ' as the ghosts themselves.

l. 652. **terrā** =in **terrā.**

soluti, ' loosened ', i.e. ' untethered '.

ll. 653 **quae gratia**—655. The order for translation is **eadem gratia currum** (=**curruum**) **armorumque quae fuit (eis) vivis, (eadem) cura pascere nitentis** (acc.) **equos sequitur (eos) repostos tellure.**

gratia =' pleasure ', and the following genitives must be rendered by ' in chariots ', etc.

quae . . . vivis, *lit.,* ' which was to them living ', i.e. ' which they felt in their life-time '.

pascere depends on **cura,** ' care to feed '.

tellure repostos, ' (now that they have been) laid to rest in earth '.

l. 657. **vescentis, canentis,** accs. pl.

paeana, acc. sg., Greek form.

l. 659. The Eridanus is the Italian river Po. Part of its course was subterranean ; hence this legend.

l. 660. **hic manus passi.** The grammar is loose. The meaning is ' here (is) a band that suffered '. Actually **passi** is a participle, ' having suffered ', and agrees not with **manus,** but with the masc. pl. members of it.

pugnando, ' in fighting ', abl. of the gerund.

l. 661. **quique,** supply **ei** and **erant,** ' and those who were '. **quique,** l. 662, is similar.

l. 662. **Phoebo digna,** ' (words) worthy of Phoebus '. The line means simply ' great poets ', for Phoebus (Apollo) was the god of poetry.

locuti =**locuti sunt.**

l. 663. ' or (those) who ennobled life through the crafts (artis, acc.), which they invented '.

l. 664. sui, ' of themselves ' objective genitive, depends on memores, acc., in agreement with alios.

fecere = fecerunt.

merendo is like pugnando, l. 660, ' by their deserving, or deserts '.

l. 665. omnibus his is a dative where a possessive genitive would be expected, depending on tempora. Cf. note on cui, l. 215. The vitta was a ribbon worn around the brows by priests.

l. 666. *Lit.*, ' whom, having been poured around, the Sibyl thus addressed '. For the first two words this comes to mean, ' These, as they gathered round '.

l. 667. Musaeum. He was a legendary poet.

medium agrees with hunc : ' him in its midst '.

l. 668 (from atque on). ' and looks up at him, towering above them with high shoulders ', i.e. ' standing head and shoulders taller than they '.

l. 670. Anchisen, acc., Greek form.

ergo is here the preposition, governing a genitive, illius.

Erebi. Erebus was one of the names of the Underworld. amnis, acc.

l. 672. huic, fem.

paucis, sc. verbis, i.e. ' briefly '.

l. 673. nulli certa domus, supply est, ' to none is there a fixed dwelling ', i.e. ' none has ', etc. nulli is a dative of the possessor. This dative, with the verb to be, is a common way of expressing ' have '.

lucis : in lucis in prose.

l. 674. riparum toros, ' couches of banks ', i.e. ' soft-cushioned banks '.

rivis belongs with recentia, ' fresh with running streams '.

l. 675. vos is nominative, subject to the imperative superate, l. 676.

si . . . voluntas, ' if the wish so leads (you) in your hearts '.

l. 676. Supply vos as object of sistam.

facili tramite : in facili tramite in prose.

l. 677. ante tulit gressum, ' carried his step before ', i.e.
' preceded them ', or ' led the way '.

nitentis, acc. pl.

l. 678. dehinc is scanned as one syllable.

l. 679. convalle virenti. Supply in.

l. 680. animas. These are souls not yet embodied. Take
inclusas after animas. et joins inclusas and ituras.

ituras, ' destined to pass ', fut. participle of eo.

l. 681. studio. This abl., *lit.*, ' with eagerness ', may be
rendered ' eagerly '.

suorum, ' of his own ones ', i.e. ' of his descendants '.

l. 682. forte, ' by chance ', ' as it chanced '.

l. 683. Notice the alliteration, to preserve which Vergil uses
for ' deeds ' or ' exploits ' the word manus, ' hand ', or here,
' handiwork '.

l. 684. tendentem adversum, ' advancing towards (him) '.

l. 685. alacris. The usual form of the nom. sg. masc. is
alacer. It is best rendered by an adverb, ' eagerly '.

l. 686. effusae, i.e. effusae sunt.

genis, abl. of route, ' down his cheeks '. Or it may be ' from
his eyes ', for which genae is sometimes put in poetry.

vox, ' speech ', as often.

ore, ' from his lips ', a common meaning of os.

l. 687. parenti, ' by thy father ', dative of the agent. See
note on tibi, l. 509. parenti goes closely with exspectata.

l. 688. vicit, ' triumphed over '.

datur tueri, ' is it given to gaze on ', i.e. ' am I permitted ',
etc.

ora, pl. for sg.

l. 689. reddere, ' to answer '.

l. 690. ' Thus for my part I considered in my mind, and thought (it) would be '.

l. 691. **tempora dinumerans,** ' counting (=as I counted) the times (say, the passing days) '.

ll. 692–693 (**accipio**). An idiomatic expression : ' borne (**vectum**) over what lands and what great seas I welcome thee '. i.e. ' what lands, what wide seas hast thou crossed ere I now welcome thee '.

l. 693. ' Buffeted by what great perils '. **iactatum** qualifies te, l. 692. Say ' what great perils have afflicted thee ! '

l. 694 **quam,** adv., ' how '.

ne quid nocerent, *lit.,* ' lest the kingdom of Libya should hurt thee some ', i.e. ' should do thee some hurt '. **quid** is adverbial accusative. Anchises had feared that Dido, in her position as the hostess and lover of Aeneas, might persuade him, as indeed she tried to do, to abandon his divine mission to found a new realm in Italy, and to remain with her as her husband and king.

l. 695. To keep Vergil's emphatic repetition of **tua** we must say ' *it was* thy sad ghost, father, thine, *which,* repeatedly confronting me, drove me to make my way to these portals '. For **haec limina,** acc. of goal of motion without preposition, see note on **locos,** l. 638.

l. 697. **stant,** i.e. ' are afloat '.

sale Tyrrheno. The Tyrrhenian sea is that part of the Mediterranean enclosed between Italy and the islands of Sardinia and Corsica.

da iungere, ' give (me) to join ', i.e. ' let me clasp '.

l. 698. **ne subtrahe :** noli subtrahere, or ne subtraxeris (perf. subj.) in prose.

l. 699. **ora rigabat,** *lit.,* ' he bedewed his face '. We should say ' his face grew wet ', in which case **memorans** must be rendered ' as he spoke '.

l. 700. **conatus,** i.e. conatus est.

collo is dative, governed by the compound **circumdare** which is here separated : ' to put his arms about his neck '. This division of a word is called tmesis.

ll. 700–701. Aeneas cannot embrace his father's shade.

l. 701. **frustra** goes closely with **comprensa.**

manus, acc. pl.

l. 705. **Lethaeum amnem.** Lethe was the river of forgetfulness, a draught from whose waters had the power to erase the memories of dead souls. See ll. 714, 715.

l. 706. **circum** governs **hunc.**

l. 707. **ac velut ubi** introduces the simile.

aestate serena, ' in cloudless summer '.

l. 709. The passive of **fundo,** ' pour ', is used almost as a deponent, in the sense ' flock '. Cf. l. 666.

murmure, i.e. with the murmur of the **gentes** and the **populi,** cf. l. 706.

l. 710. **visu subito,** ' at . . . ', abl. of cause.

l. 711. **inscius,** adverbial, ' in his ignorance '.

Take **requirit** again before the indirect questions **quae,** etc., ' asks what . . . '.

l. 712. **complerint** = **compleverint,** perf. subj., a syncopated form.

ll. 713, 714. **quibus . . . debentur,** i.e. those souls who are fated to be reborn into the world of the living. **quibus** is dat., and **fato,** abl.

l. 714. **ad,** ' at '.

l. 715. **securos latices,** not ' care-free waters ', but ' the waters that free from care '.

l. 716. The infinitives **memorare** and **ostendere,** (and also **enumerare** following) depend on **iampridem cupio,** ' I have long desired '.

coram is an adverb here.

tibi is to be taken twice, with both infinitives.

l. 717. **meorum,** ' of my (children) '.

l. 718. quo in place of ut, for which it is regularly put in a final (purpose) clause when the clause contains a comparative.

Italia reperta, abl. of cause, going with laetere : ' at Italy having been discovered ', i.e. ' at the discovery of Italy '.

laetere, 2nd sg. pres. subj.

ll. 719–721. Notice the pessimism in these lines, perhaps Vergil's own, though put into the mouth of Aeneas.

l. 719. anne putandum est, ' is it to be thought ', i.e. ' must we think '. anne is made up of -ne, interrogative particle, and an, which usually introduces the second half of an alternative question, with the meaning, ' or '. Sometimes, as here, an is prefaced to single questions the tone of which is surprised or indignant.

The rest of the sentence is acc. and infin. depending on putandum est : ' that some souls go up (ire sublimis) from here (hinc) to the world of light (caelum). . . .

sublimīs, grammatically an adjective in agreement with animas, is here used as an adverb.

l. 720. reverti, infin. passive, used as deponent.

l. 721. quae lucis, etc. Supply est. ' What so dread desire for the light (is there) to the wretched ones? ' Say ' what terrible longing for the light possesses the wretched creatures? '

ll. 724–751. In these lines, Anchises gives us a picture of the meaning and purpose of life, and of the life after death. It is drawn from several sources, but combined by Vergil into a composite scheme with slight alterations or additions of his own.

First, we have the doctrine, taken from the Stoic Creed, of the Life Spirit (Spiritus), which permeates and supports the universe. The Stoic philosophers believed it was of fire, and that all forms of life possessed a spark of it ; hence Vergil says in l. 730, ' all have the fiery vigour and the heavenly source in their seeds.'

Then Vergil borrows from Orphic and Pythagorean teaching the doctrine which regarded the body as the prison-house of the soul, for we are told that the soul is hampered by association with the sinful body (ll. 728–731), and, hence, arise the passions and desires of men. Therefore, purification is necessary (ll. 739–742), the details of which seem to be drawn from the popular mysteries and folk-lore. After the spirits have been purified by wind, or water, or fire, they then go on to Elysium, where a few only, as a reward for their virtue, possess the happy fields until the wheel of time is complete—a period which, as given in Plato, is 10,000 years.

According to Vergil, after this period in Elysium, the chosen few become the pure heavenly flame of air which they were before they entered into the wheel of birth. Anchises, himself, is one of the elect. As for the rest, the vast majority of spirits, they complete the wheel of 1,000 years in the underworld in purification and atonement, then drink the waters of Lethe, and undergo a rebirth in which it is already fated what person they will be in their new existence. This process of rebirth, life on earth, atonement in the spirit world and rebirth again, is continued until the wheel of time is complete and the spirits can rejoin the divine source from which they come.

It is obvious that the doctrine of Metempsychosis (an important element in Pythagoreanism) made a strong appeal to Vergil because of the use he could make of it for patriotic purposes, for all the souls awaiting rebirth, which Anchises parades before his son, consist of the first kings of Rome, and the famed heroes of the Republic down to Caesar, Augustus and Marcellus of Vergil's own day.

l. 724. **campos liquentis.** He means the sea.

l. 725. **Titania astra,** pl. for sg., and meaning the sun, which was fabled to be the offspring of the Titan, Hyperion.

l. 726. **intus,** an adverb, but used almost adjectivally with **spiritus ;** say ' a spirit within them '. **spiritus** is the subject of **alit.**

artus, *lit.,* ' limbs ', refers to the various parts of the universe, listed in ll. 724, 725.

l. 727. **se miscet.** Remember that such verbs as **misceo** are transitive only in Latin, and that to express the intransitive

meaning of the English 'mingle' either active + reflexive·
pronoun object, or the passive voice, must be used.

l. 728. **inde,** supply **est,** which may be rendered ' arise '.
inde = ' from this source ', i.e. the **spiritus** and the **mens** already
mentioned.

vitae. Better singular in English. **volantum,** gen. pl., less
usual form : ' of the flying ones ', i.e. ' of the birds '.

l. 729. The order is **et monstra, quae pontus fert sub marmoreo aequore.**

ll. 730–732. Vergil views the soul as dulled by an earthy
body.

ll. 731, 732. **est ollis seminibus,** ' there is to those seeds ', i.e.
' those seeds have '. The seeds are the sparks of divinity in
living creatures. **seminibus** is dative of the possessor, (cf. l. 673)
and **ollis** is old-fashioned Latin for **illis.**

l. 731. **quantum** is for **tantum quantum,** ' so far as '.

ll. 731, 732. The object of **tardant** and **hebetant** is **ea** (=se-
mina) understood.

l. 733. **hinc,** ' from this '. i.e. ' because of the flesh '.

auras. To be rendered perhaps ' the heavenly light '.

l. 734. **clausae** agrees with **animae,** the understood subject
of **metuunt,** etc.

carcere caeco. The prison is the body, which is not blind,
but blind*ing*, a sense in which **caecus** is not uncommon.

ll. 735–738. ' Nay even when, with the last light, life has
left (them), yet do not all the evil, nor all the plagues of the
body, utterly leave the hapless (creatures) and it is inevitable
(**necesse**) that many (taints), long growing (**concreta**), should
become deeply ingrained in wondrous wise '.

et is ' even '. The construction of l. 738 is **multa inolescere,**
acc. and infinitive, subject to **est** (l. 737), to which **necesse** is
complement. Notice the adverbs **funditus** and **penitus.** You
would hardly guess from the endings what part of speech they
were.

l. 739. **malorum,** ' misdeeds '.

ll. 740-743. The taint of evil is removed from the souls by exposure to wind, water and fire.

l. 740. aliae, ' some ', its usual meaning when alius is repeated, the latter forms having the meaning ' others '. aliae agrees with animae, ' souls ', understood.

The image conjured up in the irreverent mind by ll. 740-741 is comically like washing on a clothes-line !

l. 741. aliis, ' from others '.

l. 742. igni, an old form of the ablative.

l. 743. manis, acc. pl. ' We suffer, each his own ghost ', meaning, presumably, that everyone suffers what befalls to his immortal portion, his ghost (manes), in the Underworld. patimur, 1st person, and suos, 3rd, go awkwardly together.

exinde, after the before-mentioned suffering, that is.

l. 744. pauci tenemus, ' a few of us hold ', i.e. ' remain in '. Some spirits, of whom Anchises is one, require no further purification.

ll. 745-747. ' until a distant day, the cycle of time being completed, has removed the ingrown taint and leaves unalloyed (purum) the ethereal sense and the flame of the pure spirit '.

aurai is an old form of the genitive. It is a trisyllable here.

l. 748. has omnis. object of evocat, l. 749.

ubi, etc., is merely a poetical way of saying ' after 1000 years '.

rotam, the wheel of time.

volvēre, 3rd pl. perf. ind. act. Contrast the pres. infin., volvĕre. The subject of volvere is ' they ', i.e. the purified souls.

l. 749. deus, ' a god '.

agmine magno, ' in a great company ', abl. of manner.

l. 750. Begin with ut, introducing two final clauses : ' that, their memories being, of course, expunged . . . '. They have no recollection of previous incarnations. Immemores is literally ' without recollection '.

supera convexa. ' To see again the vaulted heavens ' (*lit.*,
' curved heights ') is to return to the world of the living.

l. 752. **unaque Sibyllam,** ' and together (with him) the
Sibyl '. **una** is an adverb.

l. 753. **conventūs,** acc. pl.

l. 754. **capit,** ' takes his stand upon '.

omnis, acc. pl.

posset, final subjunctive.

l. 755. **adversos,** ' facing (him) '. The spirits pass in review.

venientum, i.e. **venientium.**

l. 756–end. Vergil makes Anchises parade before Aeneas
the souls, awaiting incarnation, of some of the great men of
Roman history.   One can imagine how such a pageant, in the
noblest Latin yet written, stirred the patriotism of its Roman
hearers, and fostered the pride which Augustus hoped his court-
poet would stir.

l. 756. **age** =' come ', as before, l. 343.

ll. 756–758 contain three objects of **expediam dictis,** (with
which you should begin).   These objects are (1) the indirect
question **quae gloria sequatur** ... (2) **qui nepotes (te) maneant,**
(3) **animas inlustrīs.**

quae, (and **qui,** l. 757), ' what '.

sequatur, ' attends '.

l. 758. **nostrumque,** etc., ' and about to go into our name ',
i.e. ' and fated to bear our name '.

-que connects **inlustris** and **ituras.**

l. 760. **pura hasta.   purus** here means ' headless '.   Such a
spear, says an ancient commentator on Vergil, was bestowed
as a trophy of victory.

l. 761. *Lit.,* ' holds by lot the next place of life ', i e. ' is
fated next to enter the light of day '.

ll. 761, 762. **primus surget,** ' he first shall rise '.

l. 763. **Albanum nomen** is in apposition to **Silvius.**

Alba Longa was an Italian city near Rome over which ruled
the descendants of Aeneas and Lavinia, a native princess, until
the foundation of Rome by Romulus.

l. 764. **tibi longaevo,** ' to thee aged ', i.e. ' to thee in thine
old age '.

serum is grammatically an adjective qualifying **quem. We**
should make it an adverb, ' late ' modifying **educet.**

l. 765. **silvis,** local abl., =in **silvis.**

regem and **parentem** are nouns in apposition to **quem.**

l. 766. **unde** ' from whom ', i.e. the line of Alban kings shall
begin with him.

Longa Alba, same abl. as **silvis,** l. 765.

l. 767. Supply **est** : ' he next (is) Procas '.

l. 768. Some such expression as **deinde sequuntur,** ' then
follow ', needs to be supplied, with **Capys, Numitor** and **Silvius
Aeneas** as subjects. These are the names of other descendants
of Aeneas and kings of Alba.

qui . . . reddet refers to, and must be rendered after, **Silvius
Aeneas.**

reddet, ' shall recall '.

l. 769. **pariter** goes with **egregius,** and **pietate** and **armis** are
abls. of respect, ' in piety or warfare '. **pariter** probably means
' equally (with thee) '.

unquam. ' Ever ' after **si** is usually **quando.**

regnandam, gerundive, ' to be ruled over '. We may say
' as his kingdom '.

acceperit, fut. perf., but in such cases English uses the
present. The conditional clause records a tradition that for
long Silvius Aeneas was denied his rights as king.

l. 771. **qui,** exclamatory, ' what '.

viris, acc. pl. of **vīs.** Contrast this (**vīris**) with **virīs,** dat. or
abl. pl. of **vir,** a man.

l. 772. ' and they bear temples shadowed with the civic
oak ', i.e. ' and their temples are shadowed with the civic

wreath of oak leaves '. This is one more of Vergil's deliberate anachronisms,—the carrying back into the remote heroic past of the later Roman custom of bestowing the civic crown (**corona civica**) on those who saved a fellow citizen's life in battle. Augustus held this honour as the saviour, by ending civil strife, of many Roman lives.

ll. 773-775. The names are of those of ancient towns in **Latium**, the district of Italy near Rome.

l. 773. **Fidenam**, ' of Fidenae '. Cf. **urbs Roma**, ' city of R. '. The names in l. 773 are the objects of some suitable verb to be supplied from **imponent.** Say, ' these (shall build) for thee N. ', etc.

l. 777. **avo comitem se addet**, ' shall add himself (as) companion to his grandfather ', i.e. ' shall join his grandfather '. The grandfather is **Numitor,** (l. 767), whose daughter Ilia, or Rhea Silvia, was the mother of the twins, Romulus and Remus, by the god Mars. Romulus is called Mavortius, ' son of Mavors ', the latter being another form of the name Mars. For **Assaracus**, see note, l. 648.

l. 779. **viden** = **videsne.** It is scanned as two shorts. Thought of almost as an interjection, the expression **viden ut,** ' see you how ', is not followed by the subjunctive proper to true indirect questions.

vertice is for **in vertice,** ' upon his head '.

l. 780. **pater.** ' His father ' is Mars.

superum, acc. sg., agreeing with **eum** understood : ' for the world above ', *lit.,* ' (as) an upper one ', i.e. a dweller on earth.

suo honore. The helmet with two plumes was the badge of Mars.

l. 781. **huius auspiciis,** ' under his auspices '. The phrase = ' under his leadership ', for it was the leader's duty to ' take the auspices ', that is ascertain the divine will by divination.

l. 782. ' shall make-equal her empire with the earth, her spirit with the heaven ', i.e. ' shall spread her empire world wide, and lift her spirit heaven high '.

l. 783. **septem arces**, i.e. the Seven Hills.

una circumdabit, ' shall, a single (city), surround '.

sibi, ' for herself ', may be disregarded.

l. 784. **prole**, ' in her breed ', abl. of respect.

virum, gen. pl.

ll. 784–787. Rome is compared in these lines to the goddess Cybele, whose worship was later introduced into the city from the East.

l. 784. **qualis**, ' even as '.

' The Berecyntian mother ' is Cybele, so called because Mt. Berecyntus, in Phrygia, was a site for her worship, and because one of her titles was Magna Mater.

l. 785. **invehitur**, ' rides '. The passive of **veho** ' carry ', is used almost as a deponent in this and similar senses, such as ' drive ', ' sail '.

turrita, ' with towered diadem ', i.e. wearing a crown of which the raised portions represented towers.

l. 786. **laeta deum partu**, ' rejoicing in her brood of gods ', i.e. proud that she is the mother of so many gods, just as Rome feels pride in her heroic sons.

l. 787. **omnis** and **tenentis**, acc. pl. **caelicolas** and **tenentis** are in apposition to **nepotes**.

supera alta tenentis, *lit.*, ' possessing the high heavens ' ; say ' tenants of the sky above '.

l. 789. **hic Caesar**. Supply **est**.

l. 790. **ventura**, ' destined to pass '.

l. 791. **saepius** is often used without real distinction of meaning from **saepe**.

l. 792. **genus** =**filius** here.

Divi. The ' god ' is Julius Caesar, deified after his death.

aurea, etc. Take before this the **qui** from the next line.

l. 793. **Latio**, i.e. in Latio.

ll. 793, 794. **regnata ... quondam**. The order is **per arva**

quondam regnata Saturno. regnata, illogically, since it is an intransitive verb, =' ruled '. **Saturno** is dative of the agent. When Saturn, the father of Jupiter, ruled, the world enjoyed, according to the myths, its golden age of peace, plenty and happiness. This age Augustus is to restore.

l. 794. **Garamantas.** These were an African tribe.

ll. 795–797. The general sense is that the Earth (**tellus**) over which Augustus shall extend his sway, will reveal new regions not lying beneath the known bodies of heaven.

l. 796. **vias, '** paths '.

Atlas, the Titan, who in the myths bears the heavens on his shoulders.

l. 797. **umero,** sg. for pl.

torquet, ' revolves '.

l. 798. **in** has here a special meaning, ' in fear of '.
The three place names that follow are associated with successes of Augustus' reign.

l. 799. **responsis,** abl. of cause, ' at the oracles '.

divum, acc. pl.

Maeotia tellus. The Palus Maeotis was the Sea of Azov.

l. 800. **turbant** is here used intransitively ' are in panic '.

l. 801. **Alcides** is Hercules, himself a great traveller.

tantum telluris obivit. Notice here the flattery of Augustus, whom Vergil compares, to their disadvantage, with the hero Hercules and the god Bacchus.

l. 802. **licet** is here the conjunction, ' although ', which is regularly followed by the subjunctive. The natural position of **licet** would be first word in the line.

ll. 802, 803. These lines refer to three of the twelve labours of Hercules, the capture, after wounding it, of a brazen-footed deer of inc dible swiftness, the taking of the Erymanthian boar, and e slaying of a many-headed monster, the Lernaean Hydra.

l. 8c **pacarit = pacaverit,** perf. subj.—a syncopated form.

l. 804. **nec qui.** **Liber** (=Bacchus) is to be taken between these two words. **Liber** is a second subject to **obivit,** l. 801.

victor is often used almost as an adverb : ' triumphantly '.

pampineis. Bacchus, remember, was the Wine God.

iuga, properly ' yokes ', means here ' the team ' or ' the chariot '.

l. 805. **Nysae.** Nysa was the name of a mountain, on which Bacchus was born.

tigris, acc. pl.

l. 806. **dubitamus.** By associating himself with Aeneas, which is the effect of employing the 1st person, Anchises takes away some of the sting of the reproach which he is directing at him as being slow to win the promised kingdom in Italy.

extendere, ' to stretch ', i.e. ' give scope to '.

l. 807. **Ausonia terra,** local ablative.

l. 808. Supply **est.** **ille** is Numa Pompilius, second king of Rome. The olive bough proclaims his peaceful character.

sacra. Perhaps ' offerings '.

l. 809. **crinis,** acc. pl.

l. 810. **primam,** ' young ' or ' new '.

legibus, ' upon laws '.

l. 811. **Curibus . . . terra,** abl. of place whence. Cures was the birth-place of Numa.

l. 812. **cui.** The use of the relative after a full stop, instead of a demonstrative or personal pronoun, is very common in Latin, unusual in English : ' thereafter Tullus shall follow *him*.' Tullus, the third king of Rome, was a warlike ruler.

l. 815. **quem.** Treat similarly to **cui,** l. 812.

iactantior. The comparative can mean ' too '.

l. 816. **popularibus auris,** ' in popular favour ', abl. of cause. **aura,** *lit.*, ' breeze ', suggests the instability of popularity. Ancus Martius was the fourth king of Rome, and the conqueror of the Latins.

l. 817. **vis,** from **volo ;** **et,** ' also '.

Tarquinios. The Tarquins, of foreign (Etruscan) stock, were the 5th and 7th Kings of Rome.

l. 818. **Bruti.** Lucius Junius Brutus led a revolt against the tyranny of the last king of Rome, Tarquin the Proud, and formed a republican government, with himself as one of the two consuls who thereafter, as chief magistrates yearly elected, held what was left of the old royal power.

fascis receptos, ' the fasces which he recovered '. The fasces were the bundles of rods, which, with an axe, were carried by the consuls' lictors, or personal guards, as a sign of their right to inflict corporal and capital punishment. Vergil makes them symbols of liberty, since the consuls owed their position and this right to the popular will.

l. 819. **hic,** i.e. Brutus.

ll. 820, 821. Brutus ordered the execution of his own sons for plotting a counter-revolution to restore Tarquin the Proud.

l. 820. **natosque pater,** ' and he, their father . . . his sons '.

moventis, acc. pl., ' when they stir up '.

l. 822. **infelix,** ' unhappy man ', refers to Brutus.

ferent, ' shall report '.

minores, ' succeeding generations ', ' posterity ', subject of **ferent.** Cf. **maiores,** ' ancestors '.

The meaning of l. 822 is that history will applaud the selfless patriotism of Brutus, ignoring his agony as a father.

l. 823. **laudum** is objective genitive, dependent on **cupido,** ' passion for fame '.

l. 824. **quin.** Follow this with **aspice** from l. 825.

Decios. Two consuls of this family, father and son, each called Publius Decius Mus, deliberately sacrificed themselves in battle, in successive generations, for the victory of their armies, making a bargain as it were with the gods, that the casting away of their own lives should ensure triumph for the Romans.

Drusos. The most distinguished bearer of this name was Marcus Livius Drusus Salinator, who defeated Hasdrubal, brother of Hannibal, at the battle of the Metaurus, 207 B.C. His inclusion in this company of heroes owes something, too, to the fact that the wife of Augustus was a member of this family.

saevum securi, *lit.*, ' savage with his axe '; say ' with his ruthless axe '.

l. 825. **Torquatus.** A Roman hero who received the additional name Torquatus from the torque or necklet of twisted gold of which he despoiled a Gaulish champion whom he had slain in single combat. The allusion in the words **saevum securi** is to his having ordered, in the capacity of consul, the execution of his own son for acting in defiance of his orders.

Camillum ; another Roman hero, famous for a victory over the Gauls, in which he recovered lost Roman standards. 390 B (

ll. 826, 827. The order is **illae autem animae, quas cernis fulgere in paribus armis, concordes nunc et dum premuntur nocte.**

fulgere. The present participle is more natural than the infinitive in English.

dum nocte premuntur. The ' souls ' are those of Caesar and Pompey, the great rivals of the civil war. But they are not enemies yet. They are at peace ' now and while they are imprisoned in night ', i.e. until they are born into the world of light.

l. 828. **inter se,** ' mutual '.

ll. 830, 831. **socer, gener.** Before their final breach Pompey married Caesar's daughter Julia.

l. 830. **aggeribus Alpinis,** i.e. the Alps, which form ' ramparts ' that Caesar had to cross on his way from Gaul for the trial of strength with Pompey and the senate, in which Caesar's victory encompassed the destruction of the Republic and the senatorial oligarchy, and paved the way for the establishment of the Principate, with Augustus as 1st Roman emperor.

arce Monoeci. This ' citadel of Monoecus ' is now Monaco, on the Riviera.

adversis instructus Eois, ' arrayed with the opposing Eastern
(armies) '. Pompey, driven from Italy, met Caesar at Pharsa-
lus in Greece in 48 B.C. with troops drawn from the Eastern
provinces of the empire.

l. 832. ne adsuescite, for the prose construction nolite
adsuescere.

tanta, etc., *lit.*, ' do not accustom such great wars to your
minds ', i.e. ' accustom your thoughts to such great wars ', the
phrase being inverted according to the poet's frequent practice.

l. 833. Notice the alliteration. viris is acc. pl.

l. 834. genus qui ducis Olympo. Anchises is addressing the
soul of the unborn Julius Caesar, who ' traces his descent from
Olympus ', (i.e. is of divine stock), because he is to be a descendant of Iulus, son of Aeneas and grandson of Venus by
Anchises.

l. 835. sanguis meus, nom. used for vocative, ' thou of my
own blood '.

ille, ' that (hero) ', i.e. Mummius, who took and sacked
Corinth, 146 B.C.

l. 836. triumphata, abl. as the scansion shows, goes with
Corintho in the abl. absolute construction.

victor. See note, l. 804.

l. 837. caesis insignis Achivis, ' distinguished by Greeks
slain ', i.e. ' famous for his slaughter of the Greeks '.

l. 838. It is uncertain whether ille refers again to Mummius,
or to Aemilius Paullus, for the claims made in the next two
lines fit neither commander perfectly.

l. 839. Aeaciden, ' a descendant of Aeacus ', possibly referring to Perseus of Macedonia.

genus, ' a scion '.

The two phrases in this line refer to the same person, for
Aeacus was the grandfather of Achilles.

l. 840. ultus. See note on miseratus, l. 332.

The vengeance lay in the destruction of Mycenae and Argos,
the cities from which came the Greek leaders Agamemnon and
Menelaus.

templa et. Reverse these.

temerata. During the Trojan War Minerva's temple was defiled by Ajax, son of Oileus, when he dragged from the altar Cassandra, a daughter of Priam, who had sought sanctuary there.

l. 841. **relinquat**, potential subjunctive, ' would leave '.

tacitum, *lit.*, ' kept silent about ', i.e. ' unremarked '.

Cato (Marcus Porcius Cato) was the type of the old-fashioned Roman, a man famous in politics and literature, and as the implacable foe of Carthage. He lived from 224–149 B.C.

Cossus, one of three Romans to win the **spolia opima**, i.e. when in chief command to strip the body of the enemy leader, slain by himself in single combat. The feat was also performed by M. Claudius Marcellus, and, according to tradition, by Romulus. The victim of Cossus was Lars Tolumnius, king of the Etruscan city of Veii.

l. 842. **quis. tacitum relinquat** is understood (though it need not be again translated) from l. 841.

Gracchi. A Gracchus was consul during the war against Hannibal. More distinguished bearers of the name were the two brothers, Tiberius and Caius Sempronius Gracchus, who as tribunes of the people sought to combat senatorial misgovernment, and met their end in faction fights, 133 and 121 B.C.

l. 843. **Scipiadas.** ' the two sons of the Scipios ' are Publius Cornelius Scipio Africanus Maior, who defeated Hannibal at Zama, 202 B.C., and P. C. Sc. Aemilianus Africanus Minor, the destroyer of Carthage in 146 B.C. The latter was a Scipio only by adoption, which was much practised among the Romans.

parvo potentem, ' powerful with little ', i.e. ' poor, yet powerful '. Fabricius was a type of incorruptibility, who though a poor man, refused the bribes of King Pyrrhus, an enemy of Rome.

l. 844. **sulco, Serrane, serentem.** Vergil suggests that the name of this Roman commander is connected with the verb **sero**. The picture he draws is of a farmer turned admiral, who won a naval victory over the Carthaginians.

sulco, for **in sulco.**

l. 845. **fessum** agrees with **me** understood : ' whither, ye Fabii, are you hurrying me weary? ' The Fabii were another very distinguished family. Vergil makes Anchises select one, the most famous of all, for Aeneas to observe. This Quintus Fabius Maximus was the dictator whose cautious policy of avoiding battle with Hannibal frustrated the latter's desire to crush Roman arms in the field.

l. 846. **rem,** i.e. **rem publicam,** ' the state '. The line is almost a quotation from an earlier Latin poet, Ennius.

ll. 847–853. Some of the most famous lines in all Vergil. Others, says the poet, (and by others he means the Greeks) shall excel in the arts, in eloquence and in astronomy. The art of the Roman is to be the art of ruling others.

l. 847. **spirantia aera,** ' the breathing bronze ', i.e. bronze statues so lifelike as to seem alive.

l. 848. **vivos,** etc., i.e. ' shall fashion marble heads '.

l. 849. **caeli meatus.** Not really the movements of heaven, but of the heavenly bodies in the sky.

l. 850. **radio.** The radius or ' rod ' was used for drawing diagrams in sand by Greek teachers of mathematics and astronomy.

l. 851. **memento.** 2nd sg. imperative of **memini.**

l. 852. **tibi** is equal to **tuae.**

l. 854. **mirantibus,** ' (to them) marvelling ', i.e. ' as they marvelled '.

l. 855. **ut,** ' how ', followed by the indicative, where strict grammar would require subjunctive, since the **ut** clause is an indirect question. Cf. **stant,** l. 779.

Marcellus. A famous Roman general, M. Claudius Marcellus, who gained the **spolia opima** in B.C. 222, by slaying in battle the King of the Insubrian Gauls.

spoliis opimis. See note on **Cossus,** l. 841.

victor, adverbially, ' victoriously '.

l. 857. hic = Marcellus. rem, same sense as in l. 846.

magno turbante tumultu, ' when a great commotion troubles (it) '—abl. absolute. tumultus is the regular word for a rising or Gallic invasion threatening the home country of Italy.

l. 858. eques sternet, *lit.*, ' shall, mounted, lay low ' ; say ' shall trample beneath his charger's feet '.

Poenos. Against these, too, Marcellus gained successes.

l. 859. tertia, ' for the third time '.

arma capta, i.e. the spolia opima.

patri Quirino, ' (as an offering) to father Quirinus ', i.e. to the deified Romulus.

l. 860. hic : adverb of time. Aeneas, supply inquit.

una, adverb ; una ire, ' that there went along with (him) '.

l. 861. iuvenem. This youth is a young Marcellus, nephew of Augustus, and marked out by him as the heir to his power. He died tragically young, bringing great grief to Augustus and the Roman people as a whole.

l. 862. frons, supply erat. frons is the brow of the iuvenis of l. 861.

laeta parum, ' too little joyful ', i.e. ' most sad '.

et deiecto lumina vultu, ' and his eyes (lumina) (were) with —i.e. had—a downcast look '.

l. 863. The order is quis, pater, ille (est) qui sic comitatur virum euntem?

virum is the Marcellus of l. 855.

euntem, ' as he goes '.

l. 864. filius ' (is it his) son '.

anne. More usually the -ne would be attached to filius, and would have the same meaning as utrum, a particle serving to introduce the first of two alternative questions.

an aliquis, ' or (is it) one? '

de, ' from ', may be rendered ' of ' here.

l. 865. qui, exclamatory, ' what a '.

quantum instar (est) in ipso, ' how great a presence is in the youth (himself) '.

l. 867. **ingressus,** sc. **est.**

l. 868. **ne quaere,** ' ask not of '. Remember that **ne +** imperative is not a prose construction.

tuorum, masc., ' of thy people '

luctum. The grief mentioned is that caused by the premature death of the young Marcellus, a fate which threatens and saddens his yet unborn spirit. There is a story that the mother of Marcellus, Augustus' sister Octavia, fainted with emotion on hearing these beautiful lines about her son and upon recovery ordered that the poet be given 10,000 sesterces for each line.

l. 869. **tantum,** adverb, ' only '. **fata,** nom.

l. 870. **esse,** ' be ' in the sense of ' live '.

l. 871. **nimium** modifies **potens. visa,** sc. **esset,** ' would have seemed '.

superi, voc., = di.

fuissent, ' had been '. Remember that the pluperfect subjunctive is used in both clauses of such conditional sentences as ' if he had come he would have saved us ', i.e. conditions, relating to past time, in which events have made the assumption quite unreal.

ll. 872, 873. The order is **quantos gemitus virum ille campus aget ad magnam urbem Mavortis.**

ille campus is the Campus Martius, a plain and exercising ground outside Rome. On it Augustus built a family mausoleum, the scene of the funeral of young Marcellus.

virum, gen. pl.

Mavors is another form of Mars. ' The city of Mars ' is Rome, whose founder Romulus was a son of that god.

l. 872. **aget,** ' will waft '.

l. 873. **quae,** ' what a ', **funera** being pl. for sg.

Tiberine. Tiberinus is the god of the river Tiber.

l. 874. **praeterlabēre**, 2nd sg. fut. indic.

l. 875. **quisquam**, pronoun, ' any ', is used here for the more usual **ullus**, an adjective, and qualifies **puer**.

l. 876. **in tantum**, ' to so much ', i.e. ' so high ' **spe**, ' in hope '.

l. 877. **ullo alumno**, ' in any of her children '.

l. 878. **bello**, ' in war '.

ll. 879–880. **non . . . armato**, ' not anyone would have carried himself scatheless in-the-way-of (**obvius**) him armed ', i.e. ' none would have met him in battle, without rueing it '.

The implied protasis is ' if he had lived '. Anchises speaks of the ill-fated youth as already dead.

l. 880. **pedes**, nom. sg., ' on foot ', *lit.*, ' a footman '.

l. 882. **quā**, supply **viā** : ' by any means '.

si rumpas, a prayer : ' if only thou couldst break '.

l. 883. **tu Marcellus eris**. The sense seems to be ' thou shalt be Marcellus ' (however tragically brief thy destiny).

manibus, etc. The construction is **date spargam**, ' grant (that) I may scatter ', and the subjunctives **accumulem** and **fungar** depend similarly on **date**.

l. 884. **purpureos flores** is in apposition to **lilia**.

l. 887. **aëris**, here =' of mist '. Render by ' misty '.

l. 888. **quae per singula**, ' through them one by one '—' them ', since the relative after a full stop is unnatural in English.

duxit, (and **incendit**) require to be rendered by pluperfects in English, just as, conversely, English ' after he had done ' must be translated by **postquam fecit**.

l. 889. **famae** is a good example of the objective genitive, a use of the case in which the relation between the genitive word and the noun on which it depends (in this case **amore**) is similar to that between an object and its verb.

l. 890. **quae gerenda**, sc. **sunt**.

docet, ' tells (him) of '.

l. 891. **Laurentis**, acc. pl. ' The Laurentine folk ' dwelt in Laurentum, a native city not far from the future Rome. Latinus was its king, and his daughter, Lavinia, was later to be the wife of Aeneas.

l. 892. ' and how he is to escape, or endure, each tribulation '. The clauses are indirect deliberative questions. Notice how the double -que has to be rendered.

ll. 893–896. The passage is imitated from Homer. The sense is : dreams proceed from the Underworld ; true visions come by the gate of horn, false ones by that of ivory. It is by this that Aeneas returns to the world above.

l. 893. **fertur**, as often = ' is said '. After it supply **esse**.

l. 894. **umbris**, perhaps ' spirits '.

l. 898. **porta eburna** is ablative, and the object of **emittit is eos** understood.

l. 899. **ille** = Aeneas. **navis**, acc. pl.

l. 900. **Caietae**. This town lay on the coast of Latium.

recto litore, means ' straight along the coast '.

stant litore, ' stand (on) the shore ', i.e. ' fringe ' it.

puppes, ' ships '—synecdoche.

VOCABULARY

(N.B.—In the following vocabulary the figures (1), (2), (3), (4), after the verbs, denote the conjugation. No conjugation number is given in the case of -io verbs like capio.)

ā, ab, *prep. with abl.*, from ; after, (234).

abeō, -īre, -īvī *or* iī, itum, go away.

absisto, -ere, -stitī, -stitum, (3), withdraw, cease.

abstrūdō, -ere, -sī, -sum, (3), push off *or* away ; conceal, (7).

abstulī, *see* auferō.

absum, -esse, āfuī, am away, am absent.

ac, and.

accelerō, (1), hasten.

accendō, -ere, -ndī, -nsum, (3), kindle.

accersō, -ere, -sīvī, -sītum, (3), summon.

accingō, -ere, -nxī, -nctum, (3), gird on, arm with.

accipiō, -ere, -cēpī, -ceptum, receive, welcome ; hear (136 etc.).

accubō, -āre, -buī, -bitum, (1), lie down near ; recline, (606).

accumulō, (1), heap up, crown.

acerbus, -a, -um, sharp, bitter ; *of death, etc.,* untimely.

Achātes, -ae, *m.*, Achates, friend of Aeneas.

Acherōn, -ntis, *m.*, Acheron, a river of Hades.

Achillēs, -is, eī, and Ī, *m.*, Achilles, son of Peleus and Thetis ; a famous Greek hero, who slew Hector.

Achīvī, -ōrum, *m. pl.*, Greeks.

aciēs, -ēī, *f.*, edge ; blade, (291) ; gaze ; line of battle ; strife, (829). *In pl., sometimes* eyes.

ad, *prep. with acc.*, to, towards ; in answer to ; at, near ; **ad superos**, (481), among men.

adamas, -ntis, *m.*, adamant (*a substance remarkable for its hardness*).

addō, -ere, -didī, -ditum, (3), add, attach to.

adeō, -īre, -īvī *or* iī, -itum, approach, come to.

adeō, *adverb,* to such an extent ; indeed (498).

adferō, -ferre, attulī, allātum, bring, bring to ; bring here, (532).

adflō, (1), breathe on, inspire.

adfor, (1 *dep.*), speak to, address.

adforem, = adessem.

adgredior, -ī, -gressus sum, *dep.*, go to, approach ; attack, assail ; attempt, undertake ; challenge, (387).

adhūc, as yet, still.

adigō, -ere, -ēgī, -āctum, (3), drive, urge ; hurl down, (594).

aditus, -ūs, *m.*, entrance, approach.

adlābor, -ī, lāpsus sum, (3 *dep.*), glide towards.

adloquor, -ī, -locūtus sum, (3 *dep.*), speak to, address.

admīror, (1 *dep.*), admire ; marvel at, (408).

admittō, -ere, -mīsī, -missum, (3), admit.

admoneō, -ēre, -uī, -itum, (2), remind, warn.

adnō, (1), swim towards.

adorior, -īrī, -ortus sum, (4 *dep.*), attempt.

Adrastus, -ī, *m.*, Adrastus, a king of Argos.

adsimilis, -e, like to, resembling.

adsuescō, -ere, -suēvī, -suētum, (3), make accustomed to.

adsum, -esse, -fuī, am present, come to.

adulterium, -ī, *n.*, adultery.

adventō, (1), come to, approach, draw near.

adventus, -ūs, *m.*, approach, entrance, coming.

adversus, -a, -um, opposite, fronting, facing, opposing.

advertō, -ere, -tī, -sum, (3), turn . . . towards.

advolvō, -ere, -vī, -volūtum, (3), roll towards ; roll down, (182).

adytum, -ī, *n.*, shrine.

Aeacidēs, -ae, *m.*, son (*or* descendant) of Aeacus. *Stands for Achilles, grandson of Aeacus,* (58).

aemulus, -a, -um, full of rivalry, jealous.

Aenēās, -ae, *m.*, Aeneas.

Aenēās Silvius, a king of Alba Longa.

aēnus, -a, -um, of bronze ; aēnum, -ī, *neut. used as noun,* cauldron, (218).

Aeolidēs, -ae, *m.*, son of Aeolus.

aequō, (1), make equal ; keep pace with ; match, (474).

aequor, -oris, *n.*, level surface ; sea ; floor, (729).

aequus, -a, -um, level ; impartial, just ; favouring, (129).

āēr, -ris, *m.*, (*acc. sg.* aera), air ; mist.

aeripēs, -edis, brazen-footed.

āerius, -a, -um, rising into the air ; lofty.

aes, aeris, *n.*, copper, bronze ; brazen trumpet, (165) ; figure of bronze, (847).

aestās, -ātis, *f.*, summer.

aestuō, (1), boil, (*intr.*), seethe.

aeternus, -a, -um, everlasting, deathless. *Neut. sg. as adverb,* everlastingly, (401, 617, etc.)

aethēr, -eris, *m.*, (*acc. sg.* aethera), the bright upper air, ether ; heaven, sky, (130).

aetherius, -a, -um, ethereal, heavenly.

Agamemnonius, -a, -um, of Agamemnon, *the leader of the Greeks against Troy.*

agger, -is, *m.*, mound, rampart.

agitō, (1), keep moving, move, toss about ; agitātus, (68), harassed, storm-tossed.

āgmen, -inis, *n.*, troop, band, company.

āgna, -ae, *f.*, lamb.

āgnōscō, -ere, -nōvī, -nitum, (3), recognize, acknowledge.

agō, -ere, ēgī, āctum, (3), do ; drive, move ; waft, (873) ;

spend (*time*) ; harass, (379) ; *imperative*, **age, come !** (343, 531, etc.).

āiō, say.

āla, -ae, *f.*, wing.

alacer, -cris, -cre, quick, eager.

Alba, -ae, *f.*, Alba Longa, *the mother city of Rome.*

Albānus, -a, -um, Alban, (*adjective from the above*).

Alcīdēs, -ae, *m.*, descendant of Alceus ; *stands for* Hercules, (123, 392, 801).

aliquī, -qua, -quod, *adj.*, some, any.

aliquis, -quid, *pron.*, some one, anyone.

aliter, otherwise.

alius, -a, -ud, other, another ; **aliī . . . aliī,** some . . . others.

alligō, (1), bind to, bind round.

almus, -a, -um, kindly.

alō, -ere, aluī, altum *or* **alitum,** (3) nourish, sustain.

Alōīdae, -ārum, *m.* *pl.*, sons of Aloeus.

Alpīnus, -a, -um, Alpine.

altē, on high, aloft.

alter, -era, -erum, one, *or* the other (*of two*), another ; second.

alternus, -a, -um, alternate, by turns.

altus, -a, -um, lofty, high, tall ; on high ; deep ; **supera alta,** (787), the heavens above.

alumnus, -ī, *m.*, nursling.

alveus, -ī, *m.*, boat.

alvus, -ī, *f.*, belly, womb.

amāns, -ntis, *c.*, lover.

ambāgēs, -is, *f.*, (*usually in pl.*), mysteries (29, 99).

ambiō, -īre, -īvī *or* **-iī, -itum,** go

round, surround ; flow round, (550).

ambo, -ae, -o, both ; two, (540).

amictus, -ūs, *m.*, dress, clothing.

amīcus, -ī, *m.*, friend.

amnis, -is, *m.*, stream, river.

amō, (1), love.

amoenus, -a, -um, lovely, pleasant (*to the sight*).

amor, ōris, *m.*, love, yearning.

āmoveō, -ēre, -mōvī, -mōtum, (2), move away, remove.

Amphrȳsius, -a, -um, of Apollo (*since Apollo once lived by the river Amphrysus*).

amplexus, -ūs, *m.*, embrace.

amplus, -a, -um, large, spacious.

an, or.

Anchīsēs, -ae, *m.*, Anchises, (*father of Aeneas*).

Anchīsiadēs, -ae, *m.*, son of Anchises, (i.e. *Aeneas*).

ancora, -ae, *f.*, anchor.

Ancus, -ī, *m.*, Ancus, (4th *king of Rome*).

Androgeōs, -ī, *m.*, Androgeos, (*son of Minos*).

anguis, -is, *c.*, serpent.

anhēlus, -a, -um, panting.

anima, -ae, *f.*, breath, life, soul, ghost, spirit.

animus, -ī, *m.*, mind ; heart ; spirit, courage ; inspiration, (11).

anne, or.

annōsus, -a, -um, aged, full of years.

annus, -ī, *m.*, year ; season, (311).

ante, *adv.*, *and prep. with acc.*, before, in front (of) ; ere now.

Antēnoridēs, -ae, *m.*, son of Antenor.

antequam, (sometimes divided, ante . . . quam), conj., before.

antīquus, -a, -um, old, ancient.

antrum, -ī, n., cave.

Aornos, -ī, c., Avernus.

aperiō, īre, -ruī, -rtum, (4), open, reveal.

apertus, -a, -um, open.

apis, -is, f., bee.

Apollō, -inis, m., Apollo, (god of prophecy, also the Sun-God).

aprīcus, -a, -um, sunny.

aptus, -a, -um, fit, fitted; studded, (797).

apud, prep. with acc., among.

aqua, -ae, f., water.

āra, -ae, f., altar.

arbor or arbos, -oris, f., tree.

arcānus, -a, -um, secret.

arceō (2), keep off, hold . . . aloof.

arcessō, alternative form of accerso.

Arctos, -ī, f., the Bear constellation. In pl., the North, (16).

arcus, -ūs, m., bow.

ardeō, -ēre, arsī, arsum, (2), am on fire, burn, partic. ardēns, eager, fierce, glowing, blazing.

arduus, -a, um, high, lofty.

Argos, n., (only nom. and acc. sg. occur), Argos, (Greek city in the Peloponnese).

arma, -ōrum, n. pl., arms, weapons; armour; war; gear (353); warlike prowess (769).

armātus, -a, -um, armed.

armipotēns, -ntis, powerful in arms.

armus, -ī, m., flank, side.

ars, artis, f., art.

artus, -ūs, m., joint, limb.

arvum, -ī, n., field, land.

arx, arcis, f., citadel, stronghold; height.

aspectō, (1), look at, gaze at.

aspectus, -ūs, m., sight, vision.

asper, -era, -erum, rough, cruel; rugged, 360.

aspiciō, -ere, -spexī, -spectum, view, behold.

Assaracus, -ī, m., Assaracus, (grandfather of Anchises).

ast = at.

astō, -āre, -stitī, -stitum, (1), stand by; stay; hover, (17).

astrum, -ī, n., star.

at, but, yet.

āter, ātra, ātrum, black, murky, gloomy; dark (215).,

Atlās, -ntis, m., Atlas, (the giant who supported the world on his shoulders).

atque, and.

attingō, -ere, -tigī, -tāctum, (3), touch, arrive at; attain, (829).

attollō, -ere, (3), raise up, uplift.

attonitus, -a, -um, astonished, awe-struck.

attulī, see adferō.

auctor, -ōris, m., author, founder.

audēns, -ntis, bold, daring.

audeō, -ēre, ausus sum, (2 semidep.), dare.

audiō, (4), hear; audīta, (266), what I have heard.

auferō, -ferre, abstulī, ablātum, carry away, take away, rob . . . . of.

Augustus, -ī, m., Augustus (first Roman emperor).

aura, -ae, f., air, breath, breeze; gleam, (204); sky, (733); spirit, (747); populāris aura, (816), popular favour.

aureus, -a, -um, golden.
auricomus, -a, -um, golden, (*lit.*, golden-haired).
auris, -is, *f.*, ear.
Aurōra, -ae, *f.*, Aurora, (*goddess of the dawn*).
aurum, -ī, *n.*, gold.
Ausonius, -a, -um, Ausonian ; Italian (*since Ausonia was an ancient name for Italy*).
auspicium, -ī, *n.*, auspices (*prospects for the future, divined from watching the flight of birds*) ; leadership, (*because it was the leader's duty to ' take the auspices '*).
Auster, -trī, *m.*, the South Wind.
ausus, -a, -um, *see* audeō.
aut, or.
autem, but, however.
autumnus, -ī, *m.*, autumn.
āvellō, -ere, -vellī *or* -vulsī, -vulsum, (3), tear off, pluck off.
Avernus, -ī, *m.*, Avernus (*lake near Naples*).
Avernus, -a, -um, of Avernus, (118, 564).
āvertō, -ere, -tī, -sum, (3), turn away ; āversus, (224, 469), with face averted.
avidus, -a, -um, longing, eager.
avis, -is, *f.*, bird.
avus, -ī, *m.*, grandfather, ancestor.
axis, -is, *m.*, axis ; *the axis of heaven*, pole, zenith ; heaven, (536) ; vault, (790).

bacchor, (1 *dep.*), revel.
beātus, -a, -um, blessed, happy.
bellum, -ī, *n.*, war.
bēlua, -ae, *f.*, beast, monster.

Berecyntius, -a, -um, Berecyntian.
bibulus, -a, -um, thirsty.
bidēns, -ntis, *f.*, sheep.
bīformis, -e, two-shaped, of twofold form.
bis, twice.
Bōla, -ae, *f.*, Bola, (*name of town*).
bonus, -a, -um, good (*comparative* melior, *superlative* optimus).
bracchium, -ī, *n.*, arm.
brattea, -ae, *f.*, gold leaf, gold foil, (209).
breviter, shortly, briefly.
Briareūs, -eī, *m.*, Briareus, (*a giant with* 100 *arms*).
brūmālis, -e, wintry, of winter.
Brūtus, -ī, *m.*, Brutus.

cacūmen, -inis, *n.*, summit.
cadō, -ere, cecidī, cāsum, (3), fall, fail.
cadūcus, -a, -um, fallen.
cadus, -ī, *m.*, jar, urn.
caecus, -a, -um, blind ; dark, obscure, mysterious.
caedēs, -is, *f.*, slaughter.
caedō, -ere, cecīdī, caesum, (3), cut ; slay.
caelestis, -e, heavenly ; from heaven, (379).
caelicola, -ae, *c.*, a dweller in heaven, a god.
caelifer, -era, -erum, heavenbearing.
caelum, -ī, *n.*, heaven, sky ; the upper air, (719).
Caeneūs, -eos *or* eī, Caeneus.
caenum, -ī, *n.*, mud.
caeruleus, -a, -um, dark blue ; dark.

Caesar, -āris, *m.*, Caesar.

Caiēta, -ae, *f.*, Caieta, (*now Gaeta, town on W. coast of Italy*).

calcar, -āris, *n.*, spur.

calidus, -a, -um, hot.

cālīgō, -inis, *f.*, darkness, gloom, murk.

callis, -is, *m.*, path.

Camillus, -ī, *m.*, Camillus.

camīnus, -ī, *m.*, furnace, forge.

campus, -ī, *m.*, plain, field.

candēns, -ntis, white, glistening.

candidus, -a, -um, white.

canis, -is, *c.*, dog.

cānitiēs, -ēī, *f.*, whiteness ; white *or* grey hair ; plūrima cānitiēs, abundant grey beard.

canō, -ere, cecinī, cantum, (3), sing ; *of oracles,* utter, declare.

canōrus, -a, -um, musical, tuneful.

cantus, -ūs, *m.*, song, music.

capiō, -ere, cēpī, captum, take, occupy ; receive, (377).

Capitōlium, -ī, *n.*, the Capitol (*name of a Roman hill, and of Jupiter's temple upon it.*

caput, -itis, *n.*, head ; top.

Capys, -yos, *m.*, Capys, (*a king of Alba*).

carcer, -eris, *m.*, prison, dungeon.

cardō, -inis, *m.*, hinge.

careō, (2), *with abl.,* am without, lack ; am deprived of ; carēns, deprived of, (333).

carīna, -ae, *f.*, keel ; boat.

carmen, -inis, *n.*, song, ode ; oracle.

carpō, -ere, -psī, -ptum, (3), pluck ; proceed upon, (629).

cārus, -a, -um, dear.

Caspius, -a, -um, Caspian.

castīgō, (1), chastise.

castra, -ōrum, *n. pl.,* camp.

Castrum Inuī, *name of a town.*

castus, -a, -um, chaste, holy, pure ; righteous man, (563).

cāsus, -ūs, *m.,* fall ; hazard, misfortune, lot.

catēna, -ae, *f.,* chain.

Catō, -ōnis, *m.,* Cato.

causa, -ae, *f.,* cause, reason.

cautēs, -is, *f.,* crag, rock.

cavus, -a, -um, hollow.

Cecropidēs, -ae, *m.,* son of Cecrops ; Athenian, (21), (*because Cecrops was an early king of Athens*).

cēdō, -ere, cessī, cessum, (3), yield ; abate (102) ; leave (460).

celer, -is, -e, swift.

cēlō, (1), hide, conceal.

celsus, -a, -um, lofty.

Centaurus, -ī, *m.,* Centaur.

centum, a hundred.

centumgeminus, -a, -um, hundred-fold.

Cerberus, -ī, *m.,* Cerberus.

Cerēs, -eris, *f.,* Ceres (*goddess of agriculture*).

cernō, -ere, crēvī, crētum, (3), see.

certāmen, -inis, *n.,* contest.

certō, (1), strive, contend.

certus, -a, -um, sure, fixed, certain.

cerva, -ae, *f.,* hind, deer.

cervus, -ī, *m.,* stag.

cessō, (1), am slow, loiter ; cessas in vota, (51), art thou slow to (make) vows?

ceu, as, just as ; as if.

Chalcidicus, -a, -um, Chalcidian, of Chalcis (*town in Euboea*).

Chaos, *n.,* Chaos ; the abyss.

Chārōn, -ntis, *m.*, Charon (*ferry-man of the dead*).

Chimaera, -ae, *f.*, Chimaera.

chorea, -ae, *f.*, dance, measure.

chorus, -ī, *m.*, dance; band *or* troop of singers *or* dancers.

cieō, -ēre, cīvī, citum, (2), set in motion, rouse; call forth, (468).

cingō, -ere, -nxī, -nctum, (3), surround, encircle.

cinis, -eris, *m.*, ashes.

circā, *adv.*, around.

circum, *adv.*, *and prep. with acc.*, around; in the train of, (166).

circumdō, -are, -dedī, -datum, (1), put around; surround; embrace, enfold.

circumferō, -ferre, -tulī, lātum, carry round; purify, (229).

circumfundō, -ere, -fūdī, -fūsum, (3), pour around, scatter around.

circumstō, -āre, -stetī, (1), stand around.

circumveniō, -īre, -vēnī, -ventum, (4), come round; encircle.

circumvolō, (1), fly around, hover around.

cithara, -ae, *f.*, lyre.

cīvīlis, -e, civic.

clādēs, -is, *f.*, disaster, ruin.

clāmor, -ōris, *m.*, shout, cry, war-cry, outcry.

clangor, -ōris, *m.*, clang, noise.

clārus, -a, -um, renowned, famous.

classis, -is, *f.*, fleet.

claudō, -ere, -sī, -sum, (3), shut, shut in.

cliēns, -ntis, *m.*, client, dependant.

Cōcȳtus, -ī, *m.*, Cocytus (river of Hades; the word means ' wailing '.).

coepī, -isse, *defective vb.*, began.

coerceō, (2), keep together, confine.

cōgnōmen, -inis, *n.*, name, cognomen.

cōgnōminis, -e, like-named.

cōgnōscō, -ere, -nōvī, -nitum, (3), recognize.

cōgō, -ere, coēgī, coāctum, (3), collect, compel.

Collātīnus, -a, -um, of Collatia (*town near Rome*).

collum, -ī, *n.*, neck.

color, ōris, *m.*, colour, hue.

coluber, -brī, *m.*, serpent, snake.

columba, -ae, *f.*, dove.

columna, -ae, *f.*, column, pillar.

coma, -ae, *f.*, hair.

comes, -itis, *c.*, comrade, companion.

comitor, (1 *dep.*), accompany.

commisceō, -ēre, -scuī, -stum *or* -xtum, (3), mingle . . . with.

committō, -ere, -mīsī, -missum, (3), incur, (569).

cōmō, -ere, -psī, -ptum, (3), arrange; comptus, (*of hair*) ordered.

compellō, (1), address.

complector, -ī, complexus sum, (3 *dep.*), embrace.

compleō, -ēre, -ēvī, -ētum, (2), fill up.

comprendō, -ere, -endī, -ēnsum, (3), grasp, embrace; grasp *with the mind*, comprehend; number, (626).

comprimō, -ere, -pressī, -pressum, (3), check, restrain.

concha, -ae, *f.*, shell.

concilium, -ī, *n.*, meeting, assembly.

conclāmō, (1), shout, cry.

concors, -rdis, agreeing ; in harmony, (827).

concrētus, -a, -um, innate, ingrown.

concursus, -ūs, m., assemblage.

concutiō, -ere, -cussī, cussum, shake ; smite.

condō, -ere, -didī, -ditum, (3), put together ; hide ; lay, (152) ; found, establish.

cōnferō, -ferre, -tulī, collātum, bring together, unite.

cōnficiō, -ere, -fēcī, -fectum, complete, finish ; wear away, exhaust.

cōnfundō, -ere, -fūdī, -fūsum, (3), pour together, confuse ; partic., cōnfūsus, (504), mingled.

congerō, -ere, -gessī, -gestum, (3), heap together.

coniciō, -ere, -iēcī, -iectum, throw together ; pile up, (222).

coniunx, -iugis, c., spouse ; husband or wife.

conlābor, -ī, -lāpsus sum, (3 dep.), fall, collapse.

cōnor, (1 dep.), try, endeavour, attempt, essay.

cōnsanguineus, -a, -um, of the same blood ; used as noun, m., brother.

cōnsīdō, -ere, -sēdī, -sessum, (3), settle, sink down.

cōnsistō, -ere, -stitī, -stitum, (3), stand still, halt; set foot, (807).

cōnspectus, -ūs, m., sight, aspect.

cōnspiciō, -ere, -spexī, -spectum, behold, see.

cōnstituō, -ere, -uī, -ūtum, (3), place, set up.

cōnsul, -is, m., consul.

cōnsultum, -ī, n., decree, decision.

contendō, -ere, -ndī, -ntum, (3), strive, contend.

conticēscō, -ere, -ticuī, (3), fall silent.

contingō, -ere, tigī, -tāctum, (3), touch, reach ; happen, turn out.

continuō, forthwith.

contorqueō, -ēre, -rsī, -rtum, (2), hurl, whirl.

contrā, adv., and prep. with acc., opposite, facing ; in answer to.

contus, -ī, m., pole.

convallis, -is, f., valley.

convellō, -ere, -vellī, -vulsum, (3), pluck, tear away.

conventus, -ūs, m., assembly.

convexus, -a, -um, vaulted, arched ; convexa, n. pl., (241, 750), the vault of heaven.

cor, cordis, n., heart.

Cora, -ae, f., Cora, (a Latin town).

cōram, adv., and prep. with abl., before, in the presence of ; face to face.

Corinthus, -ī, f., Corinth.

corneus, -a, -um, of horn.

cornipēs, -pedis, horny-hoofed.

cornū, -ūs, n., horn.

corporeus, -a, -um, of the body.

corpus, -poris, n., body, frame ; creature, (583).

corripiō, -ere, -ripuī, -reptum, snatch, seize ; hasten over, (634).

cortīna, -ae, f., cauldron.

Corynaeus, -ī, m., Corynaeus (a Trojan).

Cossus, -ī, m., Cossus.

crātēr, -ēris, m., mixing-bowl.

creātrix, -īcis, f., mother.

crēdō, -ere, -didī, -ditum, (3),
trust, believe, doubt not ; entrust. (*Person trusted is put in
the dative*).

cremō, (1), burn.

crepitō, (1), rattle ; tinkle, (209).

crīmen, -inis, *n.*, charge.

crīnis, -is, *m.*, hair.

crista, -ae, *f.*, crest, plume.

croceus, -a, -um, yellow.

crūdēlis, -e, cruel.

crūdēliter, cruelly.

crūdus, -a, -um, fresh, vigorous.

cruentus, -a, -um, bloody.

cruor, -ōris, blood (*from wound*),
gore.

cubīle, -is, *n.*, bed ; den, lair.

culter, -trī, *m.*, knife.

cum, *conj.*, when, since.

cum, *prep., with abl.*, with ;
(*follows and is attached to the
ablative of personal and relative
pronouns*, e.g., mecum, quibus-
cum).

Cūmae, -ārum, *f. pl.*, Cumae
(*Greek town on Italian coast
near Naples*).

Cūmaeus, -a, -um, Cumaean.

cumba, -ae, *f.*, boat.

cunctor, (1 *dep.*), delay, linger ;
resist, am reluctant, (211).

cuneus, -ī, *m.*, wedge.

cupīdō, -inis, *f.*, desire.

cupiō, -ere, -īvī, -ītum, desire,
yearn for.

cupressus, -ī, *f.*, cypress.

cūra, -ae, *f.*, care, anxiety,
trouble ; grief, sorrow.

Curēs, -ium, *m. pl.*, Cures, (*Sabine
town*).

currō, -ere, cucurrī, cursum, (3),
run.

currus, -ūs, *m.*, chariot.

cursus, -ūs, *m.*, running, course,
voyage.

curvus, -a, -um, bent, curved.

custōdia, -ae, *f.*, guardianship ;
sentinel, (574).

custōs, -ōdis, *m.*, guardian.

Cyclōps, -ōpis, *m.*, Cyclops, (*one
of a race of one-eyed giants*).

Daedalus, -ī, *m.*, Daedalus, (*the
first airman of mythology*).

damnō, (1), condemn.

Danaī, -ōrum *or* -um, *m. pl.*, the
Greeks.

dapem, -is, (*no nom. exists*) *f.*,
feast ; food, (225).

Dardania, -ae, *f.*, Troy, (*the land
of Dardanus, who founded the
kingdom*).

Dardanidae, -ārum, *m. pl.*, Trojans.

Dardanius, -a, -um, Trojan.

Dardanus, -ī, *m.*, Dardanus,
(*founder of Troy*).

Dardanus, -a, -um, Trojan, (57).

dē, *prep. with abl.*, from, down
from ; about, concerning ;
made of, (69) ; in, (70) ; of,
(757) ; de more, according to
custom, duly.

dea, -ae, *f.*, goddess.

dēbellō, (1), crush in war.

dēbeō, (2), owe, am due.

dēcēdō, -ere, -cessī, -cessum, (3),
depart.

dēcerpō, -ere, -psī, -ptum, (3),
pluck off.

Decius, -ī, *m.*, Decius, (*Roman
family name*).

decorō, (1), adorn.

decus, -oris, *n.*, ornament :
honour, glory.

dēdūcō, -ere, -xi, -ctum, (3), lead away, carry off.

dēficiō, -ere, -fēcī, -fectum, am wanting, fail ; founder, (354).

dēfīgō, -ere, -fixī, -fixum, (3), fix ; defixus lumina, (156), with eyes downcast.

dēfleō, -ēre, -flēvī, -flētum, (2), bewail, lament.

dēfungor, -ī, defunctus sum, (3 dep.), complete, finish with, end.

dehinc, (sometimes scanned as one syllable), thereafter, then.

dehiscō, -ere, -hīvī, (3), gape, open.

dēiciō, -ere, -iēcī, iectum, cast down.

deinde (usually scanned as two syllables, deīnde), thereafter, then, next ; hereafter, (756).

Dēiphobē, -ēs or -ae, f., Deiphobe, (priestess of Apollo).

Dēiphobus, -ī, m., Deiphobus, (son of Priam).

Dēlius, -a, -um, of Delos, Delian.

dēlūdō, -ere, -sī, -sum, (3), deceive, mock.

dēmēns, -ntis, mad, frantic, distraught ; as noun, madman (590).

dēmittō, -ere, -mīsī, -missum, (3), lower, send down ; of tears, shed.

dēmum, at last ; sic demum, so, and so only ; tum demum, then, and only then.

dēns, -ntis, m., tooth.

dēnsus, -a, -um, thick.

dēpendeō, -ēre, (2), hang down.

dēpōnō, -ere, -posuī, -positum, (3), lay down, lay.

dērigō, -ere, -rexī, -rectum, (3), govern, direct.

dēscendō, -ere, -ndī, -nsum, (3), go down, descend.

dēscēnsus, -ūs, m., descent.

dēscrībō, -ere, -psī, -ptum, (3), describe ; trace, (850).

dēsinō, -ere, -sīvī, -situm, (3), cease.

dēsuescō, -ere, -suēvī, -suētum, (3), render unaccustomed ; partic. desuētus, unaccustomed.

dēsum, -esse, -fuī, am wanting, am lacking, (often with dative).

dēsuper, from above.

dētrūdō, -ere, -sī, -sum, (3), thrust down, thrust away.

dēturbō, (1), drive away.

deus, -ī, m., god ; (occasional forms are : dī, nom., voc. pl. ; deum, gen. pl. ; dīs, dat., abl. pl.).

dēveniō, -īre, -vēnī, -ventum, (4), come down to, come to.

dexter, -era, -erum, right, on the right.

dextera or dextra, -ae, f., right hand ; trust, (613).

dīcō, -ere, -xī, -tum, (3), say, speak, tell, call, name, tell of, utter, recite.

dictum, -ī, n., word.

Dīdō, -ōnis, f., Dido.

diēs, -ēī, m., (occasionally, f.), day ; time.

differō, -ferre, distulī, dīlātum, put off, postpone.

digitus, -ī, m., finger.

dīgnus, -a, -um, worthy ; with abl., worthy of ; fitting, (173).

dīnumerō, (1), count, number.

dīrus, -a, -um, fearful, terrible.

Dis, Dītis, m., Dis, (god of the Underworld).

discēdō, -ere, -cessī, -cessum, (3), depart.

discessus, -ūs, *m.*, departure.

discō, -ere, didicī, (3), learn, acquaint oneself with.

discolor, -ōris, of different colour, contrasting, (204).

discordia, -ae, *f.*, dissension.

discrīmen, -inis, *n.*, distinction, difference.

dīspiciō, -ere, -spexī, -spectum, discern.

distringō, -ere, -inxī, -ictum, (3), stretch apart, stretch out; *partic.*, districtus, (617), spread-eagled.

distulī, *see* differo.

diū, for a long time.

dīva, -ae, *f.*, goddess.

dīverberō, (1), smite asunder.

dīves, -itis, rich, wealthy; precious, (195).

dīvitiae, -ārum, *f. pl.*, riches.

dīvus, -ī, *m.*, (*gen. pl. often* dīvum), god.

dō, dare, dedī, datum, (1), give, grant, allot; appoint; utter *words*; pay *penalty*; make, (76); permit, (327).

doceō, -ēre, -cuī, -ctum, (2), teach; tell; tell of, (891).

doctus, -a, -um, learned, skilled; wise, (292).

doleō, (2), grieve, grieve for.

dolor, -ōris, *m.*, grief, pain.

dolus, -ī, *m.*, guile, fraud, deceit.

domina, -ae, *f.*, mistress, queen.

dominor, (1 *dep.*), hold sway.

dominus, -ī, *m.*, lord, master.

domō, -āre, -uī, -itum, (1), tame, subdue.

domus, -ūs, *f.*, house, home, dwel-

ling, building; *pl.*, halls, (269); abodes (533).

dōnec, until.

dōnum, -ī, *n.*, gift, offering.

Dōricus, -a, -um, Doric, i.e. Greek.

Drūsus, -ī, *m.*, Drusus, (*Roman family name*).

dubitō, (1), hesitate.

dubius, -a, -um, doubtful; dubiis rebus, (196), in my perplexed fortunes.

dūcō, -ere, -xī, -ctum, (3), lead, guide, draw; fashion, shape; consider; spend (*time*); trace.

ductor, -ōris, *m.*, leader.

dulcis, -e, sweet, clear.

dum, while, until.

duo, -ae, -o, two.

dūrus, -a, -um, hard, unpitying; stout, (54, 148).

dux, ducis, *m.*, leader, guide, captain.

ē, *see* ex.

eburnus, -a, -um, *adj.*, ivory.

ecce, lo ! behold !

ēdūcō, -ere, -xī, -ctum, (3), lead out; raise; bring forth, bear.

efferō, -ferre, extulī, ēlātum, bear forth; raise; *partic.*, elatus, (23), rising.

effingō, -ere, -nxī, -ctum, (3), represent, portray.

[effor], -fārī, -fātus sum, (1 *dep.*), speak, utter, tell.

effugiō, -ere, -fūgī, -fugitum, flee, escape; flee from, elude.

effundō, -ere, -fūdī, -fūsum, (3), pour forth; *partic.* effusus, (305), streaming; (339). thrown overboard.

egēnus, -a, -um, needy ; res
egenae, (99), need.

egestās, -ātis, f., want.

ēgī, see ago.

ego, meī, I.

egomet, emphatic form of ego, I
myself.

ēgregius, -a, -um, illustrious,
peerless.

ēlātus, see effero.

elephantus, -ī, m., elephant ;
ivory.

Ēlis, -idis, f., Elis, (city and district of the Peloponnese).

ēluō, -ere, -uī, -ūtum, (3), wash
out.

Ēlysium, -ī, n., Elysium, (dwelling-
place of the blessed in Hades).

ēmicō, -āre, -cuī, (1), flash forth ;
spring forth, (5).

ēmittō, -ere, -mīsī, -missum, (3),
send forth.

ēmoveō, -ēre, -mōvī, -mōtum, (2),
move away, banish.

en, lo ! behold !

enim, conj., for ; indeed, (28).

ēnō, (1), swim forth ; fly aloft,
soar aloft.

ēnsis, -is, m., sword.

ēnumerō, (1), count over.

eō, īre, īvī or iī, itum, go, pass.

Ēōus, -a, -um, Eastern.

epulae, -ārum, f. pl., feast.

eques, -itis, m., horseman, cavalier.

equidem, truly, indeed.

equus, -ī, m., horse.

Erebus, -ī, m., Erebus, (a name
for the Underworld).

ergō, adv., therefore ; also prep.
with gen., for the sake of, (670).

Ēridanus, -ī, m., Eridanus, (name
of Italian river, the Po).

Eriphȳlē, -ēs or -ae, f., Eriphyle,
(wife of Amphiaraus).

ēripiō, -ere, -uī, ēreptum, snatch
away, rescue.

errō, (1), wander.

error, -ōris, m., wandering ; deceit ; maze, (27).

ēructō, (1), belch forth.

ēruō, -ere, -uī, -ūtum, (3), overthrow.

Erymanthus, -ī, m., Erymanthus,
(mountain range in Arcadia).

este, 2nd pl. imperative of sum.

et, and ; also, too, even ; et . . .
et, both . . . and.

etiam, also ; still, (485).

Euadnē, -ēs or -ae, f., Evadne,
(wife of Capaneus).

euhāns, -ntis, celebrating with
Bacchic cries.

Euboicus, -a, -um, Euboean ;
(from Euboea, island off E.
coast of Greek mainland).

Eumenides, -um, f. pl., the Furies.

ēvādō, -ere, -sī, -sum, (3), go up,
ascend ; go out, pass beyond.

ēvehō, -ere, -vexī, -vectum, (3),
carry out ; bear aloft.

ēventus, -ūs, m., issue ; future,
(158).

ēvocō, (1), call out, call forth,
summon.

ex or ē, prep. with abl., out of, from.

exanimis, -e, or exanimus, -a, -um,
lifeless.

exaudiō, (4), hear.

excēdō, -ere, cessī, -cessum, (3),
go out, leave, quit.

excidō, -ere, -cidī, (3), fall out,
fall from.

excīdō, -ere, -cīdī, -cīsum, (3),
cut out, hew out.

excipiō, -ere, -cēpī, -ceptum, take out, take ; catch, (173).

excolō, -ere, -uī, -cultum, (3), adorn, ennoble, (663).

excūdō, -ere, -dī, -sum, (3), beat out, fashion, forge.

excutiō, -ere, -cussī, -cussum, shake off.

exerceō, (2), exercise ; harass ; exact, (543) ; rack, (739).

exigō, -ere, -ēgī, -āctum, (3), drive out ; claim, exact ; finish ; perform, (637).

exiguus, -a, -um, small ; thin, ghostly, (493).

exim, see **exin.**

eximō, -ere, -ēmī, -emptum, (3), take away, remove.

exin or **exinde,** thereafter, then.

exitiālis, -e, ruinous, deadly, baneful.

exitus, -ūs, m., issue, end, way out.

exoptō, (1), long for.

expediō, (4), disentangle ; explain, set forth ; make ready, (219).

expendō, -ere, -endī, -ēnsum, (3), weigh out ; pay.

expleō, -ēre, -ēvī, -ētum, (2), fill up.

expōnō, -ere, -posuī, -positum, (3), disembark, (trans.).

exsanguis, -e, bloodless.

exscindō, -ere, -scidī, -scissum, (3), cut out, extirpate ; tear down, (553).

exsequor, -ī, -secūtus sum, (3 dep.), follow ; perform.

exsomnis, -e, sleepless.

exsors, -rtis, without share in (followed by gen.).

exspectō, (1), look for eagerly, await.

exstinguō, -ere, -inxī, -inctum, (3), extinguish, kill, wipe out ; blot out, (527) ; partic., exstinctus, dead, (457).

exstō, -āre, (1), stand out ; tower above, (668).

exsurgō, -ere, -surrexī, -surrectum, (3), rise up.

exta, -ōrum, n., pl., entrails.

extemplō, forthwith, at once.

extendō, -ere, -ndī, -nsum or **-ntum,** (3), stretch out ; give scope to, (806).

externus, -a, -um, outer ; foreign.

exterreō, (2), terrify, appal.

extrā, adv., and prep. with acc., outside, beyond.

extrēmus, -a, -um, outermost, utmost, last ; neut. pl. used as noun, death, (457).

exūrō, -ere, -ussī, -ustum (3), burn, burn out.

Fabius, -ī, m., Fabius, (Roman family name).

Fābricius, -ī, m., Fabricius (famous Roman general).

faciēs, -ēī, f., face ; appearance, form.

facilis, -e, easy.

faciō, -ere, fēcī, factum, do, make (fio used as passive).

factum, -ī, n., deed.

fallax, -ācis, treacherous, false.

fallō, -ere, fefellī, falsum, (3), deceive.

falsus, -a, -um, false, treacherous ; groundless, (513).

fāma, -ae, f., report, rumour ; fame, story ; glory, (889).

famēs, -is, (abl. famē), f., hunger.

fās, n. indecl., divine law ; fas est, it is lawful, it is right.

fascis, -is, m., bundle ; pl., the fasces, axe and rods carried by the lictors.

fātālis, -e, fated, of destiny, fateful.

fateor, -ērī, fassus sum, (2 dep.), own, confess.

fatīgō, (1), tire, weary, wear out ; dog, (533).

fātum, -ī, n., fate, destiny ; oracle ; pl., decrees, (376).

fātur, see for.

fātus, partic. of for.

fauces, -ium, f. pl., throat, jaws.

favilla, -ae, f., ashes.

fax, facis, f., torch.

fēcundus, -a, -um, fruitful, fertile.

fēlīx, -īcis, happy, fortunate ; of trees, etc., fruitful.

fēmina, -ae, f., woman.

fera, -ae, f., wild beast.

fērālis, -e, funereal.

feretrum, -ī, n., bier.

feriō, -īre, strike.

ferō, ferre, tulī, lātum, bear, carry, endure ; induce ; report, say, relate ; offer, (142) ; give, (198) ; pay, (213) ; cause, (464) ; produce, (729) ; fert, (675), prompts ; ferre gressum, (677), stride.

ferreus, -a, -um, of iron.

ferrūgineus, -a, -um, rust-coloured, dark-red, dusky.

ferrum, -ī, n., iron, steel ; sword.

ferus, -a, -um, wild.

fessus, -a, -um, weary, exhausted.

festīnō, (1), hasten ; perform quickly.

festus, -a, -um, festal.

fētus, -ūs, m., offspring, produce ; sprig, (141) ; growth, (207).

fībra, -ae, f., thread ; fibre, (600).

Fidēnae, -ārum, f. pl., Fidenae, (Latin town). Also sg., Fidena.

fidēs, -eī, f., faith, honour, pledge.

fidēs, -is, f., string, (of musical instrument).

fīdus, -a, -um, faithful, trusty.

fīgō, -ere, -xī, -xum, (3), fix ; transfix, pierce ; fasten ; plant footsteps ; make laws.

figūra, -ae, f., shape.

fīlius, -ī, m., son.

fīlum, -ī, n., thread.

findō, -ere, fidī, fissum, (3), cleave, split, divide.

fingō, -ere, finxī, fictum, (3), shape, mould.

fīnis, -is, m., end, frontier ; in pl., land, territory.

fīnitimus, -a, -um, neighbouring ; as noun, m., neighbour, neighbouring peoples, (378).

fīō, fierī, factus sum, am made, become, (used as passive of facio) ; fit gemitus, (220), there rises a wailing.

firmus, -a, -um, strong, stout, firm.

fissilis, -e, easily split.

flagellum, -ī, n., whip, scourge.

flamma, -ae, f., flame, fire ; torch, (518).

flectō, -ere, -xī, -xum, (3), bend, turn, turn aside ; guide, (804).

fleō, -ēre, flēvī, flētum, (2), weep, weep for.

flētus, -ūs, m., weeping, tears.

flōs, ōris, m., flower.

fluctus, -ūs, m., wave.

fluentum, -ī, *n.*, stream, current.

flūmen, -inis, *n.*, river, stream.

fluvius, -ī, *m.*, river.

fodiō, -ere, fōdī, fossum, dig; prick, (881).

folium, -ī, *n.*, leaf.

[for], fārī, fātus sum, (1 *dep.*), speak, say, utter.

fore, *fut. inf. of* sum.

forī, -ōrum, *m. pl.*, gangway, (*of ship*).

forēs, -ium, *f. pl.*, door; (*properly the two leaves of a double door*).

forma, -ae, *f.*, shape; beauty; form, (626).

formīdō, -inis, *f.*, fear, dread.

fornix, -icis, *m.*, arch.

fors, *abl.* forte, (*no other cases used*), *f.*, chance; *as adv.*, (537), perchance; forte, by chance.

fortis, -e, brave.

fortūna, -ae, *f.*, fortune.

fortūnātus, -a, um, fortunate, blessed.

frāter, -tris, *m.*, brother.

fraus, -dis, *f.*, guile, deceit; wickedness.

fraxineus, -a, -um, of ash.

fremō, -ere, -uī, -itum, (3), roar, murmur; lament, (175).

frēnum, -ī, *n.*, bridle, reins.

frequēns, -ntis, crowded, numerous.

frequentō, (1), crowd, haunt.

frētus, -a, -um, relying on, (*with abl.*).

frīgeō, -ēre, (2), am cold; *partic.*, frīgēns, the cold, i.e. dead, man, (219).

frīgidus, -a, -um, cold.

frīgus, -oris, *n.*, cold.

frondēns, -ntis, leafy.

frondeō, -ēre, (2), am in leaf; put forth leaves, (208).

frondescō, -ere, (3), put forth leaves.

frōns, -ndis, *f.*, leaf, foliage.

frōns, -ntis, *f.*, forehead, brow.

frūstrā, in vain.

frūstror, (1 *dep.*), mock, deceive.

frūges, -um, *f. pl.*, corn; meal, (420).

fugiō, -ere, fūgī, fugitum, flee, flee from, escape, avoid; *partic.*, fugiēns, *as noun*, fugitive.

fugō, (1), put to flight, rout, drive.

fulcrum, -ī, *n.*, prop, support; foot (*of couch*), (603).

fulgeō, -ēre, *or* ere, fulsī, gleam, shine.

fulmen, -inis, *n.*, thunderbolt.

fulvus, -a, -um, yellow.

fūmeus, -a, -um, smoky.

funditus, *adv.*, from the depths, utterly.

fundō, (1), found, establish; make fast, (4).

fundō, -ere, fūdī, fūsum, (3), pour, pour forth; spread out; throng, swarm, (709); *partic.*, fūsus, spreading, (440); sprawling, (423).

fundus, -ī, *m.*, bottom; fundo in imo, (581), at the bottom of the pit.

fungor, -ī, functus sum, (3 *dep.*), perform, (*with abl.*).

fūnus, -eris, *n.*, funeral; corpse; death; the dead, (510).

furiae, -ārum, *f. pl.*, the Furies, (*three goddesses of divine vengeance, Tisiphone, Megaera and Alecto*).

furō, -ere, -uī, (3), rave, rage.

furor, -ōris, *m.*, rage, madness.

furtum, -ī, *n.*, theft ; fraud, deceit ; *abl.* furtō *as adv.*, by stealth, secretly, (24).

fūsus, *see* fundo.

fūtūrus, -a, -um, future ; *neut. pl. as noun*, (12), the future.

Gabiī, -ōrum, *m. pl.*, Gabii, (*town of Latium*).

Gallus, -ī, *m.*, a Gaul.

Garamantēs, -um, the Garamantes (*African tribe*).

gaudeō, -ēre, gavīsus sum, (2 *semi-dep.*), rejoice.

gaudium, -ī, *n.*, joy, rejoicing.

gelidus, -a, -um, cold, icy.

geminus, -a, -um, double, twin, twofold ; a pair of ; two.

gemitus, -ūs, *m.*, groan, groaning ; wail.

gemō, -ere, -uī, -itum, (3), groan.

gena, -ae, *f.*, cheek.

gener, -ī, *m.*, son-in-law.

generō, (1), beget, sire.

geniālis, -e, festal.

genitor, -ōris, *m.*, father.

genitus, *see* gigno.

gēns, -ntis, *f.*, family, race, tribe ; stock, (757).

genus, -eris, *n.*, race, descent, birth ; offspring, scion, son ; progeny, (580, 648).

gerō, -ere, gessī, gestum, (3), bear, carry ; wage *war* ; have, (772).

gīgnō, -ere, genuī, genitum, (3), bring forth *children* ; dis geniti, sprung from, i.e. sons of, the gods.

Glaucus, -ī, *m.*, Glaucus.

glaucus, -a, -um, grey.

globus, -ī, *m.*, globe, ball.

glomerō, (1), gather together ; *in pass.*, flock together.

glōria, -ae, *f.*, glory.

Gnōsius, -a, -um, Cretan.

Gorgō, -onis, *f.*, a Gorgon.

Gracchus, -ī, *m.*, Gracchus, (*Roman family name*).

gradior, -ī, gressus sum, (*dep.*), stride, walk.

gradus, ūs, *m.*, step.

Grāius, *or* Grāīus, -a, -um, Greek ; *masc. pl. as noun*, the Greeks ; (*gen. pl. sometimes* Graium.)

grāmen, -inis, *n.*, grass.

grāmineus, -a, -um, grassy.

grātia, -ae, *f.*, grace, beauty ; pleasure, delight, (653).

gravis, -e, heavy ; grave ; pregnant, (516).

gravō, (1), make heavy, burden, weigh down.

gressus, (633), *see* gradior.

gressus, -ūs, *m.*, step.

grex, gregis, *m.*, flock.

gubernāclum, -ī, *n.*, rudder.

gubernātor, -ōris, *m.*, steersman, helmsman.

gurges, -itis, *m.*, whirlpool, eddy ; flood.

guttur, -uris, *n.*, throat.

habēna, -ae, *f.*, rein.

habeō, (2), have, hold.

habitō, (1), dwell.

haereō, -ēre, haesī, haesum, (2), cling.

hālitus, -ūs, *m.*, breath, exhalation.

harēna, -ae, *f.*, sand ; silt.

Harpȳīae, -ārum, *f. pl.*, the Harpies.

hasta, -ae, *f.*, spear, lance.
haud, not.
haurio, -ire, -sī, -stum, (4), drain, drink in ; drink in *sound*, (559).
hebetō, (1), blunt, dull.
Hecatē, -ēs, *f.*, Hecate.
Hector, -oris, (*acc.* Hectora), *m.*, Hector.
Hectoreus, -a, -um, of Hector.
herba, -ae, *f.*, grass.
hērōs, -ōis, *m.*, hero.
Hesperius, -a, -um, western ; Italian, (*from the Greek viewpoint*).
heu, alas !
hiātus, -ūs, *m.*, a yawning ; yawning mouth, (237, 576).
hībernus, -a, -um, wintry, of winter.
hīc, here ; hereupon, then.
hic, haec, hoc, this ; he, she, it ; *pl.* they.
hinc, hence, from here ; after this.
hiō, (1), yawn, gape.
homō, -inis, *m.*, man.
honor, -ōris, *m.*, honour ; worship, (589) ; badge of honour, device, (780).
hōra, -ae, *f.*, hour.
horrendus, -a, -um, dreadful, horrible.
horreō, -ēre, (2), stand on end, bristle (*of hair, etc.*) ; shudder.
horrescō, -ere, horruī, (3), begin to shudder.
horridus, -a, -um, dreadful.
horrisonus, -a, -um, dreadfully sounding.
hortātor, -ōris, *m.*, instigator, prompter.
hortor, (1 *dep.*), encourage, exhort.
hospitus, -a, -um, foreign,

strange ; hospitable ; *as noun,* foreigner, stranger.
hostis, -is, *c.*, enemy.
hūc, hither.
humō, (1), bury.
humus, -ī, *f.*, ground ; soil ; (*loc.* humī, on the ground).
Hȳdra, -ae, *f.*, the Hydra.
hymenaeus, -ī, *m.*, marriage-song ; marriage.

iaceō, (2), lie, am prostrate.
iaciō, -ere, iēcī, iactum, throw, fling, cast.
iactāns, -ntis, boastful.
iactō, (1), toss, toss about ; *of words,* utter boastfully ; vaunt, (877).
iam, now, already, by now ; at once, (676).
iamprīdem, now for a long time.
iānitor, -ōris, *m.*, door-keeper.
iānua, -ae, *f.*, door.
ibi, there ; then.
Icarus, -ī, *m.*, Icarus.
īcō, -ere, īcī, ictum, (3), strike.
Īdaeus, -ī, *m.*, charioteer of Priam.
īdem, eadem, idem, the same ; *nom. sg. masc.*, he too, (116, 229).
iecur, iecoris, *n.*, liver.
īgnārus, -a, -um, unaware, ignorant.
īgneus, -a, -um, fiery.
īgnis, -is, *m.*, fire.
īlex, -icis, *f.*, holm-oak.
Īlia, -ae, *f.*, Ilia.
Īliacus, -a, -um, of Ilium, i.e. Trojan.
Īlium, ī, *n.*, Ilium, a name for Troy.

ille, -a, -ud, that; the famous; *as pron.*, he, she, it; *pl.*, they.

Ilus, -ī, *m.*, Ilus.

imāgō, -inis, *f.*, phantom, spectre; form; semblance, (293); sight, (405).

imitābilis, -e, capable of imitation; *with* non, (590), inimitable.

imitor, (1 *dep.*), imitate.

immānis, -e, huge, vast, monstrous; awful.

immemor, -oris, unmindful.

immēnsus, -a, -um, measureless, boundless.

immergō, -ere, -rsī, -rsum, (3), plunge, sink, (*tr.*).

immineō, (2), overhang.

immittō, -ere, -mīsī, -missum, (3), let loose; fling into, (262).

immortālis, -e, deathless, immortal, undying.

imperium, -ī, *n.*, command, behest; rule, empire; dominion, (264, 795); power, (819).

impius, -a, -um, unholy, unnatural.

impōnō, -ere, -posuī, -positum, (3), place on, set over, impose; build up over.

impūne, without suffering punishment, scatheless, with impunity.

īmus, -a, -um, *superl. adj.*, lowest, the depths of.

in, *prep. with acc.*, into, on to, towards, against; *with abl.*, in, on.

inamābilis, -e, hateful.

inānis, -e, empty, unreal, ghostly, vain; unsubstantial, (740).

incānus, hoary, grey.

incendō, -ere, -endī, -ēnsum, (3), set fire to, kindle.

incertus, -a, -um, uncertain, doubtful.

incestō, (1), pollute, defile.

incipiō, -ere, -cēpī, -ceptum, begin.

inclūdō, -ere, -sī, -sum, (3), shut in, shut up, imprison.

inclutus, -a, -um, famous, glorious.

incohō, (1), begin; set up, (252).

incolō, -ere, -coluī, -cultum, (3), inhabit, haunt.

incolumis, -e, safe, unharmed.

increpō, (1), rebuke, upbraid.

incubō, -āre, -buī, -bitum, (1), brood over, (+ *dat.*).

incultus, -a, -um, untrimmed, unkempt.

inde, thence; thereafter, then.

indēbitus, -a, -um, not owed.

indīgnus, -a, -um, unworthy; undeserved.

indulgeō, ēre, -lsī, -ltum, (2), yield to, give scope to, indulge in, (+ *dat.*).

Indus, -a, -um, Indian; *masc. as noun*, an Indian.

inextrīcābilis, not to be unravelled.

īnfāns, -ntis, infant, babe.

īnfectus, -a, -um, *see* īnficiō.

īnfēlīx, -īcis, unhappy, ill-fated.

īnfernus, -a, -um, infernal, of the lower world.

īnferus, -a, -um, low; (*comp.* īnferior, *superl.* īmus, *or* īnfimus).

īnficiō, -ere, -fēcī, -fectum, stain, dye; infectum scelus, dyed-in wickedness, i.e. stain of guilt. (742).

informis, -e, shapeless ; unsightly, (416).

infundō, -ere, -fūdī, -fūsum, (3), pour in ; infusa per, permeating, (726).

ingemō, -ere, -uī, -itum, (3), groan over *or* at.

ingēns, -ntis, huge, mighty, vast ; deep, (491).

ingrātus, -a, -um, thankless, ungrateful.

ingredior, -ī, -gressus sum, (*dep.*), enter ; advance ; begin, (867).

inhonestus, -a, -um, shameful.

inhumātus, -a, -um, unburied.

inimīcus, -a, -um, unfriendly, hostile.

inīquus, -a, -um, unfair, hard ; cruel.

iniciō, -ere, -iēcī, -iectum, fling on.

iniussus, -a, -um, unbidden.

inlustris, -e, renowned.

innectō, -ere, -nexuī, -nexum, weave in, entwine ; devise against, (+ *dat.*), (609).

innō, (1), swim in, swim over ; voyage upon.

innumerus, -a, -um, countless.

innuptus, -a, -um, unmarried.

inolescō, -ere, -lēvī, -litum, (3), become ingrained.

inopīnus, -a, -um, unexpected.

inops, -opis, without resources, poor ; helpless, (325).

inremeābilis, -e, that can be passed but once.

inrumpō, -ere, -rūpī, -ruptum, (3), burst in.

inruō, -ere, -ruī, (3), rush in, rush on.

īnsānus, -a, -um, mad.

īnscius, -a, -um, ignorant.

īnsidiae, -ārum, *f. pl.*, ambush ; plot.

īnsīdō, -ere, -sēdī, -sessum, (3), sink down, settle.

īnsīgnis, -e, distinguished, marked out ; famous.

īnsistō, -ere, -stitī, (3), stand on ; tread on ; enter on.

īnsomnium, -ī, *n.*, dream.

īnsōns, -ntis, guiltless, innocent.

īnspīrō, (1), breathe . . . into (+ *acc.* . . . *and dat.*), (11, 12).

īnstar, *n. indecl.*, presence, majesty.

īnstaurō, (1), renew.

īnstituō, -ere, -uī, -ūtum, (3), set up, establish, ordain.

īnstruō, -ere, -xī, -ctum, (3), arrange, draw up ; array against, (831).

īnsuētus, -a, -um, unaccustomed.

īnsultō, (1), leap upon ; taunt.

īnsum, -esse, am in.

intāctus, -a, -um, untouched.

intentō, (1), stretch towards ; thrust out, (572).

inter, *prep. with acc.*, among, between ; in, (513, 658).

intereā, meanwhile.

interfundō, -ere, -fūdī, -fūsum, (3), pour between ; *pass.*, flow between, (439).

intexō, -ere, -xuī, -xtum, (3), interlace.

intonō, -āre, -uī, (1), thunder, thunder at.

intrā, *prep. with acc.*, within.

intrō, (1), enter.

intus, *adv.*, within.

Inuus, -ī, *m.*, Inuus, (*the Roman god of increase, especially among the herds*).

invādō, -ere, -sī, -sum, (3), enter,
enter upon ; attack.

invalidus, -a, -um, weak, feeble.

invehō, -ere, -xī, -ctum, (3),
carry upon ; invectus, (587),
drawn in a chariot.

inveniō, -īre, -vēnī, -ventum, (4),
find, discover.

invergō, -ere, (3), pour . . . upon
. . . , (with acc. and dat.), (244).

invictus, -a, -um, unconquered,
invincible.

invīsus, -a, -um, hateful.

invītus, -a, -um, unwilling.

invius, -a, -um, pathless, track-
less.

involvō, -ere, -volvī, -volūtum,
(3), wrap, shroud, (100) ; en-
gulf, (336).

Iovem, etc., see Iuppiter.

ipse, -a, -um, emphasizing pronoun,
-self ; (myself, himself, themselves, etc.).

īra, -ae, f., anger.

is, ea, id, that ; he, she, it, pl.
they.

iste, -a, -ud, that, that of yours.

istinc, from there, from where you
are.

ita, thus.

Ītalia, -ae, f., Italy.

Italus, -a, -um, Italian ; masc. as
noun, an Italian (gen. pl. sometimes Italum).

iter, itineris, n., road, path, way ;
journey ; course, (240).

iterum, again, for a second time.

ītō, 2nd sg. imperative of eo, (95).

iubeō, -ēre, -iussī, iussum, (2),
order, bid, command.

iucundus, -a, -um, pleasant.

iūdex, -icis, m., judge.

iūgerum, -ī, n., acre.

iugum, -ī, n., yoke ; thwart,
cross-bench, (411) ; ridge, (676,
etc.).

Iūlus, -ī, m., Iulus.

iungō, -ere, -nxī, -nctum, (3),
join ; clasp, (697).

Iūnō, -ōnis, f., Juno.

Iuppiter, Iovis, m., Jupiter.

iūrō, (1), swear ; swear by, (with
acc.), (324, 351).

iussum, -ī, n., command.

iustitia, -ae, f., justice.

iuvencus, -ī, m., bullock, steer.

iuvenis, -is, m., youth.

iuvō, -āre, iūvī, iūtum, (1), help ;
3rd. sg., impersonally, it pleases.

iuxtā, adv., and prep. with acc.,
next, close to, near by.

Ixīon, -ionis, m., Ixion.

lābēs, -is, f., spot, stain, taint.

lābor, -ī, lāpsus sum, (3 dep.),
glide ; glide down, (202) ;
slip, (602).

labos or labor, -ōris, m., labour,
toil ; trouble, tribulation ; en-
terprise, (135).

Lacaena, -ae, f., a Spartan
woman.

lacer, -era, -erum, torn, mangled,
mutilated.

lacrima, -ae, f., tear.

lacrimō, (1), weep.

lacus, -ūs, m., lake, mere.

laetor, (1 dep.), rejoice, take
pleasure in, (+abl.).

laetus, -a, -um, glad, happy, joyful.

laevus, -a, -um, left, on the left ;
f. sg. laeva, with manus understood, left hand ; with via

understood, (542), the left-hand road.

lampas, -adis, *f.*, torch.

laniō, (1), tear, mangle.

Lāodamīa, -ae, *f.*, Laodamia.

Lapithae, -arum, *m. pl.*, the Lapithae.

lāpsūrus, -a, -um, *see* lābor.

largus, -a, -um, plentiful, ample, copious.

lātē, widely, far and wide.

lateō, (2), lie hid.

latex, -ĭcis, *m.*, water.

Latīnus, -ī, *m.*, Latinus.

Latīnus, -a, -um, of Latium, Latin.

Latium, -ī, *n.*, Latium.

lātrātus, -ūs, *m.*, barking.

lātrō, (1), bark, howl.

latus, -eris, *n.*, side.

lātus, -a, -um, broad, spreading, (549).

Laurēns, -ntis, of Laurentum.

laurus, -ūs, *f.*, laurel.

laus, -dis, *f.*, praise, renown.

Lavīnia, -ae, *f.*, Lavinia.

Lavinium, -ī, *n.*, Lavinium, (*town in Latium*).

lavō, -āre, lāvī, lavātum, lautum *or* lōtum, wash ; drench, (227).

laxō, (1), loosen ; clear, (412).

legō, -ere, lēgī, lectum, (3), pick out, choose; survey, scan (755) ; gather up, (228) ; lectus, (39), chosen.

lēniō, (4), soothe.

lēnis, -e, gentle.

lentus, -a, -um, pliant.

Lerna, -ae, *f.*, Lerna, (*in Greece, near Argos*).

Lēthaeus, -a, -um, of Lethe.

lētum, -ī, *n.*, death.

Leucaspis, -is, *m.*, Leucaspis.

levis, -e, light.

lex, lēgis, *f.*, law.

lībāmen, -inis, *n.*, libation, offering.

Līber, -ī, *m.*, Liber, (*name of the wine-god, Bacchus*).

lībertās, -ātis, *f.*, freedom.

Libya, -ae, *f.*, Libya, Africa.

Libycus, -a, -um, African.

licet, -ēre, -uit, *or* licitum est, (2 *impers.*), it is permitted. licet *as conj., with subjunctive mood*, although, (802).

līlium, -ī, *n.*, lily.

līmen, -inis, *n.*, threshold ; door.

līmes, -itis, *m.*, boundary ; path.

līmus, -ī, *m.*, mud.

lingua, -ae, *f.*, tongue.

linquō, -ere, līquī, (3), leave.

liquēns, -ntis, watery.

liqueō, -ēre, (2), am liquid.

liquidus, -a, -um, liquid ; bright, clear.

lītus, -oris, *n.*, shore, coast.

lituus, -ī, *m.*, trumpet.

līvidus, -a, -um, leaden-hued.

locus, -ī, *m.*, place, region, (*pl. sometimes* loca, *n.*).

longaevus, -a, -um, aged.

longē, afar ; longē latēque, far and wide.

longus, -a, -um, long, distant ; lasting, (715).

loquor, -ī, locūtus sum, (3 *dep.*), speak, utter.

lūceō, -ēre, luxī, (2), shine, gleam

luctor, (1 *dep.*), wrestle.

luctus, -ūs, *m.*, grief.

lucus, -ī, *m.*, grove.

lūdibrium, -ī, *n.*, sport.

lūdus, -ī, *m.*, game, sport.

lūgeō, -ēre, luxī, luctum, (2), grieve, bewail, mourn.

lūmen, -inis, *n.*, light; day; *often,* eye.

lūna, -ae, *f.*, moon.

lūstrō, (1), purify; pass over, traverse; pass in review, review, regard; survey, (681, 887).

lux, lūcis, *f.*, light.

luxus, -ūs, *m.*, luxury, magnificence.

Lycius, -a, -um, Lycian.

mactō, (1), sacrifice.

madidus, -a, -um, wet, dripping.

Maeōtius, a, um, Maeotian.

maestus, -a, -um, sad, sorrowful.

magis, more.

magister, -rī, *m.*, master.

māgnanimus, -a, -um, great-souled.

māgnus, -a, -um, great, mighty, noble; *of voices,* loud; (*comp.* melior, *superl.* optimus).

malesuādus, -a, -um, ill-counselling.

malīgnus, -a, -um, grudging, scanty.

malum, -ī, *n.*, evil, misfortune; crime (527, 739).

malus, -a, -um, bad, evil; (*comp.* pēior, *superl.* pessimus).

mandātum, -ī, *n.*, trust; command.

mandō, (1), commit to, entrust to.

maneō, -ēre, mānsī, mānsum, (2), remain; last, endure; wait for, await.

mānēs, -ium, *m. pl.*, the shades of the departed, ghosts.

manus, -ūs, *f.,* hand; band, company.

Marcellus, -ī, *m.*, Marcellus.

mare, -is, *n.*, sea.

marmor, -oris, *n.*, marble; *in poetry, sometimes,* sea.

marmoreus, -a, -um, of marble; marble *as adj.*

Marpēsius, -a, -um, Marpesian, (= *of Marpesus, mountain famous for its marble*).

Mars, -tis, *m.*, Mars.

Massȳli, -ōrum, *or* -um, the Massyli.

māter, -tris, *f.*, mother.

māternus, -a, -um, mother's, maternal

Māvors = Mars.

Māvortius, -a, -um, of Mars.

māximus, *see* māgnus.

Māximus, -ī, *m.*, *cognomen of* Q. Fabius, *Roman dictator.*

meātus, -ūs, *m.*, wandering movement.

mēcum = cum mē.

medicātus, -a, -um, drugged.

medius, -a, -um, mid, middle of, central, intervening; media omnia, (131), all the space between; media inter cornua, midway between the horns.

Medōn, -ntis, *m.*, Medon.

mel, mellis, *n.*, honey.

melior, *see* bonus.

melius, *comp.* of bene, better.

membrum, -ī, *n.*, limb.

mementō, 2nd sg. *imperative of* memini.

meminī, -isse, *defective vb.*, remember.

memor, -ōris, mindful; heedfully, (377).

memorō, (1), relate, speak of, mention, say.

Menelāus, -ī, m., Menelaus.

mēns, mentis, f., mind.

mēnsa, -ae, f., table.

mēnsis, -is, m., month.

mentum, -ī, n., chin ; beard, (809).

mereor, (2 dep.), deserve, merit.

mergō, -ere, -rsī, -rsum, (3), sink, (tr.), immerse, plunge, bury, (267) ; overwhelm, (615).

metallum, -ī, n., mine ; metal.

metuō, -ere, uī, -ūtum, (3), fear.

metus, -ūs, m., fear, dread.

meus, -a, -um, my.

mi = mihi, (123).

mille, indecl., thousand ; plural, declinable, neut., milia, -um.

minae, -arum, f. pl., threats.

Minerva, -ae, f., Minerva.

minimē, least, very little, not at all, by no means.

ministerium, -ī, n., service.

ministrō, (1), attend to, tend, (with dat.).

Mīnōius, -a, -um, of Minos.

minor, -us, smaller, less, (comp. of parvus) ;

Mīnōs, -ōis, m., Minos.

Mīnōtaurus, -ī, m., the Minotaur.

minus, adv., less.

mīror, (1 dep.), wonder, wonder at.

mīrus, -a, -um, wonderful, wondrous.

misceō, -ēre, -cuī, mixtum or mistum, (2), mix, mingle.

Misēnus, -ī, m., Misenus.

miser, -era, -erum, wretched.

miserandus, -a, -um, pitiable, unhappy.

misereor, (2 dep.), pity.

miseror, (1 dep.), pity.

mittō, -ere, mīsī, missum, (3), send ; let go ; dismiss, (85).

modus, -ī, m., measure ; method, way, manner.

moenia, -ium, n. pl., walls ; a fortress, (549).

mōlēs, -is, f., mass, bulk.

mōlior, (4 dep.), toil at, undertake ; toil along, (477).

molliter, gently, smoothly ; comp., mollius.

moneō, (2), warn, advise.

monimentum, -ī, n., memorial, token.

monitus, -ūs, m., warning, behest.

Monoecus, -ī, m., Monoecus, (a name of Hercules).

mōns, montis, m., mountain, rock, boulder.

monstrō, (1), show, point out ; display, (440).

mōnstrum, -ī, n., monster.

mora, -ae, f., delay ; haud mora, (177), (there is) not delay, i.e. at once.

morbus, -ī, m., disease.

moribundus, -a, -um, dying.

moror, (1 dep.), delay, linger ; am slow to obey, (40).

mors, mortis, f., death.

mortālis, -e, mortal, human.

mortifer, -era, -erum, deathbringing, mortal.

mōs, mōris, m., custom, manner, habit ; in pl., character.

moveō, -ēre, mōvī, mōtum, (2), move, rouse ; trouble ; of war, etc., stir up ; shake, (432).

mūgiō, (4), bellow ; groan, (256).

multum, adv., much.

multus, -a, -um, much, many a;
pl., many.

mūnus, -eris, *n.*, gift; duty, task;
service, (526, 886).

murmur, -is, *n.*, murmur; hum-
ming, (709).

mūrus, -ī, *m.*, wall.

Musaeus, -ī, *m.*, Musaeus.

Mycēnae, -ārum, *f. pl.*, Mycenae.

myrteus, -a, -um, of myrtle.

nam *or* namque, *conj.*, for.

nāris, -is, *f.*, nostril; *pl.*, nose.

nāscor, -ī, nātus sum, (3 *dep.*), am
born.

nātus, *see* nascor.

nātus, -ī, *m.*, son.

nāta, -ae, *f.*, daughter.

nāvis, -is, *f.*, ship.

nāvita, -ae, *m.*, sailor, boatman.

-ne, *enclitic particle, denoting in-
terrogation.*

nē, *adv.*, not, (*with imperative*) ;
conj., lest, that . . . not, (*with
subjunctive*).

nec, *see* neque.

necesse, *adj.*, (*neut. nom. and acc.
only*) needful; *with* est it is
necessary, it is inevitable.

nec nōn, *lit.*, nor not, =and moreover.

nefandus, -a, -um, impious, monstrous.

nefās, *n. indecl.*, something contrary to divine law; crime;
guilt; nefas est, it is forbidden.

nemus, -oris, *n.*, grove, wood,
forest.

nepōs, -ōtis, *m.*, grandson, descendant.

neque, *or* nec, neither, nor, and
not; neque . . . neque . . . (nec

. . . nec . . .), neither . . . nor
. . .

nequeō, -īre, nequīvī *or* iī, -ītum,
am unable.

nēquīquam, in vain.

nesciō, (4), know not.

neu *or* neve . . . neu *or* neve . . .,
neither . . . nor.

nī, *see* nisi.

niger, -gra, -grum, black, dark.

nigrāns, -ntis, black.

nihil *or* nīl, *n. indecl.*, nothing,
naught; as *adv.*, in no way.

Nīlus, -ī, *m.*, the Nile.

nimbus, -ī, *m.*, rain-cloud.

nimium, too much, too.

nisi, *sometimes* nī, unless, if not.

nitēns, -ntis, shining, glossy.

niteō, (2), shine, am bright.

nītor, -ī, nīsus *or* nixus sum, (3
dep.), rest on, lean on, (*with
abl.*) ; strive.

niveus, -a, -um, snow-white.

noceō, hurt, injure, am harmful
to, (*with dat.*).

nocturnus, -a, -um, of the night,
night, *as adj.*

nōdus, -ī, *m.*, knot.

nōmen, -inis, *n.*, name.

Nōmentum, -ī, *n.*, Nomentum.

nōn, not.

nōndum, not yet.

nōrunt =nōvērunt, *see* nōscō.

nōscō, -ere, nōvī, nōtum, (3), get
to know, learn; *in perf.*, know;
recognize, (809).

noster, -tra, -trum, our.

nōtus, -a, -um, well-known,
usual; familiar, (221, 499).

Notus, -ī, *m.*, the South Wind.

novem, nine.

noviēns, nine times.

novus, -a, -um, new, strange, fresh.

nox, noctis, f., night, darkness.

noxius, -a, -um, harmful, baneful.

nūbila, -ōrum, n. pl., clouds.

nūllus, -a, -um, no, not any; none.

nūmen, -inis, n., divine will; divine power; deity, divinity; consent, (266).

numerus, -ī, m., number; of music, measure.

Numitor, -ōris, m., Numitor.

nunc, now.

nūntius, -ī, m., messenger.

nūper, lately.

Nysa, -ae, f., Nysa.

ob, prep. with acc., on account of; for, (660).

obeō, -īre, -īvī or iī, -itum, go to, enter on; pass over; border, wash, (58).

obiciō, -ere, -iēcī, -iectum, throw to.

oblīvium, ī, n., forgetfulness.

obloquor, -ī, -locūtus sum, (3 dep.), play as accompaniment, (646).

obmūtescō, -ere, -uī, (3), become silent.

oborior, -īrī, -ortus sum, (4 dep.), spring up, well up.

obruō, -ere, -uī, -utum, (3), overwhelm.

obscūrus, -a, -um, dim; dark; scarcely visible (268); n. pl., (100), darkness, obscurity.

observō, (1), watch.

obstō, -āre, -stitī, -statum, (1), stand in the way of, withstand, (+ dat.)

obuncus, -a, -um, curved, hooked, (597).

obvertō, -ere, -rtī, -rsum, (3), turn . . . towards . . . , (with acc. and dat.).

obvius, -a, -um, in the way (of), opposite, to meet.

occupō, (1), seize; gain first, gain.

occurrō, -ere, -currī or -cucurrī, -cursum, (3), run to meet, meet; come before.

oculus, -ī, m., eye.

odōrātus, -a, -um, scented, fragrant.

offa, -ae, f., çake.

offerō, -ferre, obtulī, oblātum, put before, present.

oleō, (2), smell (intr.).

oleum, -ī, n., oil (of the olive).

olīva, -ae, f., olive tree.

olīvum, -ī, n., oil.

olle = ille.

Olympus, -ī, m., Olympus.

omniparēns, -ntis, all-bearing, all-producing.

omnis, -e, all, every, whole.

opācō, (1), shade, make shady.

opācus, -a, -um, shady, gloomy.

operiō, -īre, -ruī, -rtum, cover; partic., opertus, hidden; neut. pl., (140), the hidden places.

opīmus, -a, -um, rich.

optimus, -a, -um, best, (superl. of bonus).

optō, (1), desire, choose.

opus, operis, n., work, labour, toil, task; opus (est), there is need of, (261).

ōra, -ae, f., shore, coast.

orbis, -is, m., round, circuit, cycle.

Orcus, -ī, m., Orcus, (*the Lower World, Hell*).

ordior, -īrī, orsus sum, (4 *dep.*), begin.

ordō, -inis, m., order, row, array.

orgia, -orum, n. pl., revels, feasts.

orīgō, -inis, f., source, origin.

ornus, -ī, f., mountain ash, rowan.

ōrō, (1), ask, beg, pray, pray for; plead (849); supplicate, (92).

Orontes, -is, m., Orontes.

Orpheūs, -eos, m., Orpheus.

orsus, *see* **ordior.**

ortus, -ūs, m., rising.

ōs, ōris, n., mouth; face; lips; eye, (191, 604).

os, ossis, n., bone.

ostendō, -ere, -ndī, -ntum *or* **-nsum,** (3), show.

ostentō, (1), show, display.

ostium, -ī, n., mouth, entrance.

ōtium, -ī, n., rest, repose.

ovō, (1), exult, triumph.

pacō, (1), pacify, appease, tame.

paean, -ānis, m., paean.

palaestra, -ae, f., wrestling-ground, wrestling.

Palinūrus, -ī, m., Palinurus.

palla, -ae, f., *woman's* robe

palleō, (2), am pale; *partic.,* **pallēns,** pale.

palma, -ae, f., palm (*of the hand*).

palūs, -ūdis, f., marsh, marsh water; mere.

pampineus, -a, -um, of vine tendrils.

pandō, -ere, -ndī, passum *or* **pānsum,** open, unfold, spread out; reveal (267, 723).

pār, paris, equal, matched, like, similar.

parcō, -ere, pepercī, parsum, (3), spare (+ *dat.*) ; cease, refrain.

parēns, -ntis, c., parent; father, mother.

pariō, -ere, peperī, partum, (3), produce, procure, gain, bring about, (435).

Paris, -idos, m., Paris.

pariter, equally, side by side.

parō, (1), make ready, prepare.

pars, -rtis, f., part, portion, share; direction, (440) ; **pars . . . pars . . .,** *sometimes with pl. vb.,* some . . . others . . . .

Parthenopaeus, -ī, m., Parthenopaeus.

partus, -ūs, m., birth; offspring.

parum, too little.

parumper, for a little while.

parvus, -a, -um, little, small; humble; (*comp.* **minor,** *superl.* **minimus.**

pascō, -ere, pāvī, pastum, (3), feed, (*transitive*) ; *pass. as deponent,* feed, graze, (*intrans.*).

Pāsiphaē, -ēs, f., Pasiphaë.

passim, everywhere.

passus, *see* **patior.**

passus, -ūs, m., pace.

pateō, (2), am open, lie open, fly open ; yawn, gape.

pater, patris, m., father.

patera, -ae, f., bowl.

patior, -ī, passus sum ; (*dep.*), suffer, endure, bear ; *partic.* **patiēns,** (+ *gen.*) ; enduring, submissive to, (77).

patria, -ae, f., fatherland.

patrius, -a, -um, father's ; country's, native.

patruus, -ī, m., uncle.

paucī, -ae, -a, few.

paulātim, little by little.

pauper, -is, poor.

pauperiēs, -ēī, f, poverty.

pavitō, (1), am greatly afraid, cower in terror.

pax, pācis, f., peace.

pecten, -inis, n., comb; plectrum, (647).

pectus, -oris, n., breast, chest; heart.

pecus, -ūdis, f., beast; pl., cattle.

pedes, -itis, m., foot-soldier, infantryman ; on foot.

pelagus, -ī, n., sea.

Pelasgī, -ōrum or -um, Pelasgi.

pellō, -ere, pepulī, pulsum, (3), drive away.

pendeō, -ēre, pependī, (2), hang, (intr.) ; linger, (151).

pendō, -ere, pependī, pēnsum, (3), weigh ; pay, (20).

penetrāle, -is, n., shrine.

penitus, from within ; deep in ; deeply ; far distant, utterly ; far, (59).

penna, -ae, f., wing.

per, prep. with acc., through, along, over, on ; in appeals, by, (364, etc.).

peragō, -ere, -ēgī, -āctum, (3), go through ; ponder ; perform, accomplish ; continue, (384).

percurrō, -ere, -currī or cucurrī, -cursum, (3), run through ; recount, (627).

percutiō, -ere, -cussī, -cussum, strike, smite.

peredō, -ere, -ēdī, -ēsum, (3), consume.

perferō, -ferre, -tulī, -lātum, endure.

perficiō, -ere, -fēcī, -fectum, finish, complete ; perfecta, (895), wrought.

Pergama, -ōrum, n. pl., Pergama (the citadel of Troy).

Pergameus, -a, -um, Trojan.

pergō, -ere, perrexī, perrectum, (3), proceed.

perīculum or perīclum, -ī, n., danger, peril.

perimō, -ere, -ēmī, -emptum, (3), destroy, cut off.

perlegō, -ere, -lēgī, -lectum, (3), review, scan.

perōdī, -isse, -ōsus sum, vb. defect., hate, loathe.

personō, -āre, -sonuī, -sonitum, (1), make ... resound ; resound, re-echo.

pēs, pedis, m., foot.

pestis, -is, f., plague.

petō, -ere, -īvī or iī, -ītum, (3), seek.

Phaedra, -ae, f., Phaedra.

phalanx, -ngis, f., phalanx ; host, (489).

Phlegethōn, -ontis, m., Phlegethon.

Phlegyas, -ae, m., Phlegyas.

Phoebus, -ī, m., Phoebus (Apollo).

Phoenissa, -ae, f., Phoenician.

Phrygius, -a, -um, Phrygian ; fem. pl. as noun, Phrygian women, (518).

piāculum, -ī, n., offering of atonement, sin offering, expiation.

picea, -ae, f., pine-tree.

pietās, -ātis, love, dutifulness ; piety.

pinguis, -e, fat, rich ; resinous, (214).

piō, (1), appease.

Pīrithous, -ī, *m.*, Pirithous.

pius, -a, -um, pious, righteous, good.

placidus, -a, -um, calm, peaceful.

plangor, -ōris, *m.*, mourning, wailing.

plaudō, -ere, -sī, -sum, (3), beat, strike ; tread, (644).

plēnus, -a, -um, full.

plūrimus, -a, -um, (*superl. of* multus), very much, very great, very many, most ; full (659).

plūs, plūris, more (*comp. of* multus).

poena, -ae, *f.*, punishment, penalty ; vengeance ; torment, (598).

Poenī, -ōrum, *m. pl.*, Carthaginians.

Pollux, -ūcis, *m.*, Pollux.

Polyboetēs, -ae, *m.*, Polyboetes.

Pōmetiī, -ōrum, *m. pl.*, Pometii.

pondus, -eris, *n.*, weight.

pōnō, -ere, posuī, positum, (3), place, set up ; lay, (508) ; build, rear ; set aside, (611).

pontus, -ī, *m.*, sea.

populāris, -e, of the people, popular.

populō, (1), lay waste ; mutilate.

populus, -ī, *m.*, people, nation, tribe.

porrigō, -ere, -rexī, -rectum, (3), stretch out.

porrō, further ; in the distance, yonder.

porta, -ae, *f.*, gate.

portitor, -ōris, *m.*, ferryman.

portō, (1), carry.

portus, -ūs, *m.*, harbour.

poscō, -ere, poposcī, (3), demand, claim ; call for, (37).

possum, posse, potuī, am able, can ; have power.

post, *prep. with acc.* after ; *as adv.*, afterwards.

postquam, *conj.*, when, after.

postumus, -a, -um, latest, last, last-born.

potēns, -ntis, powerful.

potior, -īrī, potītus sum, (4 *dep.*), gain possession of, attain, (+ *abl.*).

pōtō, (1), drink.

praeceps, -ipitis, headforemost, headlong ; precipitous.

praeceptum, -ī, *n.*, precept, bidding, order, command.

praecipiō, -ere, -cēpī, -ceptum, teach, prescribe ; foreknow, (105).

praecipitō, (1), fall headlong.

praecipuē, especially.

praeda, -ae, *f.*, booty ; a prize, (361).

praeficiō, -ere, -fēcī, -fectum, set . . . over . . . (*with acc. and dat.*).

praemittō, -ere, -mīsī, -missum, (3), send forward.

praenatō, (1), flow past.

praepes, -ētis, swift.

praescius, -a, -um, foreknowing, (*with gen.*).

praesideō, -ēre, -sēdī, -sessum, (2), preside over, (*with dat.*).

praestāns, ntis, excellent.

praestō, -āre, -stitī, -stitum, (1), excel, am superior.

praetendō, -ere, -ndī, -ntum, (3) stretch in front ; *partic.*, praetentus, opposite, (60).

praetereā, moreover.

praeterlābor, -ī, -lāpsus sum, (3 dep.), glide by.

praetexō, -ere, -uī, -xtum, (3), fringe, border.

prātum, -ī, n., meadow.

[prex, precis], f., (acc. dat. and abl. cases only found in sg.), prayer, entreaty.

precor, (1), pray; precandō, abl. of gerund, by praying, by entreaty.

premō, -ere, pressī, pressum, (3), press, weigh down; lie heavy upon, (521); control; close (lips); check (steps); imprison.

prendō or prehendō, -ere, -endī -ēnsum (3), grasp.

prēnsō, (1), grasp.

pretium, -ī, n., price, bribe.

Prīamidēs, -ae, m., son of Priam.

prīmum, first, firstly; ut primum, when first, as soon as.

prīmus, -a, -um, first.

principium, -ī, beginning; abl. principiō as adv., in the first place, first.

prior, -us, earlier, before, first.

priscus, -a, -um, ancient, old-fashioned.

pristinus, -a, -um, ancient, former.

prius, adv., before, first, sooner.

priusquam, sooner than, before, until.

prō, prep. with abl., for, on behalf of, for the sake of.

Procas, -ae, m., Procas.

procer, -ceris, m., chieftain.

Procris, -is or idis, f., Procris.

procul, at a distance, afar, from afar.

prōcumbō, -ere, -cubuī, -cubitum, (3), sink down, fall.

prodeō, -īre, -īvī or -iī, -itum, go forward, advance.

prōdigium, -ī, n., portent.

profānus, -a, -um, unhallowed.

prōferō, -ferre, -tulī, -lātum, advance, bring forward; extend, (795).

profundus, -a, -um, deep, abysmal.

prōgeniēs, -ēī, f., offspring.

prohibeō, (2), hinder, forbid.

proiciō, -ere, -iēcī, -iectum, fling away.

prōles, -īs, f., offspring; race; breed, (784).

prōmittō, -ere, -mīsī, -missum, (3), promise.

propāgō, -inis, f., offshoot, offspring; stock, (870).

properē, hurriedly, quickly.

propinquō, (1), approach, (with dat.).

propior, -ius, nearer.

proprius, (one's) own; lasting, (871).

prōra, -ae, f., prow, bows.

prōsequor, -ī, -secūtus sum, (3 dep.), follow, escort, attend.

Prōserpina, -ae, f., Proserpine.

prōspiciō, -ere, -spexī, -spectum, discern, see before one.

prōtinus, forthwith, in succession, (33).

proximus, -a, -um, nearest, next.

pūbes, -is, f., youth; body of youths; brood, (580).

puella, -ae, f., girl, maiden.

puer, -erī, m., boy.

pūgna, -ae, f., fight, battle.

pūgnō, (1), fight.

pulcher, -chra, -chrum, fair, beautiful.

pulsō, (1), strike.

pulsus, (382), *see* pellō.

pulsus, -ūs, *m.*, trampling, beat.

puppis, -is, *f.*, stern ; boat, ship.

purpureus, -a, -um, purple ; bright, dazzling, (641, 884).

pūrus, -a, -um, pure, unsullied.

putō, (1), think ; multa putāns, deep in thought, (332).

pyra, -ae, *f.*, funeral pyre.

quā, where ; by any means, (882).

quadrīgae, -ārum, *f. pl.*, four-horse chariot.

quaerō, -ere, -sīvī, -situm, (3), seek, search, enquire about.

quaesītor, -ōris, *m.*, president.

quālis, -e, of what sort, as ; what sort of.

quam, how ; how much, (436, 694) ; than.

quamquam, although.

quandō, when ; since, because.

quantus, -a, -um, of what size, how big ; tantus ... quantus, so, *or* as, great as ; quantum, as far as.

quartus, -a, -um, fourth.

quassō, (1), shake, brandish.

quatiō, -ere, ——, quassum, shake ; assail, (571).

quattuor, four.

-que, and.

queō, -īre, quīvī, quitum, am able, can.

quercus, -ūs, *f.*, oak.

quī, quae, quod, *rel. pron.*, who, which, that ; what.

quī, quae, quod, *interrog. adj.*, what? which?

quī, quae, quod, *indefinite adj.*, any.

quid, why.

quiēs, -ētis, *f.*, rest, repose ; slumber.

quiescō, -ere, -ēvī, -ētum, (3), rest, grow calm ; find repose, (328, 371).

quīn, *conj.*, but that ; *introducing principal clauses*, nay, more ; moreover, (33, 824).

quīnquāginta, fifty.

Quirīnus, -ī, *m.*, Quirinus.

quis, quae, quid, *interrog. pron.*, who? which? what?

quis, qua, quid, *indefinite pron.*, anyone, someone.

quisquam, *neut.* quidquam *or* quicquam, anyone, anything ; *as adj.*, any, (875).

quisque, quaeque, quidque *or* quodque, each.

quisquis, quidquid *or* quicquid, whoever, whatever.

quīvī, *see* queo.

quō = ut eo, that thereby, in order that, (*introducing final clause*).

quō, whither, to which.

quod, as to which, wherefore, (363) ; quod sī, but if.

quondam, once, formerly ; ever, (876).

quoque, also ; nunc quoque, even now, (816).

quotannīs, year by year, every year.

rabidus, -a, -um, raging, frenzied.

rabiēs, -ēī, *f.*, rage, frenzy.

radius, -ī, *m.*, spoke (*of wheel*) ; rod (*for tracing diagrams*) (850).

rāmus, -ī, *m.*, bough.

rapidus, -a, -um, swift.

rapīo, -ere, -puī, -ptum, seize, snatch, tear away; hurry, (*trans.*) (845); plunder, (8).

ratis, -is, *f.*, raft; ship, boat, bark.

raucus, -a, -um, hoarse; gurgling, (327).

rebellis, -e, renewing war, rebellious.

recēns, -ntis, fresh; flowing, (635).

recēnseō, -ēre, -suī, -sum, (2), reckon up, review.

recipiō, -ere, -cēpī, -ceptum, take back, review, recover.

recolō, -ere, -coluī, -cultum, (3), reflect on; meditate, (681).

rēctus, -a, -um, right, straight.

recubō, -āre, -buī, -bitum, (1), recline, lie.

reddō, -ere, reddidī, redditum, (3), give back, restore; recall, (768); give *answer*, (672); answer, (689).

redeō, -īre, -īvī *or* iī, -itum, return.

redimō, -ere, -ēmī, -emptum, (3), buy back, redeem.

redūcō, -ere, -xī, -ctum, (3), lead back; *partic.*, reductus, (703), secluded.

referō, -ferre, -tulī, -latum, bring back; restore.

refīgō, -ere, -xī, -xum, (3), unfasten; unmake, (622).

refringō, -ere, -frēgī, -fractum, (3), break off.

refugiō, -ere, -fūgī, -fugitum, flee back, flee.

refulgeō, -ēre, -lsī, (2), shine out, (204).

refundō, -ere, -fūdī, -fūsum, (3), pour back; *in pass.*, overflow, (107).

rēgificus, -a, -um, royal.

rēgīna, -ae, *f.*, queen.

regiō, -ōnis, *f.*, district, region, quarter.

rēgnō, (1), hold rule, bear sway.

rēgnum, -ī, *n.*, kingdom, realm; sway.

regō, -ere, -xī, -ctum, (3), rule, direct, guide.

relinquō, -ere, -līquī, -lictum, (3), leave.

rēliquiae, -ārum, *f. pl.*, remains.

rēmigium, -ī, *n.*, oars, oarage.

remūgiō, (4), moan, (99).

Remus, -ī, *m.*, Remus.

rēmus, -ī, *m.*, oar.

renāscor, -ī, -nātus sum, (3 *dep.*), am born again.

reor, rērī, ratus sum, (2 *dep.*), think.

reperiō, -īre, repperī, repertum (4), find.

repōnō, -ere, -posuī, -positum, *or* -postum, (3), duly place, lay, (655).

reposcō, -ere, (3), claim, call for, (530).

repostus, -a, -um, distant.

requiēs, ētis, *f.*, rest; respite, (600).

requīrō, -ere, -sīvī, -situm, (3), seek again; enquire.

rēs, reī, *f.*, thing, matter, affair; *pl.*, fortunes; res egenae, needy circumstances, i.e. poverty.

rescindō, -ere, -scidī, -scissum, (3), tear off, tear down.

reses, -sidis, inactive.

resīdō, -ere, -sēdī, (3), settle down, sink down.

resolvō, -ere, -solvī, -solūtum, (3), unloose, unravel, unstiffen ; relax, (422).

respiciō, -ere, -spexī, -spectum, look back ; regard, look at.

respondeō, -ēre, -dī, -sum, (2), answer ; respondet, (23), balances this.

respōnsum, -ī, n., answer ; oracle, (799).

restituō, -ere, -uī, -ūtum, (3), restore.

revellō, -ere, -vellī, -vulsum, (3), tear off.

revertor, -ī, pf. revertī (active form), partic., reversus, (3), return.

revīsō, -ere, -sī, -sum, (3), revisit.

revocō, (1), recall ; retrace.

revolvō, -ere, -volvī, -volūtum, (3), roll back, change.

rēx, rēgis, m., king.

Rhadamanthus, -ī, m., Rhadamanthus.

Rhoetēus, -a, -um, Rhoetean.

rigō, (1), moisten, bedew.

rīmor, (1 dep.), explore, grope, (599).

rīmōsus, -a, -um, full of cracks, leaky.

rīpa, -ae, f., bank.

rīte, duly.

rīvus, -ī, m., brook, stream.

rōbur, -boris, n., oak-wood, oak ; strength.

rogus, -ī, m., funeral-pyre.

Rōma, -ae, f., Rome.

Rōmānus, -a, -um, Roman.

Rōmulus, -ī, m., Romulus.

Rōmulus, -a, -um, of Romulus, (876).

rōs, rōris, m., dew.

roseus, -a, -um, rosy.

rōstrum, -ī, n., beak.

rota, -ae, f., wheel.

rumpō, -ere, rūpī, ruptum, (3), burst, break.

ruō, -ere, ruī, rutum, (3), rush ; ruit, is falling, (539).

rūpēs, -is, f., rock, cliff.

rursus, back again, again, afresh, once more.

sacer, -cra, -crum, holy, sacred ; sacra, n. pl., sacred rites ; sacred vessels.

sacerdōs, -ōtis, c., priest, priestess.

sacrō, (1), make sacred, hallow, dedicate.

saeculum, -ī, n., generation, age.

saepe, often ; saepius, (frequently without comparative force), often.

saeta, -ae, f., hair, bristle.

saeviō, (4), am fierce, am wrathful.

saevus, -a, -um, fierce, cruel.

sal, salis, m., salt ; sea.

Salmōneūs, -eos, m., Salmoneus.

saltem, at least.

saltus, -ūs, m., leap, bound.

saltus, -ūs, m., glade.

salūs, -ūtis, f., safety ; deliverance.

sanctus, -a, -um, holy, reverend.

sanguis, -inis, m., blood ; descendant, offspring ; lineage, (500).

satis, enough.

Sāturnus, -ī, m., Saturn.

satus, see serō.

saxum, -ī, *n.*, rock.

scelerātus, -a, -um, guilty.

scelus, -eris, *n.*, guilt, wickedness, crime ; infectum scelus, (742), the stain of guilt.

scīlicet, doubtless, of course.

scindō, -ere, scidī, scissum, (3), split, cleave, tear.

Scīpiadēs, -ae, *m.*, son of Scipio.

scrūpeus, -a, -um, rugged.

Scylla, -ae, *f.*, Scylla.

sē *or* sēsē, suī, *reflex. pron.*, himself, herself, itself, themselves.

sēclūdō, -ere, -sī, -sum, (3), shut off ; seclusus, (704), sequestered.

secō, -āre, -cuī, -ctum, (1), cut, cleave ; trace, (899).

sēcrētus, -a, -um, set apart ; secluded, (443) ; *neut., pl.,* sēcrēta, (10), the retreat.

sectus, -a, -um, cloven, (214).

sēcum, i.e. cum sē.

secūris, -is, *f.*, axe.

sēcūrus, -a, -um, without care ; that frees from care.

sed, but ; sed enim, but indeed.

sedeō, -ēre, sēdī, sessum, (2), sit ; settle, (192).

sēdes, -is, *f.*, seat, resting-place, abode, home.

semel, once.

sēmen, -inis, *n.*, seed.

sēminō, (1), sow.

semper, always.

senecta, -ae, *f.*, old age.

senectūs, -ūtis, *f.*, old age.

senex, senis, *m.*, old man ; *as adj.*, old, *with compar.* senior.

sēnsus, -ūs, *m.*, feeling, sense.

sentus, -ā, -um, rough, ragged.

sepeliō, -īre, -īvī *or* -iī, sepultum, (4), bury.

septem, seven.

septemgeminus, -a, -um, sevenfold.

septēnus, -a, -um, seven each, seven at a time.

sepulcrum, -ī, *n.*, tomb ; āra sepulcrī, funeral altar.

sepultus, *see* sepelio.

sequor, -ī, secūtus sum, (3 *dep.*), follow, pursue ; attend, (655) ; seek, (457).

serēnus, -a, -um, clear, calm, bright, sunny.

sermō, -ōnis, *m.*, conversation, speech, talk.

serō, -ere, sēvī, satum, (3), sow ; satus, *as noun*, sprung (from), descendant (of), *with ablative.*

serō, -ere, -ruī, -rtum, (3), join ; say, (160).

Serrānus, -ī, *m.*, Serranus.

sērus, -a, -um, late ; too late.

servō, (1), keep watch, guard ; keep in view, (200) ; keep within, (402) ; keep in memory.

sēsē, *see* sē.

seu, *see* sī.

sevērus, -a, -um, stern, cruel.

sī, if ; if only, would that, (187, 882) ; sīve *or* seu ... sīve *or* seu, whether ... or.

Sibylla, -ae, *f.*, the Sibyl.

sīc, in this way, so, thus.

siccus, -a, -um, dry.

sīdō, -ere, sīdī, (3), settle.

sīdus, -eris, *n.*, constellation, star.

sīgnō, (1), mark, distinguish.

sīgnum, -ī, *n.*, sign, standard.

silēns, -ntis, silent.

sileō, -ēre, -luī, (2), am silent.

silex, -icis, *m.*, (*f.*, 471, 602), flint, rock.

silva, -ae, *f.*, wood, forest, grove.

Silvius, -ī, *m.*, Silvius.

similis, -e, like.

Simois, -entis, *m.*, Simois.

simplex, -icis, simple ; pure, (747).

simul, at the same time ; together.

simulō, (1), imitate, feign ; counterfeit, (591).

sine, *prep. with abl.*, without.

singulī, -ae, -a, one each ; *n. pl.*, singula, each thing separately.

sinister, -tra, -trum, left, on the left, ill-omened ; sinistra, *sc.* manus, the left hand, (571).

sinō, -ere, sīvī, situm, (3), permit, allow.

sinus, -ūs, *m.*, fold ; windings, (132).

sistō, -ere, stitī, statum, (3), place, set, support, establish ; stay, check ; uphold, (858).

situs, -ūs, *m.*, position ; neglect, (462).

socer, -ī, *m.*, father-in-law.

socius, -ī, *m.*, companion, comrade.

sōl, -is, *m.*, sun.

sōlācium, -ī, *n.*, consolation.

soleō, -ēre, solitus sum, (2 *semidep.*), am accustomed, am wont.

solidus, -a, -um, solid, whole.

solium, -ī, *n.*, throne.

sollemnis, -e, customary ; solemn.

solum, -ī, *n.*, ground, sward.

sōlus, -a, -um, alone, solitary, lonely.

solvō, -ere, solvī, solūtum, (3), loose ; pay.

solūtus, *adj. for adv.*, freely, (652).

somnium, -ī, *n.*, dream.

somnus, -ī, *m.*, sleep ; vision seen in dreams, (702).

sonitus, -ūs, *m.*, sound.

sonō, -āre, -uī, -itum, (1), sound, echo, rustle ; ring, (180) ; *partic.* sonāns, murmurous, (753) ; mortāle sonāns, with human utterance, (50) ; sonantia, thunderous, (551).

sōns, -ntis, guilty.

sopor, -ōris, *m.*, sleep.

sopōrō, (1), make drowsy ; make soporific, (420).

sopōrus, -a, -um, sleep-bringing, slumbrous.

sordidus, -a, -um, filthy, squalid.

soror, -ōris, *f.*, sister.

sors, -rtis, *f.*, lot, portion ; condition.

spargō, -ere, -rsī, -rsum, (3), scatter, sprinkle.

spatium, -ī, *n.*, space.

speciēs, -ēī, *f.*, appearance.

spectāculum, -ī, *n.*, sight, show.

spēlunca, -ae, *f.*, cave.

spērō, (1), hope, hope for.

spēs, -eī, *f.*, hope, expectation.

spīritus, -ūs, *m.*, breath ; spirit.

spīrō, (1), breathe.

spoliō, (1), strip, spoil, rob of.

spolium, -ī, *n.*, spoil.

sponte suā, of his, her, their, own accord.

spūmō, (1), foam.

spūmōsus, -a, -um, foaming.

squālor, -ōris, *m*, filth, dirt.

stabulō, (1), have a stall, am stabled.

stabulum, -ī, *m.*, stall, stable ; covert, lair.

stāgnum, -ī, *n.*, pool, marsh.

statuō, -ere, -uī, -ūtum, (3), set up.

stella, -ae, *f.*, star.

sterilis, -e, barren.

sternō, -ere, strāvī, strātum, (3), stretch out, lay low.

stimulus, -ī, *m.*, goad, spur.

stirps, -pis, *f.*, stock, stem.

stō, -āre, stetī, statum, (1), stand, stand firm; am anchored, (697).

strāgēs, -is, *f.*, destruction, carnage; corpses, (504).

strepitus, -ūs, *m.*, noise, din.

strepō, -ere, -uī, -itum, (3), sound; strepit, is loud, (709).

strictus, *see* stringo.

strīdeō, -ēre, -dī, (2), grate, (573), hiss, (288).

strīdor, -ōris, *m.*, grating; clank, (558).

stringō, -ere, -nxī, strictum, (3), draw, unsheathe.

struō, -ere, -xī, -ctum, (3), build.

studium, -ī, *n.*, zeal, eagerness.

Stygius, -a, -um, Stygian, of Styx.

Styx, -ygis, *f.*, Styx.

sub, *prep. with acc.*, beneath, towards, down to; before, (191); just before, (255); *with abl.*, under, deep in, beneath.

subdūcō, -ere, -xī, -ctum, (3), withdraw.

subeō, -īre, -īvī *or* iī, -itum, (*sometimes with dat.*), go under; come up to, approach, (13); enter; follow.

subigō, -ere, -ēgī, -āctum, (3), compel; push along, propel, (302).

subitō, suddenly.

subitus, -a, -um, sudden.

subiectus, -a, -um, subject; *masc. as noun*, a subject, (853)

subiciō, -ere, -iēcī, -iectum, (3), place beneath, subdue.

sublīmis, -e, lofty, aloft, on high.

subtrahō, -ere, -xī, -ctum, (3), withdraw.

subvectō, (1), carry up stream.

succingō, -ere, -nxī, -nctum, (3), gird up.

succipiō, -ere, -cēpī, -ceptum, (=suscipio), catch, (249).

sulcus, -ī, *m.*, furrow.

sum, esse, fuī, am; est, goes, (14); est + *infin.*, it is possible (to).

summoveō, (i.e. submoveo), -ēre, -mōvī, -mōtum, (2), move away, remove.

summus, -a, -um, highest, very high, topmost; tallest, (245); top of.

sūmō, -ere, -mpsī, -mptum, (3), take.

suntō, *3rd pl. imperative of* sum.

super, *adv.*, above; *prep. with acc.* on to, above, beyond; *with abl.*, on, above.

superbus, -a, -um, haughty, proud.

superēmineō, -ēre, (2), rise above, tower over.

superne, upwards.

superō, (1), traverse, pass over.

superus, -a, -um, *adj.*, above; *m. pl.*, superī *as noun*, those above, i.e. gods, *or, from the view-point of dwellers in Hades*, men.

supplex, -icis, suppliant; humble.

supplicium, -ī, *n.*, punishment, vengeance ; forfeit, (740).

suppōnō, -ere, -posuī, -positum, (-postum), (3), place beneath ; *partic.* supposta, mated, (24).

suprēmus, -a, -um, *superl. of* superus, last.

surgō, -ere, -rexī, -rectum, (3), rise ; grow, (364).

suscipiō, -ere, -cēpī, -ceptum, undertake ; answer, (723).

suspectus, -ūs, *m.*, view upwards.

suspendō, -ere, -ndī, -nsum, (3), hang up.

suspēnsus, -a, -um, hanging, (741) ; uncertain, anxious, in suspense.

suspiciō, -ere, -exī, -ectum, look up at.

sūtilis, -e, made of skins stitched together, (414).

suus, -a, -um, *reflex. possessive pron.*, his, her, its, their own.

Sychaeus, -ī, *m.*, Sychaeus.

Syrtis, -is, *f.*, Syrtis.

tābēs, -is, *f.*, decay, wasting.

taceō, (2), am silent, am silent about ; tacentia, lying silent, (265).

tacitus, -a, -um, silent ; not spoken of.

taeda, -ae, *f.*, pine-torch ; pine-wood, (214, 593).

tālis, -e, of such a kind, such.

tam, so.

tamen, notwithstanding, nevertheless.

tandem, at length, at last.

tantum, so much, as far ; only.

tantus, -a, -um, so great, so much,

as great, as much ; tantum quantum, as far as, (199).

tardō, (1), slow down ; clog, (731).

tardus, -a, -um, slow, sluggish, dull.

Tarquinius, -ī, *m.*, Tarquin.

Tartareus, -a, -um, Tartarean, i.e. of Hades.

Tartarus, -ī, *m.*, (*pl.* Tartara, -ōrum, *n.*), Tartarus, the lower world.

taurus, -ī, *m.*, bull.

tectum, -ī, *n.*, roof ; building, palace ; lair, (8).

tēcum, i.e. cum te.

tegō, -ere, -xī, -ctum, (3), cover, hide.

tellūs, -ūris, *f.*, the earth, land.

tēlum, -ī, *n.*, weapon, shaft.

temerō, (1), violate.

temnō, -ere, -mpsī, (3), despise.

templum, -ī, *n.*, temple.

tempus, -oris, *n.*, time, season ; *pl.*, temples *of the head*, (496).

tenax, -ācis, fast holding, (3).

tendō, -ere, tetendī, tēnsum *or* tentum, (3), stretch, stretch out ; come ; tendere iter, pursue their way (240), pass, (541).

tenebrae, -ārum, *f. pl.*, darkness, gloom.

tenebrōsus, -a, -um, gloomy.

teneō, -ēre, -uī, -tum, hold, clasp, grasp, reach ; possess, keep ; occupy, (131).

tenuis, -e, thin ; unsubstantial.

tenus, *prep. with abl.*, as far as ; hāc tenus, thus far, (62).

tepidus, -a, -um, warm.

ter, thrice.

teres, -etis, smooth ; shapely, rounded.

tergum, -ī, *n.*, back.

terra, -ae, *f.*, earth, land, soil, dry land ; **Terra,** Earth *personified.*

terrēnus, -a, -um, earthy.

terreō, (2), terrify, scare.

terribilis, -e, dreadful.

tertius, -a, -um, third.

testor, (1 *dep.*), call to witness ; testify, bear witness, (619).

Teucer, -crī, *m.*, Teucer.

Teucrī, -ōrum, *or* -um, *m. pl.*, Trojans.

thalamus, -ī, *m.*, marriage chamber ; marriage, (94) ; chamber, (280).

Thersilochus, -ī, *m.*, Thersilochus.

Thēseūs, -eī *or* -eos, *m.*, Theseus.

Thrēicius, -a, -um, Thracian.

Thybris, -idos, *m.*, = Tiberis, the Tiber.

Tiberīnus, -ī, *m.*, Tiberinus (*god of the Tiber*).

tīgris, -is *or* -idis, *c.*, tiger.

timeō, (2), fear.

timidus, -a, -um, fearful.

timor, -ōris, *m.*, fear.

Tīsiphonē, -ēs, *f.*, Tisiphone.

Tītānius, -a, -um, Titan.

Tityos, -ī, *m.*, Tityos.

tollō, -ere, sustulī, sublātum, (3), raise ; take ; se tollunt, raise themselves, i.e. soar, (203).

tondeō, -ēre, totondī, tōnsum, (2), shear ; feed on, (598).

Torquātus, -ī, *m.*, Torquatus.

torqueō, -ēre, torsī, tortum, (2), twist, turn ; roll along ; rotate, (797).

torrēns, -ntis, boiling, surging.

torreō, -ēre, -uī, tostum, (2), scorch, bake.

torus, -ī, *m.*, couch.

torvus, -a, -um, grim, fierce ; stern-looking.

tot, *indecl.*, so many.

totidem, *indecl.*, just so many, the like number of.

totiēns, so many times.

tōtus, -a, -um, whole, entire.

trabs, trabis, *f.*, beam.

trahō, -ere, trāxī, trāctum, (3), drag, draw, trail ; draw out, protract ; spend *time*, (537).

trāiciō, -ere, -iēcī, -iectum, throw across ; pass, (536).

trāmes, -itis, *m.*, path.

trānō, (1), swim across ; sail across, (671).

trāns, *prep. with acc.*, across.

trānsmittō, -ere, -mīsī, -missum, (3), send across.

trānsportō, (1), carry across.

tremefaciō, -ere, -fēcī, -factum, make to tremble.

tremō, -ere, -uī, (3), tremble.

tremor, -ōris, *m.*, tremble, shudder.

trepidō, (1), tremble.

trepidus, -a, -um, alarmed ; quaking, (800).

trēs, tria, three.

tricorpor, -oris, with three bodies.

trifaux, -cis, from three throats.

triplex, -icis, threefold, triple.

trīs, = trēs.

trīstis, -e, sad ; stern, gloomy.

triumphō, (1), triumph ; triumph over, (836).

triumphus, -ī, *m.*, triumph.

Trivia, -ae, *f.*, Trivia.

Trōia, -ae, *f.*, Troy.

Trōiānus, -a, -um, Trojan.

Trōius, -a, -um, Trojan.

Trōs, -ōis, *m.*, Tros.

truncus, -ī, *m.*, trunk.
truncus, -a, -um, mutilated, mangled, cut off.
tū, tuī, thou.
tuba, -ae, *f.*, trumpet.
tueor, -ērī, -itus sum, (2 *dep.*), see ; gaze at, look at.
Tullus, -ī, *m.*, Tullus.
tum, then, at that time, next.
tumeō, (2), swell.
tumidus, -a, -um, swelling.
tumultus, -ūs, *m.*, uprising, tumult.
tumulus, -ī, *m.*, mound, tomb.
tunc, then.
turba, -ae, *f.*, crowd, throng, company.
turbidus, -a, -um, confused ; muddy, thick ; loca turbida, the place of disorder.
turbō, (1), throw into confusion, disorder ; shake ; *intrans.*, am in confusion, (800).
turbō, -inis, *m.*, whirlwind, whirl.
tūreus, -a, -um, of frankincense.
turpis, -e, foul ; hideous, ugly, (276).
turris, -is, *f.*, tower.
turrītus, -a, -um, crowned with towers.
tūtus, -a, -um, safe ; guarded, (238) ; *neut. pl.*, safety, (358).
tuus, -a, -um, thy.
Tydeūs, -eī *or* -eos, *m.*, Tydeus.
Tyrrhēnus, -a, -um, Tyrrhenian, Etruscan.

ūber, -eris, *n.*, udder ; mother's breast.
ubi, where, when.
ulciscor, -ī, ultus sum, (3 *dep.*), avenge.

üllus, -a, -um, any.
ulmus, -ī, *f.*, elm.
ulterior, -ius, further.
ultimus, -a, -um, furthest.
ultor, -ōris, *m.*, avenger.
ultrā, *adv.*, *and prep. with acc.*, beyond, further.
ultrix, -īcis, *f. adj.*, avenging.
ultrō, *see notes*, ll. 387, 499.
ultus, *see* ulciscor.
ululō, (1), howl.
ulva, -ae, *f.*, sedge.
umbra, -ae, *f.*, shade, shadow ; spirit, ghost.
umbrifer, -era, -erum, shady, shadowy.
umbrō, (1), overshadow ; shadow, (772).
umerus, -ī, *m.*, shoulder.
umquam, ever.
ūnā, together.
uncus, -a, -um, hooked, clutching.
unda, -ae, *f.*, wave ; water.
unde, whence ; from whom, from which.
undō, (1), bubble.
unguō, -ere, unctum, (3), anoint.
ūnus, -a, -um, one ; alone.
urbs, -is, *f.*, city.
urgeō, -ēre, ursī, (2), press hard , oppress.
urna, -ae, *f.*, urn.
usquam, anywhere.
usque, right on, ever, still.
ut, as, when, how ; ut primum, when first, as soon as; *with subj.*, in order that ; that, so that.
utcunque, however ; whenever.
uterque, utraque, utrumque, each of two ; both.
ūtor, -ī, ūsus sum, (3 *dep., with abl.*), use.

vacca, -ae, *f.*, cow.
vacuus, empty.
vādō, -ere, (3), go.
vadum, -ī, *n.*, shallow water ; *pl.*, shallows, (320).
vāgīna, -ae, *f.*, scabbard.
vāgītus, -ūs, *m.*, wailing (*of infants*).
vagor, (1 *dep.*), wander.
valeō, -ēre, -uī, -itum, (2), am strong ; *with infin.*, am able, can.
validus, -a, -um, strong, mighty.
vallis, -is, *f.*, valley.
vānus, -a, -um, empty, vain.
varius, -a, -um, different, changing ; many-coloured.
vāstus, -a, -um, huge ; waste.
vātēs, -is, *c.*, bard ; seer ; prophet *or* prophetess.
-ve, or.
vęctō, (1), carry.
vectus, *see* veho.
vehō, -ere, -xī, -ctum, (3), carry ; *pass.*, go, voyage.
vel, or ; vel ... vel, either ... or.
vēlāmen, -inis, *n.*, covering, dress.
Velīnus, -a, -um, Velian, of Velia.
vellus, -eris, *n.*, fleece.
vēlum, -ī, *n.*, sail.
velut, just as.
vēna, -ae, *f.*, vein.
vęndō, -ere, -didī, -ditum, (3), sell.
venerābilis, -e, to be revered ; aweful, (408).
veniō, -īre, vēnī, ventum, (4), come ; *neut. of fut. partic.*, ventūrum, the future, (66).
ventōsus, -a, -um, windy.
ventus, -ī, *m.*, wind.
Venus, -eris, *f.*, Venus ; *also as common noun*, love, (26).

verber, -is, *n.*, stroke, lash.
verbum, -ī, *n.*, word.
vērē, truly.
vereor, (2 *dep.*), fear, am afraid ; scruple, (613).
vērō, in truth, indeed.
verrō, -ere, verrī, versum, (3), sweep, sweep over.
versō, (1), keep turning, keep tossing.
vertex, -icis, *m.*, top, summit ; head.
vertō, -ere, -tī, -sum, (3), turn.
vērum, -ī, *n.*, truth.
vērus, -a, -um, true.
vescor, -ī, (3 *dep.*), feed, feast, (657) ; *with abl.*, feed on.
vester, -tra, -trum, your.
vestibulum, -ī, *n.*, entrance.
vestīgium, -ī, *n.*, footstep, step.
vestīgō, (1), track ; watch for signs of, (145).
vestiō, (4), clothe ; invest, (640).
vestis, -is, *f.*, garment, raiment, robe, dress.
vetō, -āre, -uī, -itum, (1), forbid.
vetus, -eris, old.
via, -ae, *f.*, road, way, path.
vicem, *no nom.*, -is, *f.*, change, interchange.
vicissim, in turn.
victor, -ōris, *m.*, conqueror ; *as adj.*, victorious.
videō, -ēre, vīdī, vīsum, (2), see ; *pass., often*, seem.
vigor, -ōris, *m.*, vigour, force.
vīmen, -inis, *n.*, twig.
vincō, -ere, vīcī, victum, (3), conquer, overcome ; prevail.
vinculum *or* vinclum, -ī, *n.*, chain, bonds.
vīnum, -ī, *n.*, wine.

violentus, -a, -um, violent.

vīpereus, -a, -um, of vipers, snaky.

vir, -ī, *m.*, man, hero.

virectum, -ī, *n.*, lawn.

virēns, green.

vireō, (2), am green,

vīres, *see* vīs.

virga, -ae, *f.*, twig, rod, wand.

virgō, -inis, *f.*, maiden.

virgultum, -ī, *n.*, thicket, brake.

viridis, -e, green.

virtūs, -ūtis, *f.*, virtue, worth, courage.

vīs, *acc.* vīm, *abl.* vī, *pl.*, vīrēs, -ium, force, power, might ; *sg. often* = violence, *pl.*, strength.

viscum, -ī, *n.*, mistletoe.

viscus, -eris, *n.*, entrails ; carcass ; patriae viscera, your country's vitals, (833).

vīsus, -ūs, *m.*, sight.

vīta, -ae, *f.*, life.

vitta, -ae, *f.*, fillet, garland.

vīvus, -a, -um, alive, living.

vix, scarcely.

vocō, (1), call, summon, invoke ; challenge, (172).

volēns, -ntis, willing, willingly.

volitō, (1), flit about.

volō, (1), fly ; fly about, (75) ; *partic. as noun*, volantes, fliers, i.e. birds, (239).

volō, velle, voluī, wish ; mean, (318).

volucer, -cris, -cre, winged ; swift ; fleeting, (702).

voluntās, -ātis, *f.*, wish, will, desire, purpose.

volūtō, (1), ponder.

volvō, -ere, volvī, volūtum, (3), roll ; *pass.*, roll (*intrans.*), writhe, (581).

vorāgō, -inis, *f.*, abyss.

vōs, you.

vōtum, -ī, *n.*, vow.

vōx, vōcis, *f.*, voice, shout, cry ; speech, (686) ; *pl.*, words, sounds, notes, tones.

vulgō, commonly ; in crowds.

vulnus, -eris, *n.*, wound.

vult, 3 *sg. pres. ind.* of volo, wish.

vultur, -uris, *m.*, vulture.

vultus, -ūs, *m.*, countenance, face, features.

Xanthus, -i, *m.*, Xanthus.